Dave Armstrong

Debating James White
Shocking Failures of the "Undefeatable" Anti-Catholic Champion

ISBN 978-1-304-58671-1

Biblical citations are taken from the Revised Standard Version of the Bible (© 1971 by Division of Christian Education of the National Council of the Churches of Christ in the United States of America); unless otherwise noted.

Front cover photograph: Raphael, detail from *The School of Athens* (1510)

Back cover photograph: Raphael, detail from *St. Paul Preaching in Athens* (1515)

DEDICATION

To all who have ever read one of James White's books or articles on Catholicism, or listened to his oral debates or webcasts on the same topic: especially those who are open to following the truth wherever it leads them.

INTRODUCTION

An *anti-Catholic* – in scholarly usage – is not merely a person who differs with Catholicism. Nor does it refer to someone who "hates" Catholics or opposes all things Catholic simply because they are Catholic. And it doesn't refer to emotions or opposition to individuals, but rather, to Catholic theology.

The anti-Catholic is one who thinks that Catholicism is not a Christian system of theology and that to be a good Christian and get saved, one must be a *bad* Catholic; that is, reject several tenets of Catholicism that differ with Protestantism; or in the case of Orthodox anti-Catholics, with Orthodoxy.

But first let me introduce the man who is the subject of this book. James White (b. 1962) is a Reformed Baptist apologist, author, public speaker and debater, and elder at his church. He does many other things in his apologetics besides oppose Catholic theology, and many of these are good and worthwhile endeavors; for example, his critiques of Islam (his recent emphasis), the King James Only viewpoint, theological liberalism, Mormonism, and atheism.

By and large, in dealing with these topics, he does a good job, in my opinion, and I have often publicly commended him for it. When it comes to Catholicism, on the other hand, it's quite a different story. In that domain he falls into the typical (and rather outrageous) errors of anti-Catholic thought.

Mr. White is the founder and director of Alpha and Omega Ministries, which began in 1983. In 1990 he started concentrating on critiquing Catholicism, and produced his first two books on the topic: *The Fatal Flaw*, and *Answers to Catholic Claims* (both by Crowne Publications: 1990). His other books (out of 26) that are devoted wholly or largely to Catholicism, include *The Roman Catholic Controversy* (1996), *Mary – Another Redeemer?* (1998), *The God Who Justifies* (2001), and *Scripture Alone* (2004): all published by Bethany House.

White obtained an M.A. Degree in theology from Fuller Theological seminary in 1989. During the mid-90s as the Internet began to flourish, he began devoting a lot of time and energy to that medium, and he started his weekly webcast, *The Dividing Line*, in September 1998. It often deals with Catholicism. He developed a website and blog, with voluminous writings, as well.

He is probably most known (and renowned) for his formal oral debates. According to his website he has done 117 of these, starting in August 1990, including 38 devoted to various Catholic beliefs: or 32% of all his debates. He engaged in more than one debate with apologists such as Fr. Mitch Pacwa (five), Robert Fastiggi (four), Tim Staples (three), and Patrick Madrid (two).

White also has challenged me to oral debate on three occasions: 1995, 2001, and 2007. Thus, he averages a request every six years (even though – oddly enough – he constantly asserts that I am a profound imbecile and ignoramus in theological and exegetical matters), and is due to ask me again before this year is out. Perhaps this book will be the impetus.

My answer was the same in every instance: I regard oral debates as vastly inferior to written debate and I don't cultivate public speaking, in any event. I note that White is also a writer, whereas I am a writer only, so that the written medium is where we could and should best interact: the common ground.

"Debating" in the title of this volume is especially apt, as it highlights how Mr. White views himself and how he – by all appearances – especially wants to be known. I love debate and dialogue, myself, as a longtime socratic and apologist. Christian apologists (defenders of the faith: in either its Protestant, Catholic, or Orthodox forms) certainly debate; if they don't, they are surely not apologists worth their salt.

The question at hand, however, is how to *define* a debate, what one's *intentions* are in undertaking one, and whether the *truth* is being defended while debating.

Mr. White engages in habitual "boilerplate" regarding his debates and those who (for whatever reason) decline to participate in them with him. One very common theme is his notion that writers "hide behind their keyboards" – they are (he thinks) intellectual cowards and scared to death to face him -- the Terrifying and Unanswerable Scourge of Catholics – behind a podium in a public oral debate. Here are three examples:

> Dr. Stauffer: Brave Behind the Keyboard, Unwilling to Defend His Assertions (article title: 3-25-06 on his blog)

> . . . Armstrong continues to refuse to debate man to man in person, and wishes only to hide behind his keyboard where he knows that no one, and I mean no one, can possibly force him to answer a direct question. As long as you can use the written forum, you can avoid the very essence of debate, the heart of debate, which is answering direct questions that test your position for consistency. Armstrong knows he is simply constitutionally incapable of the task, but he refuses to admit it, opting instead for this kind of rhetoric. (7-12-07 on his blog)

> There are far too many folks who hide behind a keyboard on web forums . . . (2-3-09 on his blog)

Mr. White's typical treatment of yours truly (since 1995) is clearly observed above. I will try as much as is possible in this book to avoid documenting his constant juvenile and sub-Christian resort to personal insult, so as not to afflict readers with silly tedium (I wish to stick solely to theological issues). But removing White's ubiquitous insults of his Catholic opponents in written records is very often about as easy as removing the white stripe from a candy cane: it's so intermingled as to be impossible to extricate from the substance. I'll do my best!

The other frequent and annoying theme with regard to Mr. White's debates and his "spin" about them, is the notion that when an oral debate *did* occur and the other party didn't make it available in his venue, this "proves" a tacit admission of defeat. Here's an absolutely classic instance of that polemic, from a website article (9-18-00) reprinted on 12-28-12 on his blog:

7

I have seen my opponents use many tactics to cover over poor performances in debates. You will find documented on this website at least one imaginative approach taken by *Catholic Answers* back in 1993 when Patrick Madrid attempted to do damage control after our *sola scriptura* debate in San Diego by writing "The White Man's Burden" in *This Rock* magazine . . .

But never before have we seen such complete and utter admission of defeat than we are seeing from *St. Joseph Communications* regarding the July debate with Tim Staples on Papal Infallibility in Fullerton, California . . .

. . . we have learned that *Saint Joseph's* is still not selling the audio tapes of the debate, and that more than two months after the encounter. We have been making the tapes available since the week after the debate. We made it available as soon as we possibly could. . . . you cannot, as of today (September 18th, 2000), order the debate from *Saint Joseph's*. Why not?

Of course, White has never ever linked to our own first lengthy 1995 "postal debate." He gave me permission to post it on my website, but he has never linked to it. Thus, if we follow his reasoning above, how is that *not* an admission that he lost the debate (especially given the fact that he left my final 36-page single-spaced response utterly unanswered)? Otherwise, why wouldn't he encourage folks read our exchange, so they can see how marvelously he allegedly did and how miserably I did?

White would respond that our exchange was not a debate in the first place, because it wasn't moderated or live in front of an audience. It would be tough to argue with a straight face that a debate must *always* be oral and can never be in writing. That would take out, for example, many of the famous debates in the 16th century between Catholics and Protestants, such as those between Erasmus and Martin Luther, or John Calvin and Cardinal Sadoleto. It would also entail the absurd position that the ancient philosopher Plato wrote no dialogues or debates (often reconstructions of the great Socrates engaging in dialogue).

For my part, I have had a consistent track record in favor of written, point-by-point exchanges where two parties seriously *interact* with each other and engage in several rounds of back-and-forth response. I have participated in well over 700 of these on my blog and earlier website, since 1996 when I first went online. I wrote at length about the relative merits of oral and written debate in a website paper dated January 2001:

> It is said that in a public, oral debate, obfuscation, or "muddying the waters" is minimized by the other person's ability to correct errors immediately, and to "call" the opponent on this, that, or the other fact or argument. But this assumes that immediate, spur-of-the-moment corrections are more compelling than a correction which resulted from hours of careful research with primary sources, Scripture, etc.
>
> It is said that live oral debates are a better use of time; that things can be said quicker than they can in writing. But I respond that truth takes time to find and communicate. Propaganda, on the other hand (such as the norm of today's political rhetoric) is very easy to quickly spout. Evangelicalism lends itself far more easily to shallow rhetoric and slogans; Catholicism does not. It is complex, nuanced, and requires much thought and study. And thought takes time, no matter how you slice the cake. Again, truth and the acquisition of knowledge and wisdom requires time.
>
> It is claimed that there is more interest in oral public debates. I'm not so sure about that, especially with the advent of the Internet, but perhaps this is true. In any event, that has no bearing on my own objections. It is not public debate per se I am opposed to, but the perversion of it by unworthy tactics and methods, which is the usual result when one is dealing with anti-Catholics. So I am actually supporting what I consider to be true debate, not the pale imitations of it which pass for "debates."
>
> It is asserted that it's harder to get away with lies and half-truths in the public arena. Quite the contrary, I

would maintain; it is much easier to disinform and misinform, because one can put up an appearance of confidence and truth very easily, through rhetorical technique, catch-phrases, cleverness, playing to the crowd, etc. These things are by no means as "certain" as avid proponents of oral debate make them out to be.

It is stated (by anti-Catholics) that Catholics don't fare well in public oral debates. Under my thesis, I could readily agree with that. It is true that the Catholic faith is not conducive to an environment where sophistical carnival-barker, used-car salesman types try to distort, twist, and misrepresent it at every turn (and this need not be *deliberate* at all: it matters not -- the end result is the same).

In an earlier paper (11-27-00) I wrote:

The Catholic position is not well-presented at such "debates" (i.e., public, oratorical ones) because it is complex, highly interrelated, and (in its complexity, spiritual profundity, and inner logic) much more a "thinking man's religion" than Protestantism is. Presenting such an outlook can't very easily be done in a time-limited debate where our opponent is playing the audience like a carnival barker or a dishonest politician. It *can* be done in a book or a lengthy article, or in a website which deals with *all* the interrelated topics (or at least links to them), so that the inquirer can learn how they are thoroughly biblical, coherent, and true to history (and development of doctrine is also another huge and crucial, necessary factor not easily summarized or even understood by many).

Again, it has to do with the complexity and interrelatedness of the Catholic position, and the difficulty in promulgating it in sound-bytes, as is the case in so many brands of evangelicalism. Websites are uniquely designed to teach the faith, if this complexity is granted (with the technology of links). I think the only near-equivalent to this in live debate would be a series of debates, one after the other, so that the faith can be seen in its many dimensions and in its marvelous cohesiveness: what I would call a "cumulative apologetic argument."

In a debate about papal infallibility, for instance, it would be necessary to also have debates on apostolic succession, episcopacy, the nature of the Church, indefectibility, the nature of authority, NT teaching on Tradition, development of doctrine, the self-defeating nature of *sola Scriptura*, etc. I don't think the average Protestant has any hope of understanding papal infallibility (and "problems" like the Honorius case) without *some* knowledge of these other presuppositional issues.

In short, then, I think that any number of Catholic apologists could and would win such a debate on content (because our argument is true, and many apologists could convincingly present it), yet "lose" it in terms of impact on the audience, and in terms of the difficulty of persuading even those fair-minded or predisposed to be convinced of our side. We should take before and after surveys of people who attend these "debates" to see whether what I suspect is true or not (and make it a condition of the debate).

If we must debate these sophists and cynically clever men, at least we need to make sure they have to also defend *their* position and not just run ours down with the standard, garden-variety anti-Catholic gibberish, bolstered with "quasi-facts" and half-truths presented in a warped, distorted fashion. Those who don't know any better will always be taken in by those tactics (which is exactly why anti-Catholics continue to use them, consciously or not).

Most public debate formats will not allow a fair exchange to occur, due to complexity of subject matter, and the stacked deck which requires us to defend complex truths, while the anti-Catholic escapes his responsibility of defending the generally unexamined absurdities and

11

self-contradictions of his own position. Many anti-Catholics are never, ever willing to defend their own view beyond the usual trivial, sloganistic, sarcastic jibes.

It depends in large part on how one defines "debate" or being "good at it." If by that is meant that a person is able to be quick on his feet and offer both objections and answers; sure, many anti-Catholics are (especially the more educated ones). If, however, one means by being a good debater, being honest with the facts and honestly dealing with one's opponents best shots, most professional anti-Catholics are atrocious.

These are my opinions about the shortcomings of circus-like oral "debates" with anti-Catholic apologists, and the main rationale for why I don't engage in them. If someone thinks that written debate is not debate, then this book is not for them, since it will mostly consist of written debates and point-by-point critiques. But for those who agree with me that written, back-and-forth, substantive exchanges are worthy of the name "debate," this book will be a (hopefully helpful) close examination of the flawed theology of James White and his critiques of Catholicism.

In fact, despite his "oral debate only" rhetoric, Mr. White has written or contributed to at least two books that consisted of debates with others: *Debating Calvinism vs. Dave Hunt* (Multnomah: 2004), and *The Plurality of Elders in Perspectives on Church Government: Five Views of Church Polity* (Broadman-Holman: 2004). He's surely debated me, too.

I'm happy, as always, to present both sides and let the reader judge. This is the beauty of dialogue or even non-dialogical exchanges where at least one person defends a true position. The truth will always shine through if one is open to following it wherever it may lead. White's efforts at debunking Catholicism fail first and foremost because he is opposing what is *true*. "You can't make a silk purse out of a sow's ear."

The material will be presented chronologically, and Mr. White's words (excepting the first very long debate) will be italicized. If his position is so superior, it'll withstand all this close scrutiny, But if *not* . . .

TABLE OF CONTENTS

Chapter One

Is Catholicism Christian?
["postal" debate of March-May 1995]

Introduction: The following debate (uploaded long since on my website and later, blog, with the express permission of Mr. White -- e-mail letter of 2 February 2000), came about when I wrote a "snail-mail" form letter to several counter-cult researchers. It occurred almost a year before I went online.

I discovered his name and organization in *The 1993 Directory of Cult Research Organizations*, compiled by Eric Pement: who was the "cult expert" at Jesus People USA in Chicago (they put out the magazine *Cornerstone*, and I visited there in 1985), and Keith E. Tolbert: a cult researcher with whom I worked in the early 1980s. I specialized in the Jehovah's Witnesses. That was one of my first major apologetics efforts.

White responded twice and I replied twice. My final reply: a densely-argued tome of 36 single-spaced pages, was left completely unanswered, and remains so to this day. Eventually I received a short note informing me that he had no intention to ever do so.

It represents one of the most sustained, tightly-argued presentations of my contention that the anti-Catholic position is viciously self-defeating and can't *possibly* be held with logical consistency.

I have edited out White's personal attacks, where possible. I wasn't perfect, either, and got in a few shots of my own, that I later apologized for (just for the record: no such apologies ever came from Mr. White). The complete transcript (if anyone is interested in all the gory details) can be read on my blog, on the "Anti-Catholicism" web page: under White's name. I have the paper copies in my possession.

In this debate, because it is so lengthy, and not "back-and-forth" in the manner that most debates of this book will be, White's words will not be italicized.

* * * * *

23 March 1995

James White

Alpha & Omega Ministries

Dear Mr. White,

I am a cult researcher (#248 in *1993 Directory of Cult Research Organizations*, Tolbert & Pement) and Christian apologist, who converted to Catholicism in 1990 after ten years of committed evangelicalism (including five as a campus missionary).

I am disturbed by the tendency among cult researchers and other leaders in Protestantism to regard the Catholic Church as "apostate" and/or non-Christian, since it supposedly denies the gospel of Jesus Christ. This is not worthy of men of your stature and theological training, and is also uncharitable, since it is slanderous and schismatic.

I'd be interested in dialoguing with you or anyone you might know (with perhaps more time on their hands) who would be willing to do so, about this matter and any or all of the theological issues which sadly divide us (enclosed is a list of my tracts and a few samples).

I have been published in *The Catholic Answer* and *This Rock*, two of the leading Catholic apologetic journals, and will soon have a book out, *The Credibility of Catholicism* [later renamed, *A Biblical Defense of Catholicism*; at this point my much longer first draft was completed], . . . which is a defense of

Catholicism from Scripture, the early Church, and reason, as well as a very extensive critique and examination of the so-called "Reformation" (I prefer the objective term "Revolt").

Catholicism is not only Christian -- it is far superior to Protestantism on biblical, historical, and rational grounds. Secondly, I would say that a position maintaining that Protestantism is Christian while Catholicism is not, is self-defeating, incoherent, and intellectually dishonest, if thought through properly (which is rarely the case). I never had this outlook as a Protestant for these very reasons.

Among the many insuperable difficulties of anti-Catholicism:

1) The canon of the Bible was determined by the Catholic Church. Thus, *sola Scriptura* necessarily requires a tradition and Catholic (conciliar and papal) authority: not to mention the preservation of Bible manuscripts by monks.

2) At what moment did Catholicism become apostate? At John's death? In 313? With Gregory the Great and the ascendancy of papal power? In the "Dark Ages" of c.800-1100? With the Inquisition or Crusades? Or at the Council of Trent? And how can anyone know for sure when?

3) 23,000 denominations and the scandalous organizational anarchy, schism, and theological relativism inherent therein virtually disproves Protestantism in and of itself.

4) Protestantism has only been around for 477 years!

5) If the Inquisition disproves Catholicism, then the Witch Hunts and killings of Anabaptists, the suppression of the Peasants' Revolt, and early Protestantism's horrendous record of intolerance (at least as bad as Catholicism's by any criterion) disproves Protestantism as well.

6) Protestantism inconsistently and dishonestly appeals to indisputably Catholic Church fathers such as St. Auqustine (above all) St. John Chrysostom, St. Jerome, St. Ignatius, St. Irenaeus, St. Justin Martyr (also, later Catholics such as St. Francis, St. Thomas Aquinas, and Thomas a Kempis).

7) Likewise, it inconsistently appeals to Church councils which it likes (generally the first four) and ignores the rest, on questionable theological and ecclesiological grounds. Development of doctrine is accepted to an extent, and then incoherently rejected. This is largely what made me a Catholic, after reading Newman's *Development of Doctrine.*

8) Funny how an "apostate" Church has uniquely preserved traditional Christian morality such as the indissolubility of marriage, gender roles, the prohibition of contraception, euthanasia, infanticide, abortion, etc., while Protestantism is compromising these with frightening rapidity.

Sola fide is not the gospel. If so, then there wasn't a gospel to speak of for 1500-odd years, since *sola fide* was a radically novel and unbiblical interpretation of justification and sanctification. The God I serve is greater than that. His hands weren't tied until Dr. Luther figured everything out! Related to this is the slanderous assertion that Catholics are Pelagian or semi-Pelagian and believe in salvation by works.

Nothing could be further from the truth. We merely refuse to separate works from faith in a dichotomous relationship, as Luther did (which is why he wanted to throw out James -- so clear was its Catholic teaching). Catholicism condemned Pelagianism at the 2nd Council of Orange in 529 A. D., almost 1000 years before Luther. The very first Canon on Justification in the Council of Trent states:

If anyone saith that man may be justified before God by his own works, whether done through the teaching of human nature or that of the law, without the grace of God through Jesus Christ; let him be anathema.

This would seem to be sufficient to put the matter to rest. But blind prejudice and anti-Catholicism stubbornly persist.

Many other biblical proofs for Catholicism are in my apologetic works, if you're interested. Thanks for your time.

Sincerely, your brother and co-laborer in Christ,

Dave Armstrong

* * * * *

April 6, 1995

Dave Armstrong

Dear Mr. Armstrong:

I am in receipt of your letter of March 23rd, which, it seems, was sent to a number of ministries listed in the *Directory of Cult Research Organizations*. I quote what seems to be the thesis statement of your letter:

I am disturbed by the tendency among cult researchers and other leaders in Protestantism to regard the Catholic Church as "apostate" and/or non-Christian, since it supposedly denies the gospel of Jesus Christ. This is not worthy of men of your stature and theological training, and is also uncharitable, since it is slanderous and schismatic.

I am enclosing two books I have written on this subject. The thesis of the first, *The Fatal Flaw*, is seemingly, from your perspective, "uncharitable" and "slanderous and schismatic."

However, I stand by the thesis, and insist that truth is only uncharitable, slanderous and schismatic to those who have embraced a belief that is not in accordance with God's revelation. I'm sure the teachers in Galatia felt Paul was being most uncharitable in writing Galatians, but that did not stop him from doing so.

Personally, Dave, I find the Roman church's anathemas, contained in the dogmatic canons and decrees of the Council of Trent, as well as those of Vatican I, to be *most* uncharitable. What is worse, since they are in direct opposition to the truth, I find them to be most reprehensible as well, and much more accurately entitled "schismatic," since that term can only be meaningfully used with reference to a departure from *the truth*.

Before you dismiss my response as merely the ruminations of a fundamentalist "anti-Catholic," let me point out that I have studied the Roman position quite thoroughly. Indeed, I have engaged in seventeen public debates against Roman apologists such as Dr. Mitchell Pacwa, Dr. Robert Fastiggi, Gerry Matatics, and a friend of yours, Patrick Madrid (my copy of *Surprised by Truth* is even autographed!). I will be debating Robert Sungenis and Scott Butler at Boston College in a matter of weeks. I know the arguments of Catholic Answers [the organization] quite well, I assure you.

Your story in *Surprised by Truth* is almost predictable, Dave, no offense intended. Your rejection of Roman theology was not based upon a knowledge of *why*, and hence was ripe for refutation. You admit you rejected the tenets of the Reformation when you say, "I had always rejected Luther's notions of absolute predestination and the total depravity of mankind." And your involvement in Operation Rescue simply gave you the opportunity of seeing that Roman Catholics can be real nice folks who really believe in the teachings of the Church in Rome. And the feeling of "brotherhood" created by standing against a common evil, joined with the simple fact that you were not truly a Protestant to begin with, is reason enough to explain your swimming the Tiber.

You wrote in your letter,

Catholicism is not only Christian -- it is far superior to Protestantism on biblical, historical, and rational grounds. Secondly, I would say that a position maintaining that Protestantism is Christian while Catholicism is not, is self-defeating, incoherent, and intellectually dishonest, if thought through properly (which is rarely the case). I never had this outlook as a Protestant for these very reasons.

I'm sure you believe that the Roman position is superior on biblical grounds, but, of course, how could you believe otherwise? Rome claims final authority on biblical interpretation to begin with, so surely once you have accepted the claims made by Rome to ultimate religious authority, how could you believe anything other? Yet, I have to wonder about claiming biblical superiority when, in point of fact, entire dogmas, like the Immaculate Conception, Bodily Assumption of Mary, and Papal Infallibility lie, quite obviously, outside the realm of the Scriptures.

Oh yes, I know all the arguments ~ see my refutation of Patrick's attempt to come up with a biblical basis for the Immaculate Conception in our journal, *Pros Apologian* (I am enclosing a copy for you), and my debates with Dr. Fastiggi on Papal Infallibility and the Marian doctrines. What really strikes me as being "not worthy" of someone such as yourself, Dave, is stating that a system that could produce a document like *Indulgentiarum Doctrina* is in fact "biblically superior" to a system that could produce something like Hodge's *Commentary on Romans* or Edwards' sermons on the sovereignty of God.

As to being superior on "historical" grounds, I again have to beg to differ. I well know how easily Roman apologists cite patristic sources as if the early Fathers would have been subscribers to *This Rock*. However, I have found a woefully consistent practice of "anachronistic interpretation" in Roman apologetic works. I have found that normally the Roman apologist will find a phrase, say, having to do with Peter, and will read into that phrase the fully developed Roman concepts that, quite honestly, did not even exist at the time of the writing of that particular Father.

What is worse, many such apologists are dependent almost completely upon what I call "quote books." For example, when I debated Gerry Matatics for more than three hours on the patristic evidence regarding the Papacy in Denver during the Papal visit, he did not have any original source materials with him. Instead, he was utilizing compilations, such as Jurgens.

This often led him to grave errors. Indeed, one time he stood before the audience counting index entries in Jurgens and telling the audience that such-and-such number of early Fathers supported his position, and that on the basis of index entries in Jurgens! An amazing sight to behold, I assure you. Be that as it may, I believe it would be relatively easy to dispute such a broad statement as the one you made in your letter.

As to the use of the broad term "Christian" with reference to Roman Catholicism, such a term, due to its ambiguity in this situation, is less than useful. Faithful in preaching the apostolic message of the gospel? Certainly not, and that is the issue, Dave. If you feel a communion that replaces the grace of God with sacraments, mediators, and merit, can be properly called "Christian," then please go ahead and use the phrase. But please understand that if a person shares the perspective of the epistle to the churches of Galatia they will have to hold to a different understanding, and hence may not be as quick to use the term "Christian" of such a system.

You then listed a number of what you called "insuperable difficulties of anti-Catholicism." I would like to briefly comment on each one.

> 1) The canon of the Bible was determined by the Catholic Church. Thus, *sola Scriptura* necessarily requires a tradition and Catholic (conciliar and papal) authority: not to mention the preservation of Bible manuscripts by monks.

That is a common argument, but it is a sadly misinformed argument, Dave. The canon of the NT may have been recognized by the Christian Church (note I specifically limited that statement 1) to the NT, as the OT canon long pre-existed the Christian church, and 2) to the passive voice, "recognized" not "determined" as you used it), but that is a *long* stretch from the point you and your compatriots not only would *like* to make, but *must* make to establish your position.

First, the canon of the NT pre-existed either Hippo or Carthage, see Athanasius' 39th Festal Letter for just one example. Secondly, your entire argument falls apart when we ask if your theory holds true for the Old Testament. If the OT did not require conciliar and papal authority, why would the NT? And what is more, please note how easily, and yet without any basis, you insert the capitalized form of Tradition into your argument. Are you saying the canon is an apostolic tradition? If so, which apostle gave the canon? If not, are you not admitting that it was derived at a later time?

Roman apologists take all sorts of different positions on these topics, especially when it comes to the nature and extent of tradition. In light of your third point I think you might seek to do some "house-cleaning" before condemning Protestants for their variety of opinions. Oh, one other item: the Catholic Church of the fourth century was a far cry from the Roman Catholic Church of the 20th, wouldn't you agree? I mean, you constantly mentioned Newman's theories in your *Surprised by Truth* article, and it would seem to me that anyone who recognizes the necessity of embracing Newman's hypothesis recognizes the vast differences between primitive and modern beliefs on many important subjects.

> 2) At what moment did Catholicism becomes apostate? At John's death? In 313? With Gregory the Great and the ascendancy of papal power? In the "Dark Ages" of c.800-1 100? With the Inquisition or Crusades? Or at the Council of Trent? And how can anyone know for sure when?

What's even more important, *why does it matter?* It was obviously a process, just as the papacy developed, changed, and grew over time. Do we know for sure when the Pharisees became corrupt? Do we need to know? Of course not.

> 3) 23,000 denominations and the scandalous organizational anarchy, schism, and theological relativism inherent within virtually disproves Protestantism in and of itself.

Does the theological relativism in modern Roman Catholicism disprove it on the same grounds, Dave? Does the fact that you can get about as many opinions from Roman priests as you can get from Protestant ministers mean something to you? As you well know, the Watchtower Society makes a similar claim. Why is their claim invalid and yet yours is not?

> 4) Protestantism has only been around for 477 years!

And modern Romanism, replete with such theological novums as Papal Infallibility and the Bodily Assumption of Mary, has been around for less time than that, Dave. It really doesn't seem like your arguments are very consistent, does it?
In your fifth point you mention the Inquisition "disproving" Catholicism. The problem with your point is this, Dave: we Protestants don't claim infallibility. Rome does. There is a big difference. Please note the following comparison:

IV LATERAN COUNCIL

> Convicted heretics shall be handed over for due punishment to their secular superiors, or the latter's agents. . . . Catholics who assume the cross and devote themselves to the extermination of heretics shall enjoy the same indulgence and privilege as those who go to the Holy Land.

This freedom means that all men are to be immune from coercion on the part of individuals or of social groups of any human power, in such wise that in matters religious no one is to be forced to act in a manner contrary to his own beliefs.

Not only do we see the obvious conflict between these two "ecumenical" councils, but we see that the IVth Lateran Council specifically taught that those who would take up the cross in the effort to exterminate heretics would enjoy the same indulgence as those who went to the Holy Land. Now, Dave, surely you can see the vast difference between the silliness of, say, a "Protestant" like Benny Hinn teaching his ideas as facts, and an ecumenical council of the Roman Catholic Church teaching that indulgences would be given to those who took up the cause of *exterminating* the heretics (i.e., simple Christian folks who were slaughtered at the behest of the Roman hierarchy). What is more, is not the granting of indulgences based upon the exercise of the keys? Does this not then touch upon the very faith of the Roman church? I believe it does.

Your sixth point was little more than a statement that you feel Protestants "inconsistently and dishonestly appeal" to various of the early Fathers. Well, I feel that Roman Catholics "inconsistently and dishonestly appeal" to the very same Fathers. So? What do you do with citations such as the following?

Regarding the Papacy itself, and Matthew 16:18, Oscar Cullmann said:

He who proceeds without prejudice, on the basis of exegesis and only on this basis, cannot seriously conclude that Jesus here had in mind successors of Peter. . . . On exegetical grounds we must say that the passage does not contain a single word concerning successors of Peter . . . The intent of Jesus leaves us no possibility of understanding Matthew 16:17ff. in the sense of a succession determined by an episcopal see.

(*Peter, Disciple, Apostle, and Martyr* [Philadelphia: Westminster Press, 1953], 207, 236)

On page 162 of the same work Cullmann said: "We thus see that the exegesis that the Reformation gave . . . was not first invented for their struggle against the papacy; it rests upon an older patristic tradition."

Johann Joseph lgnaz von Dollinger, in his work *The Pope and the Council* (Boston: Roberts, 1869), 74, asserted:

Of all the Fathers who interpret these passages in the Gospels (Matt 16:18, John 21:17), not a single one applies them to the Roman bishops as Peter's successors. How many Fathers have busied themselves with these texts, yet not one of them whose commentaries we posses -- Origen, Chrysostom, Hilary, Augustine, Cyril, Theodoret, and those whose interpretations are collected in catenas -- has dropped the faintest hint that the primacy of Rome is the consequence of the commission and promise to Peter! Not one of them has explained the rock or foundation on which Christ would build His Church of the office given to Peter to be transmitted to his successors, but they understood by it either Christ Himself, or Peter's confession of faith in Christ; often both together. Or else they thought Peter was the foundation equally with all the other Apostles, the twelve being together the foundation-stones of the church (Apoc. xxi.1 4). The Fathers could the less recognize in the power of the keys, and the power of binding and loosing, any special prerogative or lordship of the Roman bishop, inasmuch a -- what is obvious to any one at first sight -- they did not regard the power first given to Peter, and afterwards conferred on all the Apostles, as any thing peculiar to him, or hereditary in the line of Roman bishops, and they held the symbol of the keys as meaning just the same as the figurative expression of binding and loosing.

Karlfried Froehlich wrote,

The earlier exegetical history of Matt. 16:18-19, Luke 22:32, and John 21:15-17 was largely out of step with the primatial interpretation of these passages. . . . The mainstream of exegesis followed an agenda set by patristic precedent, especially Augustine, but also other Western Fathers. . . . The understanding of these Petrine texts by biblical exegetes in the mainstream of the tradition was universally non\-primatial before Innocent III . . . . It was the innovative exegetical argumentation of this imposing pope which began to change the picture.

(*St. Peter, Papal Primacy and the Exegetical Tradition 1151-1350*). Found in Christopher Ryan, ed., *The Religious Role of the Papacy: Ideals and Realities 1150-1300* (Toronto: Pontifical Institute, 1989), 42, 4)

One truly wonders about blanket statements regarding *Protestant* misuse of patristic sources, Dave.

As to point number seven, I would direct you especially to my discussion of the "development of doctrine" in the enclosed book, *Answers to Catholic Claims*, pp.63-73. I would also like to ask if you have read Salmon's refutation of Newman in his work, *The Infallibility of the Church*?

Finally, do you really feel point number eight carries sufficient weight to establish anything?

You write that *sola fide* is not the gospel. Yet, it is the clear record of the NT that it *is* the gospel. Let's say you are right that there wasn't a gospel around for 1 500 some odd years for the sake of argument. Would this be sufficient reason for you to reject the NT witness to that gospel, Dave? You are, of course, not right to say that there was no gospel for those 1500 years. Even if you were to ignore Wycliffe and Hus, and all those murdered by Rome in the intervening centuries, what do you do with Clement of Rome?

They all therefore were glorified and magnified, not through themselves or their own works or the righteous doing which they wrought, but through His will. And so we, having been called through His will in Christ Jesus, are not justified through ourselves or through our own wisdom or understanding or piety or works which we wrought in holiness of heart, but through faith, whereby the Almighty God justified all men that have been from the beginning; to whom be the glory for ever and ever. Amen (Clement of Rome, 32)

You then repeated some well-worn slogans regarding Luther along with the first canon of the Council of Trent on justification, and concluded, "This would seem to be sufficient to put the matter to rest. But blind prejudice and anti-Catholicism stubbornly persist." The problem, Dave, is that you need to also quote canons 4, 5, 9, 12, 14, 1 5, 1 7, 24, 30, 32, and 33. I quote just a few of these:

Canon 24: If anyone says that the justice received is not preserved and also not increased before God through good works, but that those works are merely the fruits and signs of justification obtained, but not the cause of its increase, let him be anathema.

Canon 32: If anyone says that the good works of the one justified are in such manner the gifts of God that they are not also the good merits of him justified; or that the one justified by the good works that he performs by the grace of God and the merit of Jesus Christ, whose living member he is, does not truly merit an increase of grace, eternal life, and in case he dies in grace, the attainment of eternal life itself and also an increase of glory, let him be anathema.

Canon 33: If anyone says that the Catholic doctrine of justification as set forth by the holy council in the present decree, derogates in some respect from the glory of God or the merits of our Lord Jesus Christ, and does not rather illustrate the truth of our faith and no less the glory of God and of Christ Jesus, let him be anathema.

This kind of teaching has led Roman Catholic theologians to conclude:

> Man, for his part, in order to arrive at full sanctification, must cooperate with the grace of the Holy Spirit through faith, hope, love of God and neighbor, and prayer; but he must also perform other "works." It is a universally accepted dogma of the Catholic Church that man, in union with the grace of the Holy Spirit must merit heaven by his good works. These works are meritorious only when they are performed in the *state of grace* and with a *good intention.*
>
> (Matthias Premm, *Dogmatic Theology for the Laity*, p.262)
>
> We have shown that according to the Holy Scripture the Christian can actually merit heaven for himself by his good works. But we must realize that these works have to be performed in the *state of grace* and with a *good intention.* (*Ibid.*, p.263).

Again we find that having an allegedly "infallible guide" does not result in unanimity of opinion. The point that you seem to have missed as a "Protestant," Dave, and now miss as a Roman Catholic, is that the Reformation was never about the *necessity* of grace. Did you ever read such monumental works as Calvin's *Institutio* when you were a Protestant, or as you were seeking "answers" to the claims of Rome? If you had, you would know that no one has ever said that Rome teaches that grace is *unnecessary.* That is not the issue. The issue, Dave, is the *sufficiency* of God's grace apart from man's works. That, my friend, is the issue that you *still* have to face (see pp. 36-37 of *The Fatal Flaw*).

29

Just today my seventh book came out, *The King James Only Controversy*. I will be quite busy for some time due to the release of the book. However, I may be making an East Coast swing to do some debates with KJV Only advocates, and I am always willing to engage Roman apologists as well. Would you be willing to defend the statements you made in your letter in public debate, Dave? Your letterhead included the phrase "Catholic Apologist" (I note in a font very reminiscent of that used by Catholic Answers). If that is the case, might you be interested in engaging in some very practical apologetics? I would be happy to debate *sola scriptura*, the Papacy, justification by faith, the Marian doctrines, etc. Shall we discuss the possibility?

I am sending this letter to you along with the noted materials in the US Mail. However, I am also going to fax it to you so that you will receive it quickly. I am also sending a copy to Eric Pement, should anyone contact him regarding your mailing to the individuals in the cult directory. In fact, I would be more than happy to make this letter available to anyone who wishes to see a brief response to the claims you made in your letter.

I have added your name to our mailing list. Our next *Pros Apologian* will be a full-length rebuttal of Patrick Madrid's article, *The White Man's Burden*, replete with a defense of the doctrine of *sola scriptura*. That edition has already been written, and is simply in the proof-reading stage.

I am sure, Dave, that you are quite happy right now in the bosom of Rome. There is a wonderful feeling, I'm sure, that accompanies being told with infallible certainty what to believe. But I simply hope, Dave, as I hope for those who have embraced the same kind of authoritarian claims from the Prophet in Salt Lake City or the Governing Body in Brooklyn, that you will realize that your decision to embrace that allegedly infallible authority was in and of itself not infallible. You might well be wrong. Think about that my friend.

Justified by faith and hence at peace,

James White

Recte Ambulamus ad Veritatem Evangelii

* * * * *

22 April 1995

James White

Dear James,

I hope this letter finds you well. Thank you very much for your extensive reply (dated April 6, 1995) to my letter – the most in-depth response I've yet received from a Protestant after more than four years as a Catholic (not for lack of trying, believe me). Let me commend you on one of the many areas of agreement which we do indeed share -- your work with regard to the King James Only crowd. Gail Riplinger is a true nut. I'm happy that you've taken on this serious error. Keep it up! Would that all of your "crusades" were so worthwhile and useful for the Body of Christ.

I agree with your first point about "uncharitability" and "schismatic" words and actions. Truth is often seen as uncharitable. We feel similarly about each other's outlook. I claim your views possess this trait precisely because I believe them to be untrue. You return the favor. If indeed I'm a Christian, then your words about my beliefs violate several clear biblical injunctions, such as, "Thou shalt not bear false witness."

Thus we are inexorably brought back to square one: What is a Christian?, Is *sola fide* the gospel?, Is *sola Scriptura* the eleventh commandment ("Thou shalt have no authority except Scripture")?, Is sacramentalism idolatrous and Pelagian?, etc. One major distinction, however, should be duly noted. We Catholics -- notwithstanding harsh Trent language -- still officially regard Protestants as our "brothers in Christ," whereas

31

so many of you regard us as non-Christians. Thus, the issue of charity would seem to favor us, at least at first glance.

Thank you for your three books and newsletter. I always (sincerely) appreciate free reading materials. . . . I'll read your stuff provided you're willing to interact with my refutations. I can confidently defend all of my works and always welcome any critiques of them.

I'll admit that you're by far the most intelligent of the anti-Catholics, . . . At least you seek to achieve some modicum of objectivity by citing legitimate sources, to your great (almost unique) credit. How you misinterpret and misunderstand and argue against these sources constitute your own logical "fatal flaw." James Akin, in his critique of your book ("Fatally Flawed Thinking," *This Rock*, July 1993, pp.7-13) points out several of the book's many egregious errors, even in the basic *understanding* of Catholic positions (see, e.g., p. 13).

Let *me* point out that I too have studied the Wittenberg and Genevan and Amsterdam and Tulsa and Downers Grove and Grand Rapids position(s) quite thoroughly; and have lived (some of) them wholeheartedly for ten years, half of which as an intensely-committed evangelist willing to endure great hardships and misunderstanding for the sake of Christ and His call on my life. So we're even there, too. Again, I think I get the edge since I've actually **been** on both sides of the fence, whereas you haven't (this isn't to say that one cannot know a position from the outside - e.g., my Jehovah's Witness research). . . .

You get the edge on debates. I've sought in vain to engage Protestants in both conversation and by letter, but no one has yet shown the willingness to continue after reading any of my in-depth critiques of Protestantism. Perhaps you'll be the first. I would have *relished* just this opportunity when I was Protestant, so I'm truly perplexed at the weak knees of evangelicals. My perspective is constructively ecumenical, not destructively adversarial. Evangelicals are fairly decent at published self-criticism, but apparently not very willing to face biblical, historical and reasoned critiques from across the Tiber. This is most unfortunate and curious.

I know the arguments of anti-Catholicism quite well, I assure you (also those of ecumenical Protestant apologists). Your arguments in *Fatal Flaw* and your letter are almost predictable, no offense intended. Let me respond to the latter, if I may. You claim I didn't have an adequate knowledge of "Roman" theology, hence I was open prey for clever, devious papists who easily reeled me in by means of Babylonish guile, because I had indeed already "rejected the tenets of the Reformation" and was "not truly a Protestant to begin with." . . .

First of all, your information as to the state of my knowledge of Catholicism prior to my conversion is far too inadequate to justify your wild speculations, based as they are on a twelve-page conversion story (the shortest in the book). What do you know about the extent of my studies, or how well-read I am, or who I've talked to? Next to nothing. I know it's necessary for you to come up with wishful and baseless theories, since it's unthinkable for you to accept the possibility of a thoughtful and genuine conversion to Catholicism based on Scripture, Church history and reason.

But this doesn't make said theories hold any water if they lack the appropriate facts and analysis. Your "reasoning" here is exactly analogous to that of outright atheists who "explain" away Protestant conversions, ignoring the sincere self-reports of people who have undergone "born-again salvation" (they think *God* a crutch, rather than *infallibility*). Having personally experienced both types of conversions, I need not denigrate either one by means of foolish speculation. I merely reinterpret the first theologically. You could do that, too, but instead you resort to unfounded, condescending scenarios of my alleged ignorant gullibility.

Secondly, you denigrate my being impressed with Catholics in Operation Rescue. Now, how is this any different from the observance of committed "born again" Protestants, talked about all the time in the "testimonies" of evangelical circles as a means of "getting people saved," of "being a good witness," "walking the walk," "letting your light shine," being "epistles read of men," etc.? There *is* no difference. It's silly for you to criticize this element in my odyssey when it is so much a part of your own evangelistic, conversionist theology and ethos, as you are surely aware.

As I stated in my book, I had never seen such commitment among Catholics. It is to be expected in order for one to believe in any way of life which claims to transform human beings. But this was only one fairly minor factor. The primary initial reasons for my change were the moral bankruptcy of Protestantism (e.g., contraception and divorce), its anti-historical essence (as shown in Newman's *Development*), and the absurdity and unbiblical nature of Luther's many novel fancies (gleaned from reading his own words).

The only possible way in which I could formerly be described as some sort of "Catholic" would be my longstanding beliefs in (like Wesley) progressive sanctification, and (like the best Protestant scholars such as Geisler, Colson, Lewis, and Pelikan) strong advocacy of both history and reason, elements largely frowned upon by Protestantism. But clearly you don't accept my story at face value.

Instead, like a true ideologue in the worst sense of that term, you grasp for straws in order to bolster your *interpretation* of what you would like to *believe* about my supposed journey from semi-Pelagianism to Pelagianism, rather than from dim to bright light, as I see it, or from skeletal, "mere" Bible Christianity to full-bodied, historical, incarnational Christianity grounded in tradition and a real Church, not merely subjective whims and fancies, abstractions, and countless arrogant counter-charges and self-proclaimed "authorities."

Thirdly, it's news to me that belief in supralapsarian double predestination and total depravity (man is a worm on a dunghill) constitutes the quintessence of true Protestantism and hence, Christianity. This opens up a gargantuan can of worms both theologically and logically.

Akin pointed out how (as I suspected) your five-point Calvinism leads you to exclude from the Body anyone denying even limited atonement alone (p.8). Then, he recounts (p.9, note 12) how you tried to weasel your way out of the unavoidable implications of your own position by denying this. Which is it? Was I a Protestant or not, since I most certainly denounced "such things as the Mass, purgatory, and indulgences," which you told James Akin were necessary for Christianhood?

I was in very good company as a Protestant: Melanchthon (whom Luther hailed as the greatest theologian that ever lived, and his *Loci* as second only to the Bible) rejected Luther's denial of free will as early as 1527 in his *Commentary on Colossians*, and did not include this falsehood in the *Augsburg Confession* (1530), the authoritative Lutheran document approved by Dr. Luther himself. Strange, then, if he wasn't a Christian. John Wesley is thought by most Christians to be among their number -- at least as eligible as you, if I do say so. Likewise, . . . C. S. Lewis, and Dietrich Bonhoeffer, and Newman, Chesterton, Knox and Richard John Neuhaus before their conversions. I believe all of these men were Arminian.

Whole denominations, such as Methodists, Lutherans, the majority of Anglicans, Free Will Baptists, most pentecostals and many non-denominationalists are also out of the fold, by your definition. Even Keith Tolbert, a major cult researcher and now sole author of the *Directory*, is an Arminian (Assembly of God). So I guess he isn't a Christian either, and is in danger of becoming a papist (which prospect would be quite surprising to him, I'm sure!). Why, then, don't you write books about all *these* erring non-Christians too, since people will go to hell, according to you, by following their Pelagian doctrines just as us poor papists will? What's good for the goose . . .

Spare me. No reputable pastor or evangelist openly presents Five-Point Calvinism as the gospel. Billy Graham (whom I greatly respect) tells me I merely need to give my life over to Christ to be saved. It's ridiculous enough to present *sola fide* as the gospel (as Sproul, MacArthur and Ankerberg do), let alone TULIP, which excludes the great majority of Christians at all times through history. . . .

This is absolutely blasphemous and one of the most abominable lies from the pit of hell ever devised [double predestination and supralapsarianism]. That's why I always rejected it, but this had no bearing on my former firm belief in *sola Scriptura* and *sola fide*. Those are the two true (albeit weak) pillars of Protestantism, as illustrated in the very rallying-cries of

Luther and other "Reformers." Who ever cried "Predestination to hell alone for the reprobate"?! I've always held that Calvinism was *consistent*, but unscriptural . . .

Because of the dreadful, ghastly teachings of Calvinism [i.e., certain elements of it, noted above], men could not suffer it for long, so that, typically, error in turn bred even worse error. We see this clearly in the history of New England, where the Puritans evolved into Unitarians by 1800. Host of the founders of the cults, such as Russell, Eddy, Joseph Smith, and Wierwille, started out as Calvinists and found the teachings so revolting that they went to the other extreme and embraced Pelagianism and rejected the Trinity. Both the Lutherans and (most) Anglicans came to their senses and rejected Calvinism early on.

But another insuperable difficulty remains with this intolerable position of yours. Who are *you* to say whether I am a Christian or not? You're just one little old cult researcher with a pulpit, a para-church ministry and a Master's from Fuller -- hardly in the same league with the many stalwart figures mentioned above. Are you a Magisterium of one? Are you your own pope (which, I argue, is pretty much true for every individual Protestant)? Why should I trust your word on this (and my eternal destiny) rather than that of Wesley, or C. S. Lewis, or the "great" Melanchthon, or a host of others, not to mention Augustine, Irenaeus, Athanasius, Ignatius, Aquinas and the massive structure of the Catholic Church, the fathers, Christian tradition, the councils, etc.?

Thus you subtly set *yourself* up, for all intents and purposes, as the sort of Infallible Guide you chide me for embracing ("there is a wonderful feeling, I'm sure, that accompanies being told with infallible certainty what to believe"). Your whole enterprise presents a quite humorous (but tragi-comic) episode in self-delusion and blindness to the absurdity of one's own position. Can't you see it? Your argument collapses on your own head (but since it is a house of cards in the first place, I guess it won't hurt too much!).

You say, "You might well be wrong." Of course! What else is new? But . . . I'd much sooner place my trust in Catholicism (in terms of *human* authority – not meant to exclude

Christ!) in all its glory than in the foul-mouthed, emotionally-unstable and contradictory Luther and the calculating, self-righteous and ruthless Calvin, both of whose teachings are full of holes theologically, lacking precedent historically, and gravely deficient morally.

Everyone trusts in *someone* or *something*, whether it's tradition or Protestant "Reformation mythology" ("Luther lit a candle in the darkness...") or Billy Graham or an infallible Bible (but which *interpretation*?) or Pastor Doe down the street or J. Vernon McGee, or whatever I feel the "Spirit" is telling me up in my attic, surrounded by the infallible, "perspicuous," and trustworthy guidance of the Bible and James White books, which refute all others. The Protestant position is self-defeating, indeed full of "organizational anarchy, schism, and theological relativism," as I write in my letter. Who could fail to see that? You yourself admit in your book that most evangelicals have gone astray (as if this is something unexpected!).

You make a silly remark about "how could you believe otherwise?" about the superiority of Catholic biblical support since I am not permitted to doubt this as a Catholic. The reply is simple. If I'm *shown* otherwise, then most certainly I will renounce Catholicism, just as I left evangelicalism for higher things. You assume I am shackled like a prisoner in a "Roman" dungeon for all eternity. But we believe in free will -- you are the ones who deny that. You act like I accept the proposition that Catholicism is more biblical only because I am taught this from Mother Church, and not on the basis of actually considering the merits of each side.

In a sense this is true because the Catholic is not arrogant enough to assume that he is the arbiter and final judge of all truth given him from any source (see my arguments above about the inevitability of trusting something outside oneself). We submit to a tradition which includes all the great Christian minds who have reflected upon that deposit of faith, received from Jesus and the apostles and developed as a result of battle with heretics for nearly 2000 years. I am very proud to do this, and not in the least ashamed.

I did accept the authority of the Church *initially* because of clear superiority over the absurdity and historical implausibility of the Protestant a-historical, Docetic-like, "mystical" conception of the Church and its tradition, and desperate reliance on *sola Scriptura*: an unbiblical, man-made, self-defeating, arbitrary tradition. But once I thoroughly familiarized myself with all the apologetic literature and biblical arguments for the Catholic distinctives I could find (in the four-year course of writing my book), I became absolutely convinced that Catholicism is the most biblical position, as I stated in my letter.

I guess you'll just have to read some of my book (with your consent, you might start with the *sola fide* and *sola Scriptura* chapters), to understand why I believe as I do, and feel fully justified intellectually and biblically in placing my trust in the Church for doctrines I may not yet totally understand as well as those which I do grasp (see Newman's *Grammar of Assent* for the full treatment of Catholic intellectuality). My challenge to you is to *refute* my arguments therein and elsewhere.

Ever since I studied Socrates (from whom I derive my preferred method of discourse) in college in 1977 I have consistently sought to strongly believe in ideas, based on evidence, unless and until I am shown otherwise -- and I am always willing to change my mind in such cases, as I have done on numerous occasions throughout my life (which is one reason I am a Catholic, pro-life, politically conservative, and against divorce and contraception -- all views which I used to oppose). In this aspect I haven't changed a whit since "poping." How can you blame me for remaining Catholic when no Protestant has shown a willingness for over four years to show me how my apologetic arguments fail?

Where is the concern for my soul from these people, if indeed I'm on a terrible hellbound path, as many of them think (or at least drastically wrong on many points, if not "unsaved")? I'd be glad to encounter and confront any of these opposing views in continuing dialogue, . . . It looks like you might be that person. I'll have to wait for your response to see if this is the case. So, I am open-minded in every sense of the word. Are you willing to convert to Catholicism if shown that it is superior to Protestantism? If not, then it is you who have profoundly "blind faith" (or, stubborn pride), not me. As the saying goes, "a man convinced against his will, retains his original belief still."

As for recourse to the fathers, there can be no doubt that Protestants (like *their* fathers Luther and Calvin) are selectively dishonest -- no question whatsoever. I myself engaged in this same tactic when fighting for Protestantism in 1990. I tried to squeeze the fathers into my own mold, for my own polemical purposes. This was devious, but it is done all the time by evangelicals, particularly in espousing St. Augustine as one of their own, which is patently ridiculous.

Although what you describe as "anachronistic interpretation" among Catholic apologists happens, I'm sure, at times (all people being biased), usually the Protestant misunderstands the concept of *development*, in which any given doctrine is not required to be in place in its fullness in the first, second, or sometimes third and even fourth centuries.

Rather than trading horror stories of "patristic abuse," I would prefer to actually pick a topic and see what the fathers indeed taught. I've compiled this evidence in all my theological chapters in my book, so I'm already prepared for such a debate. How about the Eucharist, or the authority of bishops, for starters? I stand by Newman's statement, "to be deep in history is to cease to be a Protestant." In this sense I was predestined to become a Catholic, as I have always loved history (including Church history). As soon as I studied the fathers, it was all over.

Your letter goes from bad to worse at the bottom of p.2. Now "sacraments . . . replace the grace of God"!!! How preposterous! . . . You are again on the slippery slope of excluding almost all Christians who disagree with you from Christianity. Even your hero and mentor Calvin (*Inst.*, IV, 14, 1) defines a "sacrament" as, "a testimony of divine grace toward us," and cites St. Augustine in agreement: "a visible form of an invisible grace," which is, of course, the standard Catholic definition, known to any Catholic child with any catechetic instruction whatever. Luther, of course agrees. Even in his *Babylonian Captivity*, a critique of Catholic sacramentalism, he still upholds the Catholic view for baptism and the Eucharist, and in this case is much closer to my view than yours.

He regards baptism as a regenerative sacrament, in opposition to your typical Baptist anti-sacramental opinions:

> [Infant] Baptism is a washing away of sins . . . the sacrament of baptism, even with respect to its sign, is not a matter of the moment, but something permanent . . . We must therefore beware of those who have reduced the power of baptism to such small and slender dimensions . . .

> (*Three Treatises*, Fortress, Philadelphia, pp. 191-2).

For Luther, baptism not only does not "replace the grace of God," it *imparts* it sacramentally in a most real and profound way, even to an infant, and "washes away sins," as Catholics, Anglicans, Lutherans, Methodists and Presbyterians (the last two in a somewhat lesser, symbolic, but still sacramental sense) believe. Again, why don't you write books condemning all these folks (including your two primary founders) for "adding to the completed work of Christ on the Cross," etc.?

Luther, of course, believed in the Real Presence as well (and even -- egads - *adoration* of the Host -- see, e.g., *Table Talk*, ed. Hazlitt, no. 363, p. 207). Thus, according to you, Luther must be both a "works-salvationist" and an idolater (even Calvin called him "half-papist" for this very reason), not to mention his belief in the Immaculate Conception and other "unbiblical" Marian doctrines (see my enclosed article).

One of Luther's two favorite works (along with, appropriately, *Bondage of the Will*) was his seminal *Commentary on Galatians*. Yet you would now have me to believe that the correct perspective on this book, contrary to Luther's, excludes the use of sacraments! Your theological landscape is indeed a strange one, full of mysterious and unexpected detours and astonishingly contradictory backwaters.

Do you mention these beliefs of Luther when you extoll him in *Fatal Flaw*, chapter 1, and leave the impression that he was opposed to the "Roman system" *in toto*? Of course not, because such straightforward honesty would be fatal to your case and would fail to rouse the anti-Catholic "ignorant armies of the night" (Luther is misused just as much as the fathers are). This is "anachronistic interpretation" par excellence, and it happens all the time.

For precisely this reason I was really shocked to learn about Luther's errors and considerable shortcomings as well as his many agreements with Catholicism. I had swallowed the myth, spoon-fed from Protestant legatees who in turn have taken in the fairy-tales with their mother's milk for 474 years (the Diet of Worms remains that to this day!). The truth is always more interesting, and particularly so in Luther's case.

Your treatment of the canon of Scripture misses the point, which is that the Catholic Church, and "extrabiblical authority" was necessary for you guys to even have your Bible, let alone construct with tortured "logic" myths such as "perspicuity" and *sola Scriptura* from this book which you would never even *have* but for the Catholic Church, which, inexplicably, preserved it even though it supposedly destroys that same Church's belief system -- evident to any "plowboy." . . .

It's the oldest rhetorical trick in the book to simply dismiss an important question as irrelevant, when one can't answer it, as you did with my query as to when Catholicism became apostate. You say, "do we need to know? Of course not." Of course every anti-Catholic *does* need to know, in order for his "Church history," to the extent that he has any at all, to have any shred of plausibility. There must have been a Church all those years when all "true believers" waited with baited breath for Messiah-Luther to be born in Eisleben (no less improbable than Nazareth for such a momentous figure, I guess).

You have no case, pure and simple, since all the Catholic distinctives appeared early, at least in kernel form, as far as records reveal to us (already strikingly so in St. Ignatius and St. Clement). Anti-Catholics are so desperate for a quasi-history, that, e.g., Dave Hunt is ready to embrace the Catholic and Albigensians as brothers before he would ever think of accepting me!

Ken Samples writes in a recent *Christian Research Journal* (Spring 1993, p. 37) that if Catholicism is a cult,

> . . . then there was no authentic Christian church during most of the medieval period. Contrary to what some Protestants think, there was no independent, nondenominational, Bible-believing church on the corner (or in the caves) during most of the Middle Ages. Additionally, the schismatic groups who were around at the time were grossly heretical. So much for the gates of hell not prevailing against the church (Matt. 16:18).

I couldn't agree more. For you to blithely ignore this massive crack in the facade of your anti-Catholicism (it's no problem for ecumenical Protestants, as I once was) with, in effect, a smirk and wave of the hand is, at best, quixotic, and at worst, intellectually dishonest. The burden of proof for this remains with you, and so my challenge still awaits a reply, rather than an evasive dismissal.

Likewise, you scoff at my disdain for the indefensible existence of 23,000 denominations [later, I questioned this number and usually phrase it as "many hundreds"]. You don't dare admit that this is a valid point against Protestantism (perhaps your "fatal flaw") because you would obviously then be in big trouble. Yet it certainly *is* without question (e.g., Jn 17:20-23, Rom 16:17, 1 Cor 1:10-13, Gal 5:19-21 and many other passages). Thus you are bound by the outrageous and scandalous situation of Protestant sectarianism, in clear opposition to Scripture. About all Protestants can do here is mutter incoherently about agreement on "central issues," which falsehood I deal with in my refutation of Geisler's defense of *sola Scriptura* (also enclosed), or else they can take the path of citing the existence of liberals within Catholicism.

This won't do either, for the simple reason that we have dogmas and councils and papal encyclicals and infallible utterances which constitute our teaching -- definite, observable, and documented for all to see, even the most wild-eyed liberals such as Kung and Curran and McBrien. It doesn't matter a hill of beans what these people *say* they or the Catholic Church believe. . . . I despised liberal Protestantism when I was among your number and I have even more contempt for Catholic liberalism, as it has far less excuse. Your side, of course, has neither any authority nor a sensible, workable method for determining truth in doctrine. In rare instances where someone is disciplined, they just go to another sect or start a new one (e.g., Swaggart).

In Catholicism, on the other hand, a liberal like Kung can be (and was) authoritatively declared as no longer a Catholic theologian, and not to be trusted for correct doctrine. By the nature of the beast you guys can't do that. Hence my apt description of "anarchism" and "relativism." This is why your analogy is like comparing apples and oranges. It simply won't wash.

As for the Watchtower, it denies both the Bible and consistent Christian Tradition and many beliefs which even you and I share, such as the Trinity, bodily resurrection of Christ, the omnipresence and omniscience of God the Father and the fact that He is a Spirit (they think He has a body), etc. [White later questioned that they claimed God the Father had a body, and I documented it]. Obviously, there is no comparison. This is why their claim is invalid, along with their paltry 115-year existence, which is only 359 years less than the existence of your [sect] -- both being grossly inadequate in terms of passing on the true apostolic tradition (without Catholicism).

Since you brought up the cultic comparison, I will also note that both cults and Protestantism are man-centered, whereas Catholicism is Christ-centered. Even your names betray this: Lutherans, Calvinists, Wesleyans, whereas ours simply means "universal." Where our sub-groups bear the name of individuals (Franciscans, Thomists, Benedictines, etc.) this is clearly understood as a branch of the larger tree, not as mutually-exclusive (in important aspects) systems, as in Protestantism. Luther and Zwingli and their ilk start new [sects]. St. Francis and St. Ignatius Loyola merely start *orders*, always in obedience to the Catholic Church.

Your remark about the supposed recent origin of "modern Romanism" is yet another instance of the incomprehensibility of development to the Protestant dichotomizing, "either-or" mind (which Luther had already perfected to a tee). It's pointless to respond to it other than to refer you to my various tracts about development or to Newman's essential work on the subject.

You gleefully note the divergent views of Lateran IV and Vatican II on religious tolerance. Yes, there has been a change of opinion here, but unfortunately for you, the teachings involved are not religious *dogmas* of the faith, but rather, disciplinary measures. I detest as much as you corruptions in the Inquisition, the indefensible sacking of Constantinople in 1204, etc., indeed all persecution. This argument was my main one against Catholicism when I was still fighting against it.

The Church has learned from its errors, as have the Protestant sects, which have an even worse history of intolerance and persecution, since your crimes are greater and more inconsistent with your supposed "freedom of conscience" for all to follow God in whatever way is deemed best by the "individual with his Bible alone" . . . If all Christian groups who have persecuted are ruled out of the faith, then about all that is left are the Quakers, Mennonites, and Amish, and whoever else descended from the Anabaptists.

You may count yourself among these, but your theological fathers are still Luther and Calvin, who are horribly stained with the blood of dissenters. Your *founders* were guilty of abominable crimes, whereas no one in Catholicism (even popes) have a place as high and lofty as these Protestant Super-Popes, who dictated infallible revelations which had to be believed under pain of death (yes, literally).

So, as almost always, what you think is a knockout punch to your detested "Romanism" rebounds back to you with much more force, for the reasons just recounted. What I call the "reverse Inquisition" argument stands accepted Protestant mythology on this topic on its head and shocks the daylight out of evangelicals who are invariably ignorant of the history of their own group (which is par for the course). The documentation for my contentions is so compelling as to be denied only by someone with his head in the sand. The "out" here is to simply deny that one is a "Protestant." "I'm not one of *them*," you often hear; "I'm a *Bible* Christian." But this will not do, as it is intellectually-dishonest to a nauseating degree in its a-historical delusion, which is a trademark of classic Protestantism. You love to claim you're "one" when it comes to denominationalism, but not when it comes to the skeletons in your closet.

As for your lengthy attempted refutation of papal claims and their biblical justification, I refer you to my chapter on the papacy and infallibility, which runs 98 pages, single-spaced. Again, you ignore the factor of *development*, which is nowhere more apparent and necessary than in the understanding of the evolution of the papacy. Your three long quotes, which you obviously thought were so unanswerable, have little or no force against my position.

You blithely dismiss my points 7 and 8 with your by-now familiar hit-and-run tactic of glib avoidance when you have no answer. Your section in your *Answers* book on development has little to do with the specific question I raised -- the inconsistent appeal to councils. Funny, too, how I managed to find and read both Salmon and Dollinger's books when I was vigorously fighting infallibility in 1990.

Now how could this be if I wasn't a Protestant and was already some sort of proto-Catholic mutation, according to your theory? Somehow I found the very books that you are enamored with. If you had communicated with me then, I think you would have found me quite a kindred (Protestant) spirit, with Salmon and good old Dollinger under each arm (Dollinger, by the way remained doctrinally Catholic in every sense except in accepting papal infallibility and in submitting to the Magisterium), even though I never denied that Catholicism was Christian.

For, in the anti-Catholic mentality, every co-belligerent against the great Beast and Whore is accepted as a brother almost without question (witness Dave Hunt and the Albigensians), much like your "feeling of 'brotherhood' created by standing against a common evil," which you posited as a reason for my conversion.

Salmon consistently misinterprets development to mean "evolution" in the sense of the *essential change* of doctrines, which of course it is *not*. He states,

> The old theory was that the teaching of the Church had never varied (p.33).

I got news for Salmon and you -- it still *is* the teaching, i.e., the essence never changes, but the subjective understanding and binding authority can. Development was clearly taught at least as far back as St. Augustine and St. Vincent of Lerins. In the latter's work, the concept is found in the same context as his famous statement (which Salmon loves to cite): "everywhere and always the same," thus proving that the two concepts are harmonious and *complementary* -- another difficult concept for the Protestant to grasp -- not *contradictory*, as Salmon seeks to prove, with great rhetorical flourish and straw-man triumphalism.

He doesn't, however (much like you), actually deal with Newman's brilliant *analogical* arguments, which comprise the heart of his classic work, since they are unanswerable from the Protestant perspective. I was honest enough (and granted enough light and grace) to accept this, and it was a crucial component in my conversion, as you correctly note. Salmon, on the other hand, is content to quixotically repeat over and over something which isn't even relevant, in a mere *appearance* of strength.

One brother of a friend of mine . . . also made much of Salmon and early on waxed eloquently about his debating ability. When I gave him my *sola Scriptura* paper and informed him that I had not only read but would also devour Salmon for lunch, he promptly vanished, never to be heard from again, presumably crushed because his champion was not unanswerable. Oh well, such is life for a lonely Catholic apologist. I also tried for four long years to "recruit" Protestants into my ecumenical discussion group, but failed. Apparently the prospect of being refuted by Catholics, who aren't supposed to know anything of the Bible or the Christian life, is horrifying. But if we're so wrong, where was the evangelistic zeal to save our souls?

You pass off my point number 8 with a 14-word sentence. Yet it is absolutely crucial. How, indeed, could such an anti-Christian system be so dead-right about morality -- far better than any particular Protestant sect and immeasurably superior to Protestantism as a whole, which is profoundly compromised, especially on sexual, marital and gender issues. The very fact that you don't regard this as of any "weight" merely confirms in my mind the Protestant tendency of unconcern for holiness and morality (also clearly observed in Luther's life and teachings - e.g., the bigamy of Philip of Hesse), one of the primary reasons for my abandoning it. Here again you are radically a-historical and anti-incarnational. I suppose your reason would be that my statement is not immediately scriptural, therefore, of no import for "Bible alone" followers. Or, as I suspect, because you don't know how to answer it. One or the other.

I'm delighted that you cite St. Clement of Rome on justification, as if he was a "faith alone" adherent. Nothing he says here is against Catholic teaching whatsoever, as proven by Trent's Canon I on Justification, which I cited, and the decrees of Second Orange. I included this very passage in my book when I dealt with justification. But I went on to quote from the next two sections as well, where St. Clement talks about good works ("the good worker receives the bread of his labor confidently" - 34, 1). Later, in 58, 2 he states that the ones who have "kept without regret the *ordinances and commandments* given by God" will be "enrolled and included among the number of those who are saved through Jesus Christ." So this is what I "do" with St. Clement, whose letter is just as easily interpreted as in harmony with Catholic teaching as Protestant (I think more so).

He merely reiterates the ("works-salvation"?) teachings of Jesus (Mt 5:20, 7:16-27, 25:31-46, Lk 18:18-25), which Protestants so downplay when they talk about justification, bypassing the Lord and immediately rushing to St. Paul, who is made out to be a proto-Luther figure. But St. Paul, like St. James' "epistle of straw," also stresses the organic connection between faith and works in our salvation, as in Catholicism (Rom 2:5-13, 1 Cor 3:8-9, Gal 5:6, 6:7-9, Eph 2:8-10, Phil 2:12-13, 3:10-14, 1 Thess 1:3, 11, 1 Tim 6:18-19). Evangelicals, in their propensity for selective presentation of verses and neglect of context, conveniently ignore all these passages when talking about justification.

Your Canons 24, 32 and 33 from Trent and others, and comments about the "sufficiency of God's grace apart from man's works" prove nothing. These canons are in harmony with the one I quoted and others in that same vein. When will you Protestants stop making your false dichotomies when there is no necessity to do so? This is so irritating because it's almost impossible to convince you that you are constantly doing it. You can believe in all your "solas" and contradictions if you so desire. But please understand that our view does not operate on those principles. So in Trent's canons on justification, faith and works, God's preceding grace and man's cooperating action are not seen as contradictory, as you believe.

You act like merely adding up numbers of decrees with which you disagree, over against mine, with which you may agree, somehow proves that the Church is Pelagian (which it has always condemned) rather than Christian. This is not reasonable. It isn't even your methodology with Scripture. Neither the Virgin Birth nor original sin are mentioned very often there, yet they are firmly believed by all evangelicals. Why? Because they are true, and *harmonize* with the rest of Scripture. Likewise with the Immaculate Conception, yet you rail against it by virtue of its implicit presence in Scripture.

In order to overcome the "dichotomous tendency of Protestant thought," I highly recommend Louis Bouyer's *The Spirit and Forms of Protestantism*, which also has an excellent treatment of the absolute preeminence of God's preceding and enabling grace in Catholic soteriology, over against your misguided assertions here.

Since you brought up the Fathers, how about St. Ignatius, writing about 14 years after St. Clement:

> May none of you be found a deserter [so much for Calvinism] . . . Let your works be as your deposited withholdings, so that you may receive the back-pay which has accrued to you. (*Letter to Polycarp*, 6,2)

Gee, I used to think that Catholics only learned to talk like that in the corrupt era of Tetzel and Eck, with all the drivel about the "treasury of merits" and all, so irrefutably demolished in Luther's *Feces*. If Clement and Ignatius were heretics and Arminians, then the Church was already off the rails within a generation of John's death! How quickly do things collapse! What a shame! And this is how the Protestant attempt to co-opt the Fathers always ends up -- an entirely futile and fruitless endeavor.

You also mention Wycliffe and Hus as purveyors of the "gospel," certainly the favorite "proto-Protestants" of the Middle Ages, second and third only to St. Augustine in this regard, who is Luther and Calvin's favorite "Protestant." As usual, there seems to be little effort to actually study the opinions of these fellow "anti-Catholics." They are seized upon because of their rebellious beliefs.

Indeed Wycliffe comes about as close as you will get, but according to the learned Protestant historian Latourette in his *A History of Christianity*, vol. 1, (p.664), Wycliffe believed in a type of Real Presence (remanence) in the Eucharist (his view was similar to Luther's), seven sacraments (although he denied the *necessity* of confirmation), and purgatory. These views are more than enough to exclude him from "Christianity" and the "gospel," as defined by you, but no matter -- you inconsistently cite him anyway because his legend is a revered Protestant tradition -- all anti-Catholics must be canonized and venerated as saints in Protestantism.

You might say, "heck, nine out of ten correct beliefs ain't bad," but this misses the point. If even your best examples of "Protestants" in the B. L. so-called "dark ages" era of history ("Before Luther") fail to meet the "gospel" criterion, then what becomes of your overall case for non-Catholic Christian continuity for 1500 years? I don't think you're ready to espouse Eastern Orthodoxy as the answer to your dilemma! Your a-historical view clearly fails miserably, for extreme lack of evidence, which comes as no surprise to anyone acquainted with this period of Church history.

Hus, too -- generally regarded as less radical than Wycliffe -- believed in sacramental baptism and transubstantiation, and held, according to Protestant Roland Bainton (*Christendom*, vol. 1, p. 239) that "the sacraments at the hands of the unworthy are nevertheless valid and efficacious" (Catholicism's *ex opere operato*), so he's outside "orthodoxy" as defined by . . . you. You keep cutting off the limb you're sitting on by your extreme judgments as to who is and isn't a Christian, making many of your own positions utterly contradictory, if not downright nonsensical.

Why would you send your reply to my letter to Eric Pement? Don't you think that my arguments can easily be overcome by your cult research comrades? Why would they need your reply if my arguments are often so insubstantial as to merit one or two-sentence "refutations," as you believe? I take this as a (probably unintended) compliment -- thank you. In fact, it may help my cause, since if they mention your "rebuttal," I could then send them this (otherwise I wouldn't have).

Finally, I am delighted and (I think) honored that you are eager and "happy" to debate me in public. I love debate, but much prefer informal, conversational Socratic dialogue or written point-counterpoint exchanges to the mutual monologues and often antagonistic and disrespectful affairs which pass for "public debates." I am not particularly skilled as an orator and lecturer, nor do I have the requisite desire to participate in that type of forum. That said, I would not want to publicly represent the Church to which I give my allegiance, but would rather defer to someone with more abilities for formal debate than I possess, so that we are best represented.

I am pleased to report, however, that my friend Gary Michuta, another apologist who started our group called "Thy Faith," which puts out a magazine called *Hands On Apologetics* (similar to *This Rock*), immediately and enthusiastically accepted this challenge when I inquired about it yesterday. His phone number and fax are the same as my fax number: [deleted], and he can be reached at the following address: [deleted]. He eagerly awaits your reply.

I must, regretfully, inform you of another reason for my declining: the widespread intellectual dishonesty, evasiveness, and uncharitability of anti-Catholic debaters. Akin in his article on your book starts out by recalling how you have refused to shake hands with your Catholic opponents, or even pray the Lord's Prayer with them. This is contemptible, petty behavior. Madrid's article "The White Man's Burden" concurs, by citing your rude treatment of him and of Dr. Art Sippo, whom apparently you no longer wish to debate, having been "beaten," according to Pat's account, anyway. Like Dave Hunt, who recently "debated" Karl Keating in my area and evaded in cowardly and embarrassing fashion the topic ("Was the Early Church Catholic") all night (not even quoting a single Church father, to my recollection!), you refused, by and large, to attempt to prove *sola Scriptura* from the Bible, which was *your* topic of debate.

I find these incidents intellectually offensive and insulting to the debate opponent, the audience, and a decent sense of "fair play." Likewise, even in video presentations such as James McCarthy's *Catholicism: Crisis of Faith*, dishonest and unethical tactics were used (see Keating's article in *This Rock*, May 1993, pp. 8-17), particularly with regard to the reprehensible treatment of Fr. Richard Chilson. I also heard Keith Fournier recount on the radio very poor treatment he received at the hands of disingenuous anti-Catholics, who more or less preyed upon his good will and trapped him by inviting him to a talk which turned into a "debate" and inquisition against him (I can't remember who these people were, but my point is still valid). . . .

Lest you think I'm trying to evade you, however, I am perfectly willing, able, ready, and eager to engage you in debate on any topic you so desire either by letter or in your newsletter (if the latter, I would require prior editorial consent, due to the unscrupulous tactics recounted above). I would demand equal space in your newsletter, so that the fair inquirer could make up his own mind. You've observed my debating abilities in this letter and other writings I've given you, so I think you'll agree that timidity and fear are not my reasons for declining public oratorical debate.

Your newsletter is just as "public," and probably reaches even more people than a one-night debate would. Your next reply is crucial and will likely set the tone for the future course of your dealings with me. I hope that (at long last) you are the Protestant who will dare to actually confront my arguments, especially my numerous critiques of Protestantism. If you aren't, I will start thinking that such a person does not exist. So, I eagerly anticipate your reply, and (I hope) request for whatever of my papers you would most like to debate. I've much enjoyed writing this.

Yours, sincerely, in Christ & His Church,

Dave Armstrong

* * * * *

May 4, 1995

Dave Armstrong

Dear Mr. Armstrong:

Over the years I have attempted to establish "standards" to guide me in how I should invest my very limited time. Working, as I do, with Mormons, JWs, and now Roman Catholics and even KJV Only folks, I have to attempt to be balanced. It is not an easy task. Normally, I will admit, your letter's tone would be sufficient for it to be dismissed. I have learned to recognize sophistry when I see it, and as I grow and mature, I have learned to ignore such argumentation as falling under Paul's prohibition of 1 Timothy 2:23.

The number of simple misrepresentations, and gross caricatures, of my letter to you and the position I espouse was enough to do almost irreparable damage to your credibility and keep me from investing any of my limited time in responding to you. However, it almost seemed to me that you were hoping that would be the result of your arrogant letter, so I guess part of my reply to you is based upon a desire to deny you that very accomplishment.

Allow me to take a moment to concentrate, in one paragraph, just some of the kind, helpful, truly "Socratic" comments you included in your letter: [quotes many of my more provocative words, divorced from their context] . . .

Do you find the use of bluster and bombast helpful, Mr. Armstrong? Does it aid your case? Or is it a cover for an inability to honestly face the issues? You lamented the unwillingness of "Protestants" to correspond wth you. Seemingly you have decided that this is because you are so great, so intelligent, so well-informed and so well-read that there is none who can even begin to respond to your arguments. Might I suggest to you, Mr. Armstrong, that it *might* be because some of us have standards with reference to the behavior of those with whom we correspond? I will not debate Vinney "85% of those who hear me think I'm a lunatic" Lewis, either, and there's a reason for that: he is not worthy of being noticed on that level. [Years later, White practically begged Dr. Art Sippo: whom he insults below, to debate him again]

Seemingly you have taken at least some of your cues from Mr. Lewis, though, of course, you seem to disagree with him (and these days, Gerry Matatics) on the issue of the "separated brethren." Anyway, if you wish to get people to engage in extended conversation, Dave, try not insulting them and misrepresenting them in every other paragraph.

I mentioned above the many misrepresentations in your letter. Let me enumerate some of them for you. First, you wasted a large number of key-strokes beginning at the top of page 4. First, it didn't seem to occur to you to consider the possibility that James Akin and Patrick Madrid are fallible folks with an agenda. I have fully responded to James Akin's article (and to Patrick's blast as well), and pointed out the errors he made with reference to both my position and my actions in the past (more on that later). You are in error, as he was in error, to say that I exclude people from the kingdom on the basis of their acceptance or rejection of limited atonement.

Such is a caricature, and is unworthy of anyone who wishes to be taken seriously as an apologist. It is a misrepresentation, and if you continue to use it, you only convict yourself of dishonesty. Then you make the incredible leap (hoping no one notices the shift in terminology, perhaps?) from the term "Protestant" to the term "Christian" for the rest of this page, and on the basis of this dishonest shifting of terms, attack me on all sorts of issues, none of which are even worthy of response. This kind of argument is a mere wasting of time and effort, Mr. Armstrong. Those who have something meaningful to say don't waste their time on such things.

The exact same kind of silliness is to be found on page 7, where you write in the best style of Gail Riplinger, "Your letter goes from bad to worse at the bottom of p. 2. Now 'sacraments... replace the grace of God'!!! How preposterous! . . ." And I might add, "What dishonesty on your part!" Did you think I don't keep copies of my letters, Mr. Armstrong? I've gotten used to finding out what Mrs. Riplinger deletes with those ellipses, so did you think I would not look at what I originally wrote to see why you had to edit my words? . . .

That you chose to misrepresent my own letters not only indicates to me that you might have a difficulty defending the concept of mediation and merit in Roman theology (the two elements you conveniently deleted), but it again indicates to me that if you will dishonestly use my own words, what might you be willing to do with Irenaeus or Tertullian? Personally, Dave, I feel you not only owe me an apology for such behavior, but you have some serious work to do to restore your credibility as an honest apologist and researcher.

Finally, I mentioned the arrogance that marked your letter. I will note examples as I provide responses to your points, but one sentence that stuck in my mind came toward the end of your letter, from page 12:

> One brother of a friend of mine . . . also made much of Salmon and early on waxed eloquently about his debating ability. When I gave him my *sola Scriptura* paper and informed him that I had not only read but would also

devour Salmon for lunch, he promptly vanished, never to be heard from again, presumably crushed because his champion was not unanswerable. Oh well, such is life for a lonely Catholic apologist. I also tried for four long years to "recruit" Protestants into my ecumenical discussion group, but failed. Apparently the prospect of being refuted by Catholics, who aren't supposed to know anything of the Bible or the Christian life, is horrifying.

You are kidding, right? I mean, the above paragraph simply *drips* with an arrogance that I've seen displayed publicly by the likes of Vinney Lewis and Art Sippo, and in writing by folks like Patrick Madrid [yet White later debated him *again*, despite his dripping "arrogance"]. I have to keep reminding myself that you are the same person who has declined my challenge to publicly debate. If you would "devour Salmon for lunch," Mr. Armstrong, wouldn't that make me a mere before-dinner snack, given my obvious inferiority to Salmon as a scholar? Sort of makes your protestations about not being an orator rather empty, don't you think?

Well, having spent nearly three pages on materials that should not have even been included in a letter such as yours, I turn to responding to the actual assertions made therein. You noted that, "If indeed I'm a Christian, then your words about my beliefs violate several clear biblical injunctions, such as, 'Thou shalt not bear false witness.' " No, that would only be true if what I said about Roman theology was in fact untrue, and you did not even begin to demonstrate that *anything* I said was inaccurate on that account.

Next you noted, "We Catholics - notwithstanding harsh Trent language - still officially regard Protestants as our 'brothers in Christ,' whereas so many of you regard us as non-Christians." Yes, I'm sure the Council of Constance considered Jan Hus a "brother in Christ" as they burned him at the stake, Dave. And I'm sure the Waldensians of the Piedmont Valley were quite comforted by the fact that they were being raped and slaughtered by "brothers in Christ." . . . You can ignore such contradictions if you like, Dave, but that won't make them go away.

. . . May I respectfully suggest you remove the term "apologist" from your letterhead, then, for it is simply not possible for a person to be a serious apologist who would harbor such an attitude. I have spent literally thousands of dollars on books that attacked my faith -- I have a very respectable Roman Catholic library, a huge LDS library, shelves of Watchtower publications, books from Prometheus, even the Soncino Talmud! How in the world are you to defend your faith if you do not take the time to invest in acquiring the works of those who would refute you? You noted reading Salmon. How did you do that, if by not obtaining the book? If you borrow from a library, you are limited to how much use you can make of the book. I'm sorry, but such an attitude is very strange coming from one who claims to be an apologist.

. . . I'm a Protestant apologist, not an anti-Catholic. When you start calling yourself an anti-Protestant, I'll allow you to get away with calling me an anti-Catholic. . . .

You noted, "Again, I think I get the edge since I've actually been on both sides of the fence, whereas you haven't." Why do you find this to be an advantage, Mr. Armstrong? Gerry Matatics has often made much of the same concept, yet, I have to wonder why someone would think that way. Obviously, from my perspective, you are, to use the proper term, an apostate. To make one's apostasy a badge of honor, and to say that this gives you an "edge," bewilders me. Scripture says a double-minded man is unstable in all his ways, and we are warned about those who are blown about by every wind of doctrine. . . . I just have to point out that such instability is not an edge, but a distinct disadvantage, wouldn't you say?

You referenced your book a number of times in your letter, even using it as reference source and saying things like, "See my chapters on such and such." . . . How, may I ask, can I make reference to a book that is yet to be published and is not available to me? [obviously, I would have sent him copies of those portions if he were interested . . .]

In regards to your use of the phrase, "constructively ecumenical," what do you mean? One Roman apologist (who asked to be "off the record") confided to me just recently that "ecumenical dialogue is a joke. The only reason we are talking to you is to bring you back to Rome, nothing else." I think he has a good basis in history for such a statement, don't you?

. . . am I to conclude, Dave, that I should not take what Roman apologists say at face value? I mean, you did write the article in *Surprised by Truth*, right? And if you did, could you be so kind as to show me where in that article you give the slightest evidence of being familiar with, say, Calvin's discussions on *sola scriptura* or *sola fide*? You mentioned such biggies as Charles Colson and Hal Lindsey, but where did you give me even the slightest indication that you were, in fact, fully aware of *why* Roman theology was to be rejected? Where did you tell us that you had read, say, the Canons and Decrees of the Council of Trent, or maybe Hardon's works? If it is in your article, Dave, I must have missed it. Could you cite the page numbers to me that would give me any reason to retract what I said above? I'd appreciate it.

You asked me, "What do you know about the extent of my studies, or how well-read I am, or who I've talked to? Next to nothing." Indeed. Do forgive me for taking your own conversion story as being reflective of your actual experience. I'll try to remember not to take such writings at face value in the future. They must be meant only to lead people to consider Roman Catholicism, not to tell the truth about your background or experience. [some years later, after White kept claiming how ignorant I was of Protestant theology, I produced a lengthy list of what I had read as a Protestant. Without missing a beat, White switched from saying I was unread and ignorant, to being knowingly deceptive]

As to the idea that a person would convert to Rome based upon Scripture, Church history and reason, such a conversion will take place only when a person makes the final epistemological leap in submitting to (I might say "succumbing to") the absolute claims of Rome. Once that decision is made, the rest falls into place naturally enough. And since you gave me no reason to believe that you had ever encountered the claims of Rome in any meaningful way prior to your conversion, I can only repeat what I said before: you were ripe for conversion. I guess I should modify that a little: the Watchtower makes the same kind of final epistemological claim upon its adherents, so you had encountered it, just not dressed in the liturgy and history of Rome.

. . . I, too, was involved for a while with Operation Rescue. I left the movement because of the issue of Romanism and the implicit statement that I had to overlook fundamental differences on the gospel itself "for the good of the movement." Maybe, just maybe, it is you, Dave, who jumped to "condescending scenarios"?

. . . Next you wrote, "Thirdly, it's news to me that belief in supralapsarian double predestination and total depravity (man is a worm on a dunghill) constitutes the quintessence of true Protestantism and hence, Christianity." Of course, what I had said was that since you rejected predestination and total depravity, you were not a true Protestant (speaking in the historical sense -- *you* connected Luther with the beliefs, as you will recall), and I stand by the statement. Surely you recall Luther's admission to Erasmus that he, above all of Luther's other foes, had focused upon the *real* issue, that being the concept of "free will" versus the bondage of the will, and that, of course, brings up both predestination and total depravity. Luther was not systematic enough to get into debates about supralapsarianism or infralapsarianism -- such is not the issue.

If you always denied that man's will is bound to sin and that God has predestined a people unto himself, you may have been attending a Protestant church and may have been in the majority of what is *called* Protestantism today, but the fact remains that as to the Reformation and the heritage thereof, you were a traitor, more at home in Rome's semi-Pelagianism than in Paul's Augustinianism (to create a wonderfully anachronistic phrase that speaks volumes).

Not that you were alone: the majority of "Protestantism" today is treading water in the Tiber on that issue. Of course, I said all of that (possibly not with the same colorful terminology) in *The Fatal Flaw*. And as I mentioned, you are simply wrong to say I exclude those who reject limited atonement from the Christian faith.

Just a quick note: "Spare me. No reputable pastor or evangelist openly presents Five-Point Calvinism as the gospel." You *are* kidding, right? Well, given the twisted, contorted, Jack Chickian-Gail Riplingeresque view of the Reformed position you present in this very paragraph (page 4, at the bottom), maybe you aren't. I shouldn't expect you to know the historical realities of people like Jonathan Edwards, or Charles Haddon Spurgeon, or Whitefield, but you even mentioned Sproul, who, of course, is Reformed. You probably didn't read much of Gerstner as a "Protestant," nor would I expect you to know such names as Albert Martin. Well, anyway, I'll have to tell my pastor that you believe he is not reputable. I'm certain he will be most disappointed. :-) . . .

`I get the distinct feeling, Dave, that you don't like the Reformed gospel. No surprise, given your love for Roman theology. Those who have never realized their own helplessness often hate the gospel, I've discovered. I've seen similar paragraphs from other Roman Catholics, from atheists, from Mormons, and even from some "Protestants," too. I have to really focus my attention just to realize that the authors of such diatribes are actually referring to the gospel of grace, so plainly presented by Paul in Ephesians 1 and Romans 8 through 9: it's hard to recognize that, given how twisted is the torturous presentation. Of course, if I were to present Roman theology in such terminology (without a single reference to a single Roman source) I would be dismissed as a raving "anti-Catholic." But, I've rarely found Roman apologists to be consistent in their arguments, so I shouldn't be surprised that you would use such a double standard here, either.

Again, as a historian, I find your comments about Puritanism "evolving" into Unitarianism quite humorous (you *did* mean that to be a joke, right?). As a student of Jonathan Edwards I must say I would be one of the few folks who would get such a joke. I can tell this is a joke because of your statement that Joseph Smith began as a "Calvinist." Again, your research couldn't be *that* bad, so I must take this as a joke, too, though a not overly amusing one.

You then noted, "You're just one little old cult researcher with a pulpit, a para-church ministry and a Master's degree from Fuller - hardly in the same league with the many stalwart figures mentioned above." I have no idea *which* stalwart figures you might be referring to, but it makes no difference. A few corrections: I'm not really that old, and I don't have a pulpit. Other than that, yup, you are very much on the money. Just one little fellow out here enjoying God's blessings and being used by Him to help people see through false claims, whether those claims come from Salt Lake City, Brooklyn, Gail Riplinger, or yes, Rome itself. Of course, you, too, are just one little fellow, a novice convert to Romanism, eyes bright with the zeal of a convert, but far too young in your journey with Rome to even begin to have the whole story. I simply have to say, "So?"

Now, you managed, sadly, to miss the point of nearly every objection I raised (and, I note in passing, you skipped entire sections of my letter in your response, too). . . . you missed the weight of my objection. . . . how do you know you are in company with, say, Athanasius or Ignatius or Irenaeus? In the final analysis, is it not because Rome *tells you so*?

Oh, I know, I read the rest of your letter (even your vented hatred of Luther and Calvin) -- I know you claim to be able to analyze Rome's claims, yet, you also admitted that, "in a sense" I am right in stating that you cannot really question Rome's pronouncements. As you said, "In a sense it is true because the Catholic is not arrogant enough to assume that he is the arbiter and final judge of all truth given him from any source." Does that mean, Dave, that you are not responsible before God for what you believe? That once you sign over the title-deed to your mind to someone else (teaching magisterium, Prophet, Governing Body, whatever) you can no longer be held responsible for the truth? I wonder why the Pharisees didn't point that out to the Lord when He held them *directly responsible* for God's revelation to *them*?

Well, we can't question Rome, of course, for Rome has all authority. Instead, we must repeat what we've been taught, sort of like our mantra: "We submit to a Tradition [make sure to capitalize this term.] which includes all the great Christian minds who have reflected upon that Deposit of Faith, [not only capitalize these terms, but make sure to ignore all those Fathers who directly contradicted Roman dogmas and teachings], received from Jesus and the Apostles [but never engage in public debate to defend **that** statement!] and developed as a result of battle with heretics for nearly 2000 years [but don't bother to tell anyone why the term Roman Catholic, aside from being an oxymoron (how can something be limited-Roman-and 'universal'?), is not something that the early Fathers ever thought of using to describe themselves]." Then say that you are very proud to repeat this statement of faith. I hope you are not *too* offended if I say, Dave, that I see *precious little difference* between that kind of statement and the "testimonies" of the Mormon missionaries who speak with such enthusiasm and honesty about their trust in Joseph Smith and the living Prophet and the Book of Mormon.

I'm glad you realize that your decision to embrace Roman authority is a fallible one. That means that every time you assert Roman infallibility you will be honest and say, "I *think* Rome is infallible, but I'm not really certain of that." Most Roman apologists don't come right out and say things like that. They seem to want their audience to think that you really *can* have absolute and infallible certainty about Roman authority.

. . . Patrick Madrid, the editor of *Surprised by Truth*, even called me upon hearing my debate against Gerry Matatics on that very subject and said, "For the first time I have to admit that a Protestant clearly defeated a Roman Catholic in a debate on *sola scriptura*." Of course, I would not be the first person to suggest that you trust Patrick's opinions -- his errors in *The White Man's Burden* fill more than 20 pages of small-print, triple-column text.

Be that as it may, I again have to note that your high words sound, well, a bit "tinny," in light of your unwillingness to defend those statements in public debate. It is easy to hide behind a word-processor, Dave. You can always blow smoke in written debates -- of course, you can do the same in formal debates, too, but without as much ease, that's for certain. . . . you end your letter by referring me to someone I've never heard of before to defend your position. [that was apologist Gary Michuta, whom

White mocked as an insignificant nobody, simply because he was unfamiliar with his name. Oddly enough, he wound up debating him in May 2004 regarding the deuterocanonical books]. . . . I have no idea which of the various Roman Catholic views of "tradition" you espouse. Matatics [an ultra-radical reactionary by this time and shortly after, a sedevacantist heretic] takes one view, Madrid another. There are all sorts of different takes on the topic. You seem really enamored with Newman, so is that your view? How am I supposed to know?

You asserted that Protestant use of the Fathers is "selectively dishonest -- no question whatsoever." I do hope you don't mind my being very Protestant and questioning your pontification (pun fully intended). How about some examples, drawn, logically, from my own writings, my own debates? Surely you have listened to these debates, right? You said that you had engaged in this activity yourself in 1990. How so? Where did you do this? Did you put any of this in writing? You said evangelicals do this all the time. Such as? Who? I don't know too many evangelicals who bother to cite patristic sources to begin with, do you? Might I suggest that if you'd like to impress this upon me, you might wish to paint with a little finer brush? I've heard these arguments before, as I think you'd admit.

You said that usually the Protestant misunderstands the concept of development. Well, before Newman came up with it, I guess we had good reason, wouldn't you say? But, does that mean that those Roman Catholics I know who don't like Newman are actually Protestants, too? I'm kidding of course, but those who hang their case on Newman and the development hypothesis are liable for all sorts of problems, your eating of Salmon for lunch notwithstanding.

Might it actually be that the Protestant fully understands development but *rightly rejects it*? I addressed development and Newman in my book (written before I engaged in all the debates I've done since then), and personally, I don't think your brief dismissal was, well, worthwhile. And as for Newman's statement, "to be deep in history is to cease to be a Protestant," I would say, "to be deep in Newman is to cease to be an historically consistent Roman Catholic." I can only shake my head as I look at

Newman's collapse on papal infallibility and chuckle at his "deep in history" comment. He knew better.

. . . Next we read, "It's the oldest rhetorical trick in the book to simply dismiss an important question as irrelevant, when one can't answer it, as you did with my query as to when Catholicism became apostate." No, the oldest rhetorical trick in the book is to ignore the central parts of your opponent's arguments while accusing him of doing the same thing (that's the important part). Your question *remains* irrelevant. First, it is an improper question, since it is based upon the identification of *Roman* Catholicism with the earlier Catholic Church, and, as anyone knows, that is an improper identification. Secondly, it assumes something that is not true: that apostasy always takes place in a single act or definition of doctrine, and such is not always the case. Personally, I believe that there were believers within what even called itself Roman Catholicism for a long time -- in fact (are you sitting down?), there still are, by God's grace. So again, your question was irrelevant, and my brief response was based upon a recognition of that irrelevance.

Next you commented, "Likewise, you scoff at my disdain for the indefensible existence of 23,000 denominations. You don't dare admit that this is a valid point against Protestantism because you would obviously then be in big trouble." Do you really think, Dave, that I have not encountered this argument before? I mean, do you think that you are the only Roman apologist brilliant enough to come up with the ol', "Well, look at all the disagreements among Protestants, that proves *sola scriptura* doesn't work!" argument? You truly do flatter yourself. But to show you that you are not the first on the block with your arguments (and that your arguments are not particularly compelling), I provide you with the text of a post from *America Online* written in response to James Akin and his use of the very same argument: . . .

On one point I certainly agree with Mr. Akin: Catholic apologists often *do* use this argument. But is it a valid argument? Let's examine it.

First, and very briefly, it seems to me to be an inconsistent argument: that is, it refutes the position of the one using it. It presupposes the idea that if (in the case of Protestantism) the Scriptures are meant to be the sole infallible rule of faith for the Church, then it must follow that the Scriptures will produce an external, visible unity of doctrine on all fronts. As Patrick Madrid put it, Presbyterians and Baptists would not be in disagreement about infant baptism *if* the Bible were able to function as the sole rule of faith for the Church. I say this is an inconsistent argument because the solution offered to us by Rome – namely, the teaching Magisterium of the Roman Church, replete with oral tradition and papal infallibility – has not brought about the desired unity amongst Roman Catholics.

I have personally spoken with and corresponded with Roman Catholics -- individuals actively involved in their parishes, regular attendees at Mass, etc., who have held to a *wide* range of beliefs on a *wide* range of topics. One need only read the pages of *This Rock* magazine to know that you have conflicts with traditionalists over every conceivable topic, from the Latin Mass to modernism in Rome. I've been witness to debates between Catholics on canon laws and excommunications and Father Feeney and other items that rival any debates I've seen amongst Protestants. And I haven't even gotten to the liberals in the Roman fold! Obviously I don't need to do that, as the point is made. If *sola Scriptura* is disproven by the resultant disagreements amongst people outside of Rome, then Roman claims regarding the Magisterium are equally disproven by the very same argument.

But my main reason for addressing the common argument made by Roman apologists is that it reveals something important about Rome's view of man himself. Dr. Cornelius Van Til often commented on the errors of Rome regarding their view of man, and how these errors impacted every aspect of their theology, and he was quite right. We see an illustration right here. Rome's semi-Pelagianism (I am talking to a Roman Catholic right now in another venue who makes Pelagius look like a raving Calvinist) leads her to overlook what seems to me to be a very fundamental issue.

Let me give you an illustration: Let's say James Akin writes the *perfect* textbook on logic. It is completely perspicuous:

it is fully illustrated, completely consistent, and it provides answers to all the tough questions in plain, understandable terminology. It covers all the bases. Now, would it follow, then, that every person who consulted this textbook would agree with every other person who consulted this textbook on matters of logic?

Well, of course not. Some folks might just read one chapter, and not the rest. Others might read too quickly. and not really listen to Mr. Akin's fine explanations. Others might have read other less-well-written textbooks, and they might import their understandings into Mr. Akin's words, resulting in misunderstandings. Most often, people might just lack the mental capacity to follow all the arguments, no matter how well they are expressed, and end up clueless about the entire subject, despite having read the entire work.

Now the question I have to ask is this: is there something wrong with Mr. Akin's textbook if it does not produce complete unanimity on questions logical? Is the problem in the *textbook* or in the people *using* the textbook? In the real world it is often a combination of both: a lack of clarity on the part of the textbook and a problem in understanding on the part of the reader. But if the perfect textbook existed, would it result in absolute unanimity of opinion? No, because any textbook must be read, interpreted, and understood.

Let's say the Bible *is* perspicuous, in the sense that Westminster said, that is, that "those things which are necessary to be known, believed and observed for salvation. are so clearly propounded and opened in some place of Scripture or other, that not only the learned, but the unlearned, in a due use of ordinary means, may attain to a sufficient understanding of them." Does it follow, then, that there must be a unanimity of opinion on, say, infant baptism? Does the above even say that there will be a unanimity of opinion on the very items that "are necessary to be known, believed and observed for salvation"? No, obviously, it does not. And why? Because people -- sinful people, people with agendas, people who want to find something in the Bible that isn't really there – people approach Scripture, and no matter how perfect Scripture is, people remain people.

Now, Roman apologists may well way, "See, you've proven our point. You need an infallible interpreter to tell you what the Bible says because you are a sinful person, and hence you need a sinless, perfect guide to tell you what to believe!" Aside from the fact that such a concept itself is absent from Scripture, and is in fact countermanded by Scripture (did not the Lord Jesus hold men accountable for what *God* said to *them* in *Scripture*?), we need to observe that Rome is not solving the problem of fallible people. Once Rome "speaks" the fallible person must still interpret the supposed infallible interpretation. The element of error remains, no matter how much Rome might wish to think it has been removed. Indeed, beyond the problem of interpreting the infallible interpreter, you still have the fallible decision of following *Rome's* absolute authority rather than, say, Brooklyn's, or Salt Lake's, or Mecca 's, or whoever's -- That remains a *fallible* decision, and hence the longing for that "infallible fuzzy" that comes from turning your responsibilities over to an "infallible guide" remains as unfulfilled as ever.

Finally, the argument put forth (plainly seen in the arguments used by Karl Keating in *Catholicism and Fundamentalism*) is even more pernicious, in that it attacks the sufficiency of Scripture itself. We are seemingly told that the Holy Spirit did such a poor job in producing Scripture that while the Psalmist thought it was a lamp to his feet and a light to his path, he (the Psalmist) was in fact quite deluded, and was treading very dangerously. Instead of the glorious words of God spoken of in Psalm 119, we are told that such basic truths as the nature of God, including the deity of Christ or the personality of the Holy Spirit, *cannot* be derived solely from Scripture, but require external witnesses.

And why are we told this? Well, it is alleged that arguments can be made *against* these doctrines on the basis of Scripture passages. Of course, one could argue against *anything* if one is willing to sacrifice context, language, consistency, etc. But are we really to believe the Bible is so self-contradictory and unclear that we cannot arrive at the truth through a whole-hearted effort at honestly examining the biblical evidence? That seems to be what those across the Tiber are trying to tell us. But it is obvious that just because the Scriptures can be *misused* it does not follow that they are *insufficient* to lead one to the truth. Such is a flawed argument (no matter how often it is repeated). The *real* reason Rome tells us the Bible is insufficient is so that we can be convinced to abandon the God-given standard of Scripture while embracing Rome's ultimate authority.

I never saw a response from Mr. Akin to that post, either, but I could have missed it, too. I'd be interested in a *meaningful* (i.e., not bombastic, not filled with line after line of meaningless epithets) response from you to this post. You wrote,

> This won't do either, for the simple reason that we have dogmas and councils and papal encyclicals and infallible utterances which constitute our teaching - definite, observable, and documented for all to see, even the most wild-eyed liberals such as Kung and Curran and McBrien. It doesn't matter a hill of beans what these people say they or the Catholic Church believe.

Well, that's quite interesting. Yes, you have dogmas -- you have to pick and choose what you will *call* dogmas (like, killing heretics to receive indulgences isn't a dogma, though indulgences themselves *are*), but you have dogmas. You have councils, too -- you have to pick and choose what of the earliest councils you will and will not accept (Canon 6 of Nicea, Canon 28 of Constantinople, for example), and even what councils were "good" and which ones weren't (you don't want Sirmium or Ariminum, for example), but you have councils.

The fact that councils were called seems to cause you a problem, and the fact that they were obviously not considered infallible, even by those who attended, also causes a problem, and of course the fact that no one thought the bishop of Rome had to call councils, confirm councils, or even have an active role in councils for the first few hundred years is yet another problem, but, like I said, you have councils. And yes, you have papal encyclicals -- oodles of them, in fact, though which ones are infallible and which ones are fallible, and who is to tell, and just how binding such encyclicals are, is anyone's guess.

You say you have infallible utterances, but again, I have yet to find a simple way of finding out exactly which utterances are infallible. I have found lots of folks who want to say that Christ's Vicar has spoken infallibly an average of once a millennium, but there are all sorts of other folks who would say there are many more infallible pronouncements, though they don't infallibly known how many infallible pronouncements there are, which makes the whole infallibility issue a real mess at times. I'm sure wild-eyed liberals think of you as a wild-eyed conservative, what's even worse, the traditionalists probably think of you as a wild-eyed liberal! Ah, but I must remember: Rome is united in all things. Just ask Patrick Madrid and Gerry Matatics. Everyone is one big, happy family. No disagreements, no confusion as to what is, and what is not, infallible teaching. How truly wonderful.

Of course, all of that just points out that having an "infallible interpreter" solves nothing. Once you have an infallible interpretation, you then need an infallible interpretation of the infallible interpretation. You've simply moved your epistemological problem back a step, nothing more.

. . . You made a statement on page 10 that made me wonder. With reference to the Watchtower Bible and Tract Society you said that they deny God's omnipresence, deny that He is a Spirit, and say that He has a physical body. Really? Could you give me some references to Watchtower sources where they say this? I know the Mormons do all those things, but it's news to me that the Witnesses do that, too.

You wrote, "I will note that both cults and Protestantism are man-centered, whereas Catholicism is Christ-centered." Really? The church that allows its followers to venerate saints and Mary, instructs them to do penances lest they suffer in purgatory, directs them to priests and intermediaries, preaches indulgences, "re-presents" the sacrifice of Christ as a propitiatory sacrifice over and over again, and makes a man the Vicar of Christ on earth is "Christ-centered," while the church that cries "Christ alone," that speaks of the sufficiency of *both* His work and His Word, that proclaims that He alone is worthy of worship, veneration, service (*latria, dulia,* etc.), and says that one can have true and lasting peace with God solely through Him, is man-centered? Well, if you say so, Dave. Personally, I don't find a particle of truth in your statement.

I see a rather glaring double-standard in your sentence, "It's pointless to respond to it other than to refer you to my various tracts about development or to Newman's essential work on the subject." To which I have to respond, "Newman I know, but who is this Armstrong fellow?" :-)

I can only guess that you have a hidden TV camera in my office, Dave, because all through your letter you noted my mental state when making various comments. For example, on page 10 you write that I "gleefully note the divergent views of Lateran IV and Vatican II on religious tolerance." Gleefully, Dave? And how do you know how gleeful I might be? Be that as it may, yes, these two councils disagreed on this topic. And, of course, because you *have* to, you say, "the teachings involved here are not religious *dogmas* of the faith, but rather disciplinary measures." Really? How is that? Who told you that? You aren't engaging in "private interpretation" and providing me with a "magisterium of one" are you, Dave? Where has Rome officially said this? I'd like to see this infallible pronouncement.

What is more, where does Vatican II say, "This discussion of religious tolerance has nothing to do with faith and morals, this is a disciplinary thing"? And you utterly ignored the entire point of my argument at this point, Dave, by saying, "So, as almost always, what you think is a knockout punch to your detested 'Romanism' rebounds back to you with much more force, for the reasons just recounted." That was, quite simply, Dave, a *very* lame reply. Since this section seemed to fall right out of my letter to you, let me try it again and see if you are up to providing a meaningful response:

In your fifth point you mention the Inquisition "disproving" Catholicism. The problem with your point is this, Dave: we Protestants don't claim infallibility. Rome does. There is a big difference. Please note the following comparison [the Lateran IV – Vatican II comparison that we saw above]:

. . . Not only do we see the obvious conflict between these two ecumenical" councils, but we see that the IVth Lateran Council specifically taught that those who would take up the cross in the effort to exterminate heretics would enjoy the same indulgence as those who went to the Holy Land. Now, Dave, surely you can see the vast difference between the silliness of, say, a "Protestant" like Benny Hinn teaching his ideas as facts, and an ecumenical council of the Roman Catholic Church teaching that indulgences would be given to those who took up the cause of *exterminating* the heretics (i.e., simple Christian folks who were slaughtered at the behest of the Roman hierarchy). What is more, is not the granting of indulgences based upon the exercise of the keys? Does this not then touch upon the very faith of the Roman church? I believe it does.

Now, Dave, why didn't you deal with what I wrote to you? Where is your discussion of the difference between an organization *that claims infallibility* and Protestants who admit their fallibility? And where do you deal with the offering of indulgences for the extermination of heretics, and the fact that the granting of indulgences involves the use of the keys? And do you really want to say that statements like this are *irrelevant to faith and morals*?

Personally I think most folks can see through this, don't you? I mean, you say your church is infallible with reference to faith and morals, so when faced with evidence to the contrary you simply define those errors as having nothing to do with "faith and morals." Where can I find an infallible definition of faith and morals, Dave? It must be a pretty narrow definition, wouldn't you agree? There must not be a whole lot in the field of "faith and morals" if killing people who are "heretics" (defining who is and who is not a heretic has nothing to do with faith and morals, Dave?) and gaining indulgences for so doing is simply a "disciplinary" thing.

I was left overwhelmed yet once again by,

As for your lengthy attempted refutation of papal claims and their biblical justification, I refer you to my chapter on the papacy and infallibility, which runs 98 pages, single-spaced.

First, my comments were not lengthy -- they were a mere drop in the bucket. Secondly, I don't *have* your book which *may* be published by Ignatius Press, so how I'm supposed to refer to it is just a bit beyond me. I *may* someday publish a full-length work on *sola scriptura*, but till then I'm not going to be referring people to a source they can't even read. I could have simply said to you, "As to the papacy, simply see my debates against Gerry Matatics (Phoenix, 1990, Denver, 1993), Dr. Robert Fastiggi (Austin, 1995) and Butler/Sungenis (Boston, 1995)." Now *that* would have accomplished alot! And as for your 98 single-spaced pages, I have to admit this is the one line in your letter that made me chuckle more than anything else. [again: all I was saying was that I have made the arguments in my manuscript, if he was interested: no rocket science here. Yet white didn't get it]

You see, Patrick Madrid boasted about his being able to "bury me" under 50+ pages of quotations from the fathers on *sola scriptura*, and Scott Butler crows about his 91 citations from Chrysostom proving Petrine primacy, and you have your 98 single-spaced pages on the papacy and infallibility. Well, *that* surely finishes the debate! I mean, 98 pages! I mentioned that to a friend of mine and his response truly amused me: "Tell him to shrink his font so that you can fit more than a few words on each page and go from there." Really, Dave, think about it. If I said, "I have 196 pages of material in small print with condensed spacing that proves the papacy to be in error," would you be overly impressed? I mean, I would have twice the material you do! Wouldn't that end the debate? No, of course not. I know JW's who have "hundreds of pages documenting the Trinity is a pagan invention," too, but I have not stopped adoring the Trinity on the basis of such high-powered testimony.

You dismissed von Dollinger with a mere wave of the magical developmental wand, Dave. Your words were, "Your three long quotes, which you obviously thought were so unanswerable, have little or no force against my position." All I can say is, you might be wise to avoid publicly debating that issue if that is all you can come up with.

In light of the above it was rather hypocritical of you to then write, "You blithely dismiss my points 7 and 8 with your by-now familiar hit-and-run tactic of glib avoidance when you have no answer." Well, I'll let you think I have no answer, if you like, Dave. That's to my advantage.

Just a few more items. With reference to various moral issues you wrote, "The very fact that you don't regard this as of any 'weight' merely confirms in my mind the Protestant tendency of unconcern for holiness and morality. . . ." Having studied the lives of various of your popes, Dave, and having observed the huge mass of nominal Catholicism all around me here in the U.S., I can only remind you of the old adage about throwing stones while living in glass houses. I guess you probably didn't read Packer's *A Quest for Godliness*.

If you are going to engage in patristic debate, Dave, I would suggest sticking to contextual citations. You attempted to get around my citation of Clement's epistle by citation of 58.2. Unfortunately for your position, I'm one of those few Protestant apologists who happens to have a pretty good patristic library, a good grasp of Greek, and enough experience as a professor of church history to make me dangerous. The entire sentence is: [seven lines of Greek text which didn't scan]

To which I add my own hearty "amen" indeed. But why did this supposed Pope of Rome (of course, he was probably just the scribe for the body of elders that existed in Rome at the time) use such terminology as "the elect" like that, Dave? Perhaps he wasn't nearly as opposed to that concept as you are, maybe?

You then dismissed the central canons from Trent with yet another wave of the hand, saying they "prove nothing." Really? They prove nothing? Of what good are they then, Dave? Are they just a waste of paper or do they have some meaning? The rest of your paragraph only indicated to me that you are not very clear on the issues revolving around justification, grace, and the like. I'm tempted to say, "See my debate against Dr. Mitchell Pacwa on justification" but that wouldn't be nice. :-)

You then turned to Ignatius for a quotation, and again, demonstrated that context for the Roman apologist is an inconvenient problem. "Let none of you be found a deserter" to which you add, "so much for Calvinism." Huh? Would you mind explaining the connection here, Dave? I mean, please show me how the context here has the slightest to do with anything like the Reformed faith. Show me where Ignatius, in writing to Polycarp, refers to the bishop of Rome as the center of the Church, and that we are not to desert *him*. Good luck, as there was no single bishop of Rome at the time, which may explain why Ignatius doesn't ever refer to the bishop of Rome while writing to the Romans. If your 98 pages of material on the papacy partakes of the same kind of "here's a sentence I like, who cares if the context is relevant or not" type of citation, well, it would probably not be worth the effort of going through it, wouldn't you agree?

There is more I'd like to get to, but I've put far too much time into this already. Let me close with three items. First, I am going to import into this letter my reply to Akin's article that you don't seem to have seen. Then I will import some of the written "debate" between myself and Robert Sungenis on 2 Timothy 3:16-17. I simply don't have time to rewrite all of this for your benefit, and, given the use of the patristic sources I just went through, I have to wonder about the benefits of such an effort in the first place. You will note these posts are not exactly ancient history, as they were written fairly recently. I will attach these as sort of an "addendum" following the close of this letter, though they will be consecutively numbered along with the letter. I will close with your blanket accusations against Protestant apologists. You wrote,

> I must, regretfully, inform you of another reason for my declining: the widespread intellectual dishonesty, evasiveness, and uncharitability of anti-Catholic debaters. Akin in his article on your book starts out by recalling how you have refused to shake hands with your Catholic opponents, or even pray the Lord's prayer with them. This is contemptible, petty behavior. Madrid's article "The

White Man's Burden" concurs, by citing your rude treatment of him and of Dr. Art Sippo . . .

Of course, I feel that Roman Catholic debaters (note I don't have to define them as "anti-Protestant debaters") are far more guilty of intellectual dishonesty, evasiveness, and uncharitability than any Protestant debater I know. A few examples. You cite Akin's errors (he's admitted errors in his statements to me personally) about my not shaking hands with opponents. I refused to shake hands with Art Sippo, **period**. I have shaken hands with Gerry Matatics after every debate; the same with Dr. Mitchell Pacwa, Dr. Robert Fastiggi, Scott Butler, and Robert Sungenis. Ask them. I refused to shake hands with Dr. Sippo because he was a liar, plain and simple. He was also incredibly rude I might add. He walked off the stage while I was speaking (why should he listen to what I have to say? He didn't care what my position was to begin with), made faces at the audience, and during the question and answer period sat on his desk swinging his legs and making mocking gestures. Talk about rude! (He hasn't changed, by the way. Just this morning I received an Internet message from him, the first by that medium, that started with this line: "'Orthopodeo' . . . oh, come now, James. Isn't that handle a little bit presumptuous? It sounds to me like someone boasting of their own righteousness. But don't worry. Those of us who really know you always think of you as 'Pseudopodeo' anyway." Yes, a very kind and gracious man.) [why, then, was White trying to debate him years later? He wrote in a blog article on 8-8-05, entitled, "OK, Sippo, Let's Debate,": "So, Dr. Sippo, I'm coming to your area, to your own back yard. . . . You will not debate me on every single one of the topics your compatriots have been willing to tackle: here is your *one* subject, justification, and I will even allow you the positive position and the first word. How about it, Dr. Sippo? I await your response." If Dr. Sippos is such an insufferable imbecile, why does White – claiming to know this fact – want to challenge him to debate, *ten years* after our postal exchange?]

Next, with reference to the Lord's Prayer, that is quite true. However, if you put it in context, you might find it far less problematic. The incident took place at Boston College, April, 1993. It was at the end of the second of two debates against Gerry Matatics. The first debate had been on justification, and we had both made it quite clear that the other's position was anathema in our opinion. The second debate was on the Apocrypha. At the very end of the debate, during audience questions, a man got up and said, "I think these debates tend toward disunity. I'd like us all to stand and say the Lord's Prayer together." I explained that I could not do that for a number of reasons. First, we didn't have the unity such a prayer would pretend we had; secondly, the night before we had both agreed that the other was preaching a false gospel, and you can't sweep that under the rug with a prayer; and finally, prayer is an act of worship, and must be undertaken in spirit and truth, and this was not the context for that. Matatics, having already moved into a very traditional perspective, simply said, "If you want to know what I think about it, ask me afterwards." The moderator led in the prayer, and I, and most of the Protestants I knew of in the room, remained seated.

As to Madrid's accusations, they are groundless. I did not mistreat him in any way. He did not offer me his hand after the debate, so he says. I thought we had shaken hands, but he says we didn't. Fine, the only reason was because, as he admits, we were both surrounded as soon as the debate was over. There was nothing more to it than that. As to your assertion that I refused to attempt to prove *sola scriptura* from the Bible, that is simply untrue as well. If you are relying solely on Madrid's article, you should at least get the tape and show *some level of honesty* in your comments. Anyone who listens to the tape or reads the transcript finds a world of difference between Patrick's almost fantasy-like recollection and the reality of what took place.

In light of this, your reasons for declining a public debate are left rather hollow. Perhaps you will reconsider your refusal? I have no idea who Gary Michuta is, what his position is, what he's written, what his background is, or anything else. You wrote to the folks in the cult directory. You have the stationery that says "Catholic Apologist." You claim to eat Protestant apologists for lunch. I think you need to defend your position in a scholarly manner.

Sola scriptura, sola fide, solus Christus, soli Deo gloria,

James White

Recte Ambulamus ad Veritatem Evangelii

* * * * *

Hamlet, Act III: "The lady doth protest too much, methinks."

James White, letter of May 4, 1995, p. 1: "I have to attempt to be balanced."

Dave Armstrong, to his wife Judy, right before opening James White's letter of 5-4-95, at the dinner table: "I'll make a prediction. This letter will be filled with personal attacks and will accuse me of being scared to debate."

Proverbs 26:4-5 "Answer not an anti-Catholic according to his folly, lest thou also be like unto him. Answer an anti-Catholic according to his folly, lest he be wise in his own conceit." (*Armstrong Amplified Paraphrased Version*}

15 May 1995

James White

Dear James,

Greetings in Christ and His Church! I respond in the paradoxical spirit of Proverbs 26:4-5. . . . I stay up late at night at my word processor devising diabolical ways to distort and misrepresent your views. . . .

It couldn't be - in these instances - that I merely saw something in a different light, that I had a sincere, thought-out disagreement [?]. Animosity never needed to be introduced. . . . In light of the above, I conclude with the utmost sincerity and lack of malice, that I must have hit a nerve with you, and you simply can't deal with the possibility of your wrongness without lashing out . . . Unless and until you show some forthrightness in facing my arguments (out of common courtesy if nothing else), then can you blame me, James, for thinking that you *have no answer* in those cases? What better hypothesis explains this evasive behavior?

Much like the Pharisees, you, too, attempt to bind men to your own "Reformed," legalistic "criteria" for entrance into the Christian faith, and ignore the "weightier matters" which all Christians believe in common. You, too, can't see the log in your own eye when you hypocritically banish me (and all real Catholics) from Christianity but don't have the consistency to treat Luther, Melanchthon, Wesley, C. S. (not Vincent, whoever he is) Lewis, Wycliffe, Hus, even Calvin, in the same fashion, when they fail your various (infallible?) tests of "orthodoxy" miserably too. I am not attacking your character here. Your opposition to Catholicism is no mystery. I am merely offering a scathing attack on the false and, I believe, wicked tenets of anti-Catholicism.

The true Catholic teaching is that you are a Christian, a "separated brother." But you won't extend such graciousness to me and millions of other Catholics. Hence my disgust and anger. Just try to imagine for a moment, that you are wrong about the sub-Christian status of Catholicism. Wouldn't my anger at your schismatic and judgmental attitude towards us be completely justifiable and understandable? I know it must be difficult for you, but try to get inside my head for just a minute on just this one point. My concern is with the sinfulness of the entire anti-Catholic mentality of judgmentalism and a deluded sense of "spiritual superiority," so to speak, that is exemplified in it. My concern is the *unity of the Body*, which Jesus valued enough to make it a central theme of His prayer at the Last Supper (Jn 17:21-23). If you're wrong, you will have an awful lot to account for at the Judgment on this matter. As you say, "think about that, my friend."

Finally, I can now get to both your actual rational arguments, as well as numerous caricatures and misunderstandings of my positions. . . . I would only ask that you please consider my thoughts in their *totality* and *context*, rather than getting caught up in isolated words which stun, baffle, or offend you. Perhaps I'm not quite the Philistine and unscholarly barbarian that you make me out to be . . .

Okay, James, so you don't "exclude people from the kingdom on the basis of their acceptance or rejection of limited atonement." Very well then, I accept this correction of Akin's perspective of your belief. But I will call your bluff. Why don't you now tell me what *are* your criteria, so we can clear up this misunderstanding once and for all? I've already seen how I wasn't a Protestant according to you because of my rejection of the notion of a predestination to hell without the reprobate sinner's will being involved at all, and total depravity.

So I ask you again, just to make sure, and to avoid being accused for the nth time of dishonesty: this is your position, is it not? If so, then I merely proceeded, on this assumption, to mention other well-known Protestant Christian figures (and whole groups) who were also thereby excluded based on your own litmus test of belief: Melanchthon, Wesley, Lewis, and Bonhoeffer . . .

I fail to grasp the nature of your complaint here (see the quote from *Hamlet*). What am I missing? I will restate my arguments in basic syllogistic formulas here and elsewhere, so as to prove beyond a shadow of a doubt that I am (and always was) proceeding logically on the basis of your own stated premises, and using the famous *argumentum ad absurdum* (which infuriates most people - you apparently being no exception):

> P1) [P = Premise] Dave Armstrong was never a Protestant because he rejected absolute predestination and total depravity.
> A1) [A = Argument] But Melanchthon rejected absolute predestination and total depravity as well.
> A2) Wesley, C. S. Lewis, and Bonhoeffer also rejected absolute predestination and total depravity.
> C1) [C = Conclusion] Therefore, according to James White, Melanchthon, Wesley, C. S. Lewis, and

Bonhoeffer are not Protestants.

P2) White says Catholics (and, so it would seem to follow, Orthodox) and cults such as Mormons and Jehovah's Witnesses are not Christians.

C2) Therefore, Protestants are the only Christians, and since Arminians are not truly Protestants (C1), then only Calvinists are Christians.

C3) Therefore, according to James White, Melanchthon, Wesley, C. S. Lewis, Bonhoeffer, and Dave Armstrong (before and after poping) cannot be Christians.

P3) Calvinists are those who must accept all five points of TULIP (which are all consistent with each other).

A3) One of these five points is limited atonement.

A4) It then follows that anyone denying limited atonement is not a Calvinist.

A5) Anyone who is not a Calvinist is not a Protestant (C2).

A6) And anyone who is not a Protestant is not a Christian (C2).

C4) Therefore, anyone who denies limited atonement is not a Christian.

P4) But James White says that C4, which flows from his premises, is untrue, and is a "caricature" of his position, and "unworthy" of an apologist, a "misrepresentation," and, in fact, a position which, if used, would "convict" one of "dishonesty."

C5) Therefore, due to the contradiction of C4 and P4, White must be either illogical, or dishonest, or perhaps wishy-washy and "double-minded."

A7) We will assume James White is an honest and mentally-- and emotionally – stable guy (unlike his treatment of Catholic apologists).

A8) Assuming, then, that he is illogical, he must deny or modify one or more of his premises in order to eliminate the fatal flaw in his reasoning on this point.

Hypothetical C1) If White denies P1 (and A5 logically stands or falls with P1), then Dave Armstrong was indeed formerly a Protestant, and is owed an apology for misrepresentation and slander.

A9) By the same token, Melanchthon, Wesley, C. S. Lewis, and Bonhoeffer are also Protestants.

A10) Yet White wants to have his cake and eat it too, by maintaining implicitly and inconsistently (by an argument from silence) that Melanchthon, Wesley, C. S. Lewis, and Bonhoeffer are Protestants (hence, Christian) whereas, Dave Armstrong before poping was not.

A11) White also contradicts himself (C2) when he claims that equating the terms "Protestant" and "Christian" is an "incredible leap" and "dishonest shifting of terms."

HC2) If, in order to rectify this contradiction, White overturns P2, he stands his anti-Catholicism on its head, in which case he must repent, and apologize to Patrick Madrid, Robert Fastiggi, James Akin, Art Sippo, Fr. Mitch Pacwa, Robert Sungenis, Karl Keating et al (and all his debate and newsletter audiences). He must also renounce his book *The Fatal Flaw* and take it off the market.

P5) White maintains that Methodists, Lutherans, the majority of Anglicans, Free Will Baptists, most pentecostals and many non-denominationalists are Christians, since Dave Armstrong's *argumentum ad absurdum* to the contrary is rejected as not even "worthy of response," "a mere wasting of time and effort," and not "meaningful."

P6) But P5 contradicts P1, C1, C2, C3, P3, A4, and A5.

C6) Therefore, either P5 or (P1, Cl, C2, C3, P3, A4, A5) are false.

If the former, then James White needs to write books which rail against Methodists, Lutherans, Anglicans, and other "semi-Pelagian" / "Protestant" groups. If the latter, then Dave Armstrong was a Protestant prior to poping, and Calvinists are not the only Christians.

Final Conclusion: James White has severe reasoning disabilities, of which he is apparently blissfully unaware. Yet when Dave Armstrong points this out, his reply is characterized as "misrepresentation" and White states in parting that "those who have something meaningful to say don't waste their time on such things." Perhaps, then, James White finds basic syllogistic logic neither helpful nor "meaningful." Whether this is a *conscious* rejection or not, Dave will not rashly speculate, as it is up to James to sort out this confusion of thought and present to Dave a revised, non-contradictory system, as well as a definitive list of who is and isn't a Christian, so Dave won't be forced to make guesses obfuscated by James' frequently convoluted and inexplicable illogic.

Do I make myself clear this time? Enough to escape more of your derision upon my supposed lack of reasoning ability? One can only hope so. I am most eager to accept any clarification on your part which will explain the above seemingly insurmountable absurdities. The easy way out would be to simply admit that you blew it and have to do some major rearranging of your schema of Christian orthodoxy. I pray that you will recognize the wisdom of that course of action.

The very next paragraph makes it necessary for me to engage in some more step-by-step logic in order to explain my position to you (which was clear *enough*, I think).

> P1) James White believes that: ". . . a communion that replaces the grace of God with sacraments, mediators, and merit," cannot "be properly called 'Christian.'"
> A1) Dave merely reverses the order of this sentence, singling out "sacraments" for the sake of argument, time, and space, and deleting one "s":
> "sacraments . . . replace the grace of God".

[Dave freely admits that perhaps it would have been more advisable -- especially in retrospect, given White's now manifest propensity to attack opponents' motives -- to not rearrange the phrase in one set of quotation marks, but regards this as a trifling issue, and not "dishonest" whatsoever, certainly not intentionally, as will be demonstrated below]

P2) White calls this rephrasing "silliness," "in the best style of Gail Riplinger" (whom Dave called a "nut"), "dishonesty," "misrepresent[ation]," so bad that White feels Dave "owe[s] me an apology for such behavior," and that Dave will "have some serious work to do to restore" his "credibility as an honest apologist and researcher." Wow!!!

A2) Yet Dave's rephrasing and isolation of "sacraments" doesn't violate the meaning, logic, or intent of White's sentence in the least, because, in White's thinking:

A3) [Catholicism] "replaces the grace of God with sacraments, mediators, and merit," thus is not Christian.

A4) It follows then, that Catholicism replaces grace with mediators.

A5) And that Catholicism replaces grace with merit as well.

A6) And that, as in Dave's argument, Catholicism replaces grace with sacraments.

A7) One can rephrase A6 as: "sacraments replace grace."

C1) Thus, A2 and Dave Armstrong's argument are both true, given White's premises, and P2 and White's offense are false and improper. If you don't comprehend this, let's try an analogy:

P3) Calvin replaces the tradition of Catholic Christianity with *sola Scriptura*, *sola fide*, and private judgment.

A8) It follows then that Calvin replaces Catholic Christianity with *sola Scriptura*.

A9) And that Calvin replaces Catholic Christianity with *sola fide* as well.

A10) And that Calvin replaces Catholic Christianity with private judgment.

A11) Thus *sola Scriptura*, *sola fide*, and private judgment all replace Catholic Christianity.

C2) Therefore, *sola Scriptura* replaces Catholic

Christianity.

A12) But James White would object that C2 is a dishonest distortion of P3.

C3) Therefore, either C2 or P3 or both are false, and Calvin's views must be presented in an alternative fashion.

C4) But if this is the case, the same reasoning applies to P1 and A7, and a central tenet in White's beef against Catholic Christianity is false, and sacraments are not contrary to the grace of God.

C5) If this is true, then if other misunderstood doctrines like mediators and merits can be explained as Christian also, Catholicism may indeed be Christian and White's anti-Catholic worldview collapses in a heap of ashes. Good riddance!

P4) Dave Armstrong, operating from White's P1, and A7 -- which has been shown to logically flow from P1 -- then proceeds to make the following *argumentum ad absurdum* (completely ignored by White):

A13) Calvin believes that sacraments do not "replace" grace, but are a "testimony" of it, citing St. Augustine, who gives the standard Catholic definition of "sacrament."

A14) Thus Calvin disagrees with White on P1, and agrees with Dave on the worthwhile nature of sacraments.

A15) But Calvin is James White's mentor, and therefore must be a Christian.

C6) But Calvin cannot be a Christian according to White's P1 and its corollary A7. Therefore, White is inconsistently following a non-Christian while at the same time railing against Catholics for being non-Christian and believing in a view of sacraments not unlike Calvin's!

C7) Dave submits as a solution to this dilemma, that Calvin is indeed a Christian, albeit a grossly deficient one, and, rather, that James White is in error concerning the propriety and validity of sacraments. Furthermore:

A16) Luther believes in sacramental, regenerative infant baptism, essentially in agreement with Catholic Christianity:

> We should be even as little children, when they are newly baptized, who engage in no efforts or works, but are free in every way, secure and *saved* solely through the glory of their baptism . . . Infants are aided by the faith of others, namely, those who bring them for baptism . . . Through the prayer of the believing church which presents it, the infant is changed, cleansed, and renewed by inpoured faith. Nor should I doubt that *even a godless adult could be changed, in any of the sacraments*, if the same church prayed for and presented him, as we read of the paralytic in the Gospel, who was healed through the faith of others [Mk 2:3-12]. I should be ready to admit that in this sense the sacraments of the New Law are *efficacious in conferring grace*, not only to those who do not, but even to those who do most obstinately present an obstacle." (*Babylonian Captivity*, *Three Treatises*, Philadelphia: Fortress, rev. 1970, p. 197 / emphasis added)

A17) But sacraments, according to James White, *replace* grace (P1, A7).

A18) Whoever replaces grace with sacraments or any other "work," cannot be a Christian.

C8) Therefore, Luther (and Calvin) cannot be Christians, for this reason, as well as Luther's views on the Real Presence, adoration of the Host, and the

Immaculate Conception of the Blessed Virgin Mary, among other things.

A19) But Luther founded Protestantism and originated almost all of its distinctives (with Calvin putting the icing on the cake).

A20) And only Protestants are Christians (White's P2 and C2 above).

A21) And White is a Protestant, therefore a Calvinist, therefore able to be called a Christian. But how can non-Christians found true Christianity?

C9) Current-day anti-sacramental, "Baptist-type" Protestants have severe logical and historical problems, which are either ignored, minimized, or rationalized away by anti-Catholics such as James White, who, true to form, totally ignored the above argument as presented in Dave's letter of 4-22-95. They love to cite Luther and Calvin with evident pride and respect, except where they agree with Catholic Christianity. These instances are usually hidden from the initiate lest the evident double standard and intellectual dishonesty of this position become evident. This allows professional anti-Catholics to rail against Catholic sacramentalism and Marian devotion, but not, e.g., Lutheran (esp. Luther himself) and Anglican sacramentalism and Marian devotion. Catholics like Dave Armstrong, on the other hand, need not hide anything on these scores, and can examine the issues openly and without pretense, fear, and evasiveness.

All of the above nearly five-page treatment of basic logic would have been unnecessary if you had only given my arguments the thought and consideration that they indeed deserved in the first place, rather than taking the easy fool's course of evasion and name-calling (sorry, but you thoroughly deserve this criticism). It's your positions which are irreparably contradictory here, rather than my arguments from absurdity from your premises being "dishonest," etc. You ought to either clarify or modify them.

As to your gratuitous swipe at my declining oratorical debate, this is a vapid accusation for the following reason: you falsely assume that public spoken debate is the only (or at least far preferable) kind of debate. . . . in the spur of the moment at one of these (usually farcical) debates, I could never come up with the carefully-and tightly-reasoned responses which I have produced here as a result of hours of thought and work (I can't think of many who could, not even you yourself). Thus the audience might get the false impression that you have great reasoning at your command, whereas the truth is quite the contrary on major points under discussion, as I've clearly demonstrated (and only in your first three pages, yet!).

You claim that I "did not even begin to demonstrate that *anything* [you] said [about Roman theology] was inaccurate." This is an outright falsehood (a synonym of falsehood is "lie" -- it need not be deliberate). You have indeed borne "false witness" (I do not claim deliberately). I showed you that your view of sacraments "replacing" the grace of God is false, according to your own heroes Luther and Calvin.

True, this was not so much a theological argument (with which I deal in my Eucharist treatise) as an analogical *argumentum ad absurdum*, which I love to use (if you haven't noticed that already). But it still demonstrated that what you said created insuperable problems not only for Catholicism (assuming your correctness) but also for the Christian status of Luther, Calvin, Anglicanism, Wycliffe, Hus, etc. as well.

Likewise, I demonstrated the same thing concerning free will. It is a simple matter of logic once again (I've always admired Calvinists for their logic, at least -- such frequent lapses on your part are exceedingly curious to me). If you state that the denial of one or more parts of TULIP is non-Christian, then you are indirectly dealing with "Roman" theology, which opposes this in major ways. Ditto also for denominationalism. In attacking that (and citing four biblical passages among many) I was criticizing your view that this was okay and that the opposite view (the "oneness" of Catholicism) is troublesome, since it supposedly creates clones who parrot back "Roman" infallible teachings by rote, rather than with biblical and patristic support.

Thus I was indirectly demonstrating that what you said about "Roman" theology was indeed inaccurate. My comments on St. Clement (who was, by the way, a bishop. Do you have a bishop? If not, why do you claim St. Clement as one of your own when he himself would say you weren't: 44:2, 59:1?) also delved into questions of justification, with much scriptural citation, thus critiquing your assertions about the bankruptcy of "Roman" theology.

Furthermore, I enclosed my critique of Geisler's article on *sola Scriptura*, (a counter to the Catholic idea of tradition), and my article on Luther's devotion to Mary, which is contrary to your assertions as to what is and is not proper for a good Protestant to believe and do. So your statement at the top of this paragraph is obviously false.

I do know that it is current Catholic teaching that all validly baptized Protestants are indeed "incorporated into Christ," "Christians," and "brothers" (Vatican II, *Dec Ecumenism*, I, 3). You ought to rejoice that this is the case. But I guess, given your anti-ecumenical and schismatic mentality (e.g., rampant denominationalism is no problem), it rather saddens you that the Beast regards you as more of a brother than an enemy.

Since this is our official teaching, you can only repeatedly cite people like Gerry Matatics, who, apparently (and sadly) has become a schismatic. For you to insist that separatists and anti-Vatican II types are still Catholic is almost as silly as me saying that The Way International is Protestant since it still operates on the principles of private judgment and *sola Scriptura*. It just ain't so. It doesn't take much for the *essence* of a position to change. Many *outward* factors may still remain the same, just as in the Protestant sects. A "Catholic" who rejects a true ecumenical council is dishonestly using the name, and ought to become a Protestant, since he has adopted private judgment as his final arbiter.

How can I possibly not read anti-Catholic books since I am a Catholic apologist? Very simple! I employ the same reasoning that you use with regard to Vinney Lewis:

Might I suggest to you . . . that . . . some of us have standards with reference to the behavior of those with whom we correspond? I will not debate Vinney Lewis either, and there's a reason for that: he is not worthy of being noticed on that level.

You make similar remarks about Art Sippo . . .. Well, I am merely extending such reluctance to the written page. You yourself say that there are:

> . . . far too many "anti-Catholic" books and works around that show *little or no concern for accurate citation or presentation*." (*The Fatal Flaw*, p. 20)

Why should I waste my time in *reading* such material when you were tempted to cease *writing* to me and wasting your "limited time" because of *my* alleged "almost irreparably damaged credibility?" Until you debate Sippo and Lewis again, I will not read Chick, Alamo, Boettner, Hislop, Hunt, Ankerberg, or Brewer. Catholic Answers staff do that because they have made it part of their function (for obvious reasons). But not every Catholic apologist is so constrained (thank God!). I content myself with going back to the roots of Protestantism and reading Calvin and Luther. You surely can't be asserting that one must read *anti-Catholics* in order to understand either Protestantism or its disagreements with Catholicism!

Of current writers I will read people like Geisler, Samples and Miller, Pelikan, the Passantinos, Packer, etc. (i.e., on Catholicism) since they are ecumenical and immeasurably more logical than the anti-Catholics. I would certainly eagerly purchase and read their works, with the greatest interest. You are pretty much in a class by yourself (perhaps also Morey and Ankerberg) - anti-Catholics who show some measure of concern for sources and accuracy, and some semblance of respect for the mind and Christian history (even cogent theology).

I already stated that I would make an exception for your works, since they are obviously far and away the best of a bad lot, and since you were nice enough to send them to me free, provided you'll interact with my rebuttals. You should be pleased about that, rather than criticizing me unduly and saying that I may therefore not be an apologist. Tsk, tsk, James.

As for Salmon, I read him because he was perfect for my needs at the time as an evangelical Protestant apologist -- a scathing attack on infallibility (i.e., I was on *his side* when I read the book). I would certainly snatch up his book today if I saw it since (like your stuff) it is about the best you guys can come up with and not *immediately* dismissable as absurd and laughable hogwash. I am still proud today that as a Protestant I did not rely on blithering idiots (i.e., on Catholicism) like Boettner and Chick for my polemics, but rather, the smartest anti-Catholics, Dollinger and Salmon (I would have utilized you, too, if I had been aware of you).

I use the term "anti-Catholic" in a very basic sense – someone who is opposed to the Catholic Church (not its members per se) and does not consider it as Christian. He may or may not regard it as a consciously heinous Beast and Whore (the spectrum runs the gamut from Jack "Jesuits killed Lincoln" Chick to Dave "one million Reformation martyrs" Hunt to you). There is nothing improper or offensive in this usage whatsoever. It is the objective stating of a fact, such as the term "anti-abortion activist" (I accept that description, though I much prefer "pro-life"). It's curious that you reject a title which so accurately portrays what you *are*. But I guess I'd be embarrassed too to be in the fraternity of Catholic-bashers you're in.

Throughout my book and tracts I argue that anti-Catholicism is almost (but not quite) essential for all Protestants (in order to justify their own very existence). You go on to compare apples and oranges by stating that I should consistently call myself an "anti-Protestant." You're smarter than this (so many pages and hours taken up -- for both of us – in all these corrections of fact and logic). I say you're a Christian; you say I'm not, therefore there is no logical symmetry here. I'm not anti-Protestant by my own criterion above. I'm a seriously ecumenical Catholic who does, however, criticize Protestants as rebellious sons within the family, not enemies.

You might call me a Catholic "polemicist" or "controversialist," but not an anti-Protestant, at least according to my objective definition of terms. If merely disagreeing with Protestant positions makes me "anti-Protestant," then the denominations would have so many "anti-Lutherans," "anti-Arminians," "anti-pentecostals," etc. as to be utterly countless. With me, it's a family squabble and in-house fight, whereas you are taking on the foreign infidels, whose views are well-nigh worthless and contemptible. This leads to two entirely different attitudes, . . . I'm quite willing to call you a Protestant apologist too. The two titles are not mutually exclusive.

Being on both sides of any major disagreement is self-evidently a benefit (this was a minor point of mine and I did take pains to qualify it). The very fact that you guys trot out your Bart Brewers ("he was a Catholic priest for xx years," etc.) proves that you agree with this. Much is made of Luther's having been a monk and "understanding the Catholic position from the inside" too. Not all of us are so enlightened or blessed with the right upbringing so as to arrive at theological truth at such an early age, and stick with it through thick and thin, as it would appear from your remarks about others, you believe about yourself (a "cradle Calvinist"?). Real or so-called "traitors" are always despised by the groups they leave. That's why civil wars are the bloodiest. This is human nature, I suppose.

I might add as a parting shot that if anything is "double-minded," it is your numerous contradictory views and selective double standards of criticism, as painstakingly exhibited throughout this letter (these could rightly be called "wavering" – Jas 1:6). I would never say this unprovoked, but since you stoop to it, I only point out that one might see some hypocrisy in *you* using this charge.

Merely changing positions, even repeatedly, is not necessarily "double-minded," nor hypocritical nor "unstable," provided there is a true developmental progression from lesser truth to greater truth, and an increase in knowledge and wisdom. I would say that the phrase "double-minded" refers more to the simultaneous holding of contradictory views, or vacillation, such as in your two letters, as I've proven several times already.

Another trivial matter: I referred to my book since I gave you (unless I overlooked this) my list of tracts, which describes it. Obviously, I was speaking in the sense of the *potential* for you to read various chapters as an answer to your arguments. Why should I reiterate views which I have already expressed elsewhere? Whatever you want to read, I will give to you (several are already enclosed). I didn't want to bombard you with hundreds of pages -- I just wanted you to know that I've done this work and that it is at my disposal in manuscript form should it become necessary to refute your assertions. . . .

By "constructively ecumenical" I mean striving for increased *understanding* among Christians. I don't know what apologist told you ecumenism is a "joke" (although I agree much of what *passes* for ecumenism indeed is). I'd like to hear the context of that remark, and what he thinks of the documents of Vatican II. If the only reason I talked to Protestants (particularly of the anti-Catholic bent) was to convert them, I'd be one frustrated camper indeed, as the only ones I've helped to pope were already my friends.

No; my immediate, realistic goal (aside from simple, innocent friendliness) is simply to build bridges, and to engage in the ceaseless and almost thankless task of explaining Catholicism and defending it from the ever-present disinformation and prejudice with which we Catholics have to deal as a matter of course. In this, my attitude is little different from my campus evangelist days. I was content to let the Spirit do the work of conversion - it was my privilege to be used in some small way as a vessel of Christian truth.

Likewise, in my attempts at bridge-building, perhaps occasionally someone will convert, which I regard as a great improvement in one's spiritual status, of course, since more truth is espoused than formerly. This was also the philosophy of my ecumenical discussion group, and it never changed, even though I started it as a Protestant (the dynamic is the same on either side). Lacking that, I would be ecstatic to convince Protestants with obvious zeal and abilities such as yourself that Catholicism is Christian. This would be fulfilling the "mandate" of John 17 -- a quite worthwhile endeavor and the primary purpose of ecumenism.

Strictly speaking, if I am *actively* seeking to convert someone (which is rare, anyway) I am functioning as a Catholic evangelist and apologist. When I am seeking to understand others and to explain my views (i.e., almost all the time), I am playing more the ecumenist's role. This involves no duplicity or contradiction. Anyone with strong views wishes that others could be convinced of them, too. But given inherent divisions, we all have to get to know each other's opinions also, and charity demands this.

Okay, James, so I took some liberties in speculating on your opinions as to the means and process of my conversion (er, apostasy). Perhaps my acerbic wit got the best of me. But you go beyond that. You must accuse me of (what else?) "misrepresentation." But this time I was not attempting to quote you directly, and thought that you would realize I was writing "tongue-in-cheek," being the sharp guy (I mean that sincerely) that you are. Mainly, I was reacting to the condescension of you thinking that you know so much about my theological knowledge (or lack thereof) prior to poping, which was a bit much to take -- hence the sarcasm.

. . . Now, having accepted your rebuke on this point, why don't you then elaborate on what you meant by my lack of knowledge of the "why" of "Roman" theology, and the supposed "ripeness" of my views for "refutation." Since you (quite presumptuously) feel you know so much about this, I'd like to know what you know about me too, then I won't have to speculate excessively.

I'd be especially delighted to learn that you in fact *don't* regard the Catholic Church and its proponents as "clever," "devious," and characterized by "Babylonish guile." These are classic anti-Catholic charges, perfected in our day by Dave Hunt (following Pope Luther -- *Babylonian Captivity*...). If you disagree with this, I wish you'd write to Hunt and set him straight. We could use a guy like you to run interference for us on occasion. If you do accept this description, then where's the beef with my witticisms?

As for the precise written content of my conversion story, how in the world is that relevant here, or even any business of yours? A conversion story is just that -- a conversion story, not a treatise on theology or a library list or pro-Protestant controversialism (my prior stance), just as the Gospels have a specific purpose, and Proverbs and Psalms and Amos all have their own *raison d'etre* too. This is getting really ridiculous, and you force me to go back to my flow charts:

> P1) Dave Armstrong writes a 12-page conversion story in *Surprised by Truth* (the shortest in the book).
> P2) James White apparently thinks that it does or should present an exhaustive survey of Dave's grasp of Catholic theology prior to his conversion. In so thinking, James assumes that Dave would list all or most of what he has read and studied about Catholicism and Protestant critiques in this 12-page story.
> C1) James White thereby concludes that whatever is not listed has *not* been read or studied by Dave Armstrong.
> C2) White further concludes that this means Dave had not read Calvin's diatribes and defenses, nor Trent, nor even the catechisms of Fr. John Hardon prior to conversion.
> C3) White concludes, with little grounds, that Dave Armstrong therefore was quite lacking in his understanding of Protestantism and why it opposes Catholicism, hence was "ripe for refutation" theologically.
> C4) In other words, Dave was so lacking in knowledge of his own prior beliefs that his "conversion" is of little significance. In fact, Dave wasn't Protestant at all, since he was never a five-point Calvinist, which is the litmus test.

So then, what *was* I, anyway? A Pelagian? A Druid? A Rastafarian? All this based on 12 pages and a few short tracts and letters. You still don't know what and how much I've studied, yet you persist in this fatuous analysis and say things like, "am I to conclude, Dave, that I should not take what Roman apologists say at face value?" Why are you so concerned about this factor, anyway? Is it not simply a diversionary tactic? You can try to poke holes in my conversion odyssey if you like (I rather enjoy these analyses for humor's sake, much as musicians despise and chuckle at dead-wrong critical reviews of their work), but this won't get you off the hook of refuting what I know *now*, regardless of what I knew or didn't know then.

I didn't even mention *Surprised by Truth* in my first letter (strange, if I'm as arrogant as you think). You started this whole line of reasoning. But I fail to see how it is relevant. If you keep trying to prove that you were not presumptuous, I don't believe it is likely you will succeed.

Now, if you'll pay me labor costs, I'll write a 300-page autobiography on the precise nature of my theological knowledge and progress at every step of the way from 1977 to 1990, so I can "tell the truth" about my "background" and "experience." It would make pretty dull reading, I think, to reel off scores of book titles so as to satisfy your strict requirements for self-revelation! But if you paid me, I would do it. C'mon! I wish we'd get to some *real* issues. I value my time as much as you do yours, I'm sure. I want some real, substantive dialogue.

As for "epistemological leaps" (you must have taken some philosophy, too), Protestantism is replete with them -- for starters, *sola Scriptura*, a-historicism, private judgment, a stultifying tendency of dichotomizing ideas unnecessarily, anti-sacramentalism, anti-materialism, anti-clericalism, paper (without papal) infallibility, perspicuity, assurance of salvation, etc. You keep railing against infallibility, as if it is a totally untenable position. Well, which bucket would you pick: the one with one hole (easily patched up by Catholic apologist handymen), or the one with ten (which are denied by the Protestant apologists, who just keep filling up the bucket regardless of its leaks)?

Yes, I stand by my opposition to how you paint the picture of my being impressed by Catholics in Operation Rescue. It's not a matter of seeing "nice folks" who are sincere and consistent in their beliefs (big wow; if that was it, I'd surely be either a Mormon or a conservative Methodist!). No, it's being impressed with godly men and women of great Christian integrity. . . .

I find another thing very troubling. You would rather insist on evangelizing Catholics at *every opportunity* rather than standing together with them against the greatest evil of our age (which you admit). You think this "principle" more important than (given the reasonable opportunity at a Rescue) the very saving of babies' lives (Ecclesiastes 3:7 applies, I would say ["a time to rend, and a time to sew; a time to keep silence, and a time to speak"]).

I can think of many legitimate reasons for not participating in Rescues (I haven't since 1990 myself), but yours is certainly not one of them. I regard it as an astounding and indefensible instance of tragically blind legalism to the exclusion of the "weightier matters" of love and compassion for both the babies and the state of both a divided Christianity and a decadent civilization. It is as morally contemptible as Corrie Ten Boom saying that she would not assist in saving Jews unless she could convert them, too.

It's disgusting and abominable that Protestants such as Bill Gothard, John MacArthur and even Norman Geisier (who said on a talk show that he would not save a five-year-old from a legal death camp down the street unless it was his own), cannot even give *sanction* to the tactic of Rescue, let alone (God forbid) sit with Catholics in them. MacArthur said on Ankerberg's anti-Catholic series of broadcasts recently that we should not even participate together in non-Rescue pro-life activities! Perhaps this is your view, too. Divide and conquer.

You didn't have to compromise or "overlook" anything as a Rescuer. I didn't compromise my evangelicalism. All you had to do was shut your mouth at the clinic entrances and in the jails. Was that really too much to ask of you for the sake of the babies about to be killed? Couldn't you just pray for the infidels (and, egads, *with* them) and be a shining example of a righteous Calvinist? I talked at length with the Catholics in other venues. No one could stop me from engaging in dialogue elsewhere. The leaders only had authority over me at the Rescues, not in my private life. Even in the jails, though, I talked theology, but since I was ecumenical rather than anti-Catholic, this was no hindrance to the movement. I had a Socratic attitude of being willing to learn, not just to share everything I knew with poor, ignorant papists. It's all in the approach.

If you think that the situation of 23,000 denominations is the equivalent of the "modern state of Roman apologetics in the U.S. today" I would love to see you elaborate on this contention with some real arguments, not just desperate salvos for lack of any real reasoning or response. And please leave out the separatist "Catholic" examples, if you would, for my sake, since I don't buy it.

I challenge you once again (I am at your p.6): please tell me who is and who isn't a Christian. Are Arminians Christians? You mention "Protestantism." Who are these Protestants-in-quotes? It would seem that, at a bare minimum, Methodists, Lutherans, Anglicans, pentecostals, some Baptists, and many non-denoms are excluded right off the bat, as I earlier stated. Please tell me for sure so I can know. Surely you know, since you are quick to read others out of the faith (like the early "Reformers," especially Luther).

And again, I declare to you: if these Protestants-in-quotes are not Christian, then they are far more wicked than us poor papists, under the yoke of Rome, as there is a strong element of deception (from your standpoint) in their position. They are fake Protestants, fatally-compromised, hypocritical and nominal Protestants, "treading water in the Tiber." And who are those who reject limited atonement yet remain Christians? I'm especially curious as to Melanchthon and Wesley. Finally, St. Paul wasn't a Calvinist any more than St. Augustine was. This is made clear in my *sola fide* treatise.

Very well, then, James. I'll call your bluff again. Please send me an example (please pay close attention to what I am requesting) of a sermon intended for evangelization and as a prelude to an altar call whereby people get "saved," where TULIP is presented as the center and essence of the whole enterprise. If you can produce one (preferably more) of these, I will recant this position (it isn't as though my whole worldview rests on it, anyway). The key words were "openly presents" and I was referring to missionary-crusade type settings (or sermons, anyway), obviously not to the fact that someone might believe in TULIP. Even if you are correct on the factual point, I would still deny theologically that TULIP is the gospel. I maintain that it is a schema of heavily philosophical theology.

The gospel, as I have always believed, is, as W. E. Vine defines it:

> . . . the good tidings of the Kingdom of God and of salvation through Christ, to be received by faith, on the basis of His expiatory death, His burial, resurrection, and ascension, e.g., Acts 15:7; 20:24; 1 Pet 4:17.
>
> (*Expository Dictionary of New Testament Words*, under "Gospel")

As a (")Protestant(") evangelist, I located the apostolic proclamation of this gospel in Acts 2:6-11, 3:13-15, 18-21, 26, 4:8-12, 5:30-32, 10:34-43, 13:23, 26-33, 38-39, 16:31, 17:22-31, and 22:3-16, 21 . . . One can hardly by any stretch find TULIP in these presentations, and this was my point. It's strange to me that *sola Scriptura* adherents would redefine the gospel message when it is clearly defined in the pages of Scripture, by example of both preaching and teaching. . . .

When will you guys stop claiming the "best and brightest" Catholics as your own, when it is clear that they are not? Again, St. Augustine was a bishop, who believed in ecumenical councils and the authority of the pope, and, of course, the sacraments, and many other doctrines you find reprehensible and unChristian. Do you have a bishop? Or sacraments? Do you believe in ecumenical councils? How could he *possibly* be a "Protestant," even one of your fake ones in quotes? To claim him as one of your own is sheer ludicrosity.

And the same is true of all the other fathers, if the truth be known (with the possible exception of Tertullian in his heretical Montanist period). You might better and more consistently embrace (at least partially) the Donatists, Montanists, Novationists, Nestorians, Marcionites and even the Orthodox as your forerunners, if someone must be found to fill in the missing links of 1500 years. This constant dishonest recourse to the fathers (e.g., your implication that you are more "in company" with St. Athanasius, St. Ignatius, and St. Irenaeus than I am) only goes to show that thoughtful Protestants recognize the incumbent necessity of finding some figment of an historical "church" during the so-called "dark ages" (whenever *that* began -- you don't want to tell me).

The evolution of Unitarianism in New England is an indisputable fact of history. You can only attempt (legitimately) to deny the direct *causal* connection. You're welcome to do so with my blessing. The same thing happened to English Presbyterianism at the same time. As to my "joke" (you miss much of my *intended* humor) about Puritanism evolving into Unitarianism, I cite in my defense no less a reputable scholar of Puritanism than Perry Miller:

> By the middle of the 18th Century there had *proceeded from* it [Puritan philosophy] two distinct schools of thought . . . Certain elements were carried into the creeds and practices of the evangelical religious revivals, but others were perpetuated by the rationalists and the *forerunners of Unitarianism* . . . Unitarianism is as much the *child of Puritanism* as Methodism . . . Descendants of the Puritans who *revolted against what they considered the tyranny and cruelty of Puritan theology* . . . substituted taste and reason for dogma and authority.
>
> (*The Puritans*, New York: Harper & Row, vol. 1, revised 1963, pp. 3-4; from the Introduction. by Perry Miller / emphasis mine)

I guess if my views here are a "joke," then Miller's are, too (I'll bet you even have his biography of Jonathan Edwards. I do. Surprised?). So why don't you write to him (if he's alive) in the same mocking manner about the same topic? His research couldn't be *that* bad, could it?

Warning: another of my arguments from historical implausibility: If Calvinism is so great, and so guided by God's Providence, why is it so hard to find, both historically in Christian history, and geographically at present? Where are the great numbers of Calvinists today, even in Scotland, the Netherlands (where euthanasia is touted) and Switzerland, its historical "strongholds" (if any areas can be so described)? Are you reduced to western Michigan and Grand Rapids these days, in terms of any significant and palpable strength? If you guys are the only Christians, yours is a miserably and pitifully small "church" indeed, with scarcely little staying power (i.e., as a significant influence).

This is hardly a plausible or convincing evidence of the hand of God, in my opinion. Catholicism, on the other hand, flourishes in full splendor, as it always has (even surviving several bleak periods, humanly speaking). Much more could be said, but you don't seem to appreciate very much my historical and analogical arguments, so I'll stop.

Good news and bad news! I concede that I made a (partial) boo-boo, but the bad news is that it is an exceedingly minor point in our overall discussion. You're right about Joseph Smith not starting out as a Calvinist. I did not phrase this quite as accurately as I should have. In my book, in the "Protestant errors" chapter, I put it this way: "many founders of religious cults had Calvinistic backgrounds."

Stated this way, my remark to you is at least half-true. Brushing up on my research (which wasn't originally *mine* on this point, since I first heard and "inherited" the argument from a prominent evangelical Protestant cult researcher friend), I couldn't confirm that Joseph Smith himself was a card-carrying Calvinist. As it turns out, he may not have even tiptoed through TULIP.

Yet I found some things that likely led to the origin of this whole argument: Four members of Joseph Smith's family became officially associated with *Presbyterianism*; his mother, brothers Hyrum and Samuel, and sister Sophronia, according to his own account (as confirmed by documentation: Hoekema, *Four Major Cults*, p. 9 / Robert L. Millet, editor, *Joseph Smith: Selected Sermons and Writings*, New York: Paulist Press, 1989, p. 13 (Introduction) / Marvin S. Hill and James B. Allen, editors, *Mormonism and American Culture*, New York: Harper & Row, 1972, p. 30). Furthermore, *Joseph Smith's ancestral background was Puritan*, according to Kenneth Scott Latourette:

> Joseph Smith was born in Vermont of old New England stock. So far as the family had a religious background it was Puritan.
>
> (*The 19th Century Outside Europe*, New York: Harper & Row, 1961, p. 113)

As to my whole scenario of his reacting against Calvinism, etc., I will suspend judgment on that until such time as I see some proof (I do recall, however, this being a significant factor in C. T. Russell's heretical development, so it *does* happen among the heresiarchs). So, although partially inaccurate, I think this point of mine is a bit more worthy than, again, a "joke," as you characteristically mock it. I'd like to see you back up many of your contentions with any evidence, let alone as much as I present for even my partial errors. . . .

I get the distinct feeling, James, that you don't like the apostolic, biblical, patristic, historical and Catholic gospel. No surprise, given your love for Calvinist theology. Those who have never realized their own helplessness often hate to submit to the ecclesiastical authority established by Christ, I've discovered. I've seen similar paragraphs from other "Protestants," from snake handlers, Shakers, Quakers, Dake-ers, the Bakkers, fakers, tithe-takers, TULIP-makers, Coplandites, Mennonites, Scofieldites, "Israel"-whites, Swaggartites, Church of Christ, Church of God, United Church of Christ, Church of God in Christ, Disciples of Christ, and the Christian Church, and eponymous "Christians," even from some "Catholics" too.

Your second paragraph on p. 8 is an absolutely astonishing rapid-fire assault on my (and others') character. I *should* ignore it, but I'll comment due to its incredible nature:

1) You say I wouldn't have talked (or written) a certain way in 1990 ("that's for *certain*" -- because you have my 12-page story to prove it, I guess you'd say).

2) You object to my use of epithets, in the midst of your use of countless ones yourself!

3) Then you brag about your abilities in defending a logically indefensible position.

4) You throw in some gratuitous digs at Madrid and Matatics for good measure (I'd love to see your 60 pages of refutation of Madrid's five-page article. Gee, I wonder if there are any "epithets" in there? What tedium it must contain!).

5) Then it's back to my style, which is "tinny" (I've been called much worse, thank you).

6) The "scared-to-debate" charge rears its ugly head again. I've already disposed of that above.

7) I "hide behind a word-processor" (so asinine that my satirical affinities fail me this time).

8) I "blow smoke" (exactly what you're doing here).

9) Then it's back to the "but how can I read your book if I don't have it?" lament.

10) Then there are multiple views of Catholic "tradition" (how many? 23,000? Why don't you be precise when you make these wild charges, for once?). Are Kung's and Dollinger's and Curran's and Wilhelm's and McBrien's views included in your tally? Is Newman's view of tradition mine? Yes, since his is the Catholic view. I really don't think Patrick Madrid disagrees with Newman, who will in all likelihood be a saint one day and possibly a Doctor of the Church. Again, if Matatics is a schismatic, his view is irrelevant to my work as a *Catholic* apologist. If 90 to 95% of Protestants-in-quotes don't speak for

you, then don't make schismatics speak for *me* and *my* Church. This is silly. You say there are many views of tradition. I say there is only one, and you can discover it in the standard Catholic sources. If you think there are "all sorts of different takes" on tradition, the burden of proof is on you to *demonstrate* this, not just *talk* about it for rhetoric's sake alone.

All of this in one paragraph! Yet you wonder why I refuse to engage a person who "argues" in such a way in public debate. You can rail against me all you want about that (it will fall on "deaf ears" from now on), but I'll tell you one thing. You're sure gonna get a run for your money in this writing debate. Your constant resort to vilification of me and the ignoring of many of my arguments only proves that your oft-proclaimed debating abilities are already failing you. Call *that* statement pride if you want. I don't care.

I've only heard one of your debates -- with Fr. Pacwa on *sola Scriptura*, but I don't have a copy of it. Rather, since you issued the challenge, I will make a similar type of argument to those I utilized earlier with flow charts:

P1) X, Y, and Z are regarded by all as Church fathers.
P2) James White thinks X, Y, Z are either outright Protestant or more so than Catholic, and therefore are not Catholic, and can't be "claimed" by Catholics.
A1) But X, Y, and Z's views on A, B, and C, etc. are contrary to White's conception of what Christianity is, and ought to be.
C1) Therefore, X, Y, and Z are in fact Catholics, as in Dave Armstrong's view.
A2) But this contradicts White's P2.
C2) Therefore, White must either give up citing X, Y, and Z as "his own" and consider them infidels or apostates or else become a Catholic so as to avoid historical contradictions.

We will select (a random choice), the three fathers you cited:

How do you know you are in company with, say, Athanasius or Ignatius or Irenaeus? In the final analysis, is it not because Rome tells you so?

We will examine some of their "unprotestant" and "Romish" views. Now, if I was out of the fold of Protestantism due to the rejection of just T and U of TULIP, then the multiple errors in the views of these fathers which I will prove certainly render them infidels all the more so. I'm pleased you want to do this, . . . All emphases will be added. The battle can finally be joined. Amen!

St. Ignatius (d.c.110)

1) Denominationalism:

It is, therefore, advantageous for you to be in *perfect unity*, in order that you may always have a share in God. (Eph., 4,2)

Let there be *nothing* among you which is capable of *dividing you* . . . (Mag., 6,2)

Flee from *divisions*, as the beginnings of evils. (Sm., 8,1)

Focus on *unity*, for there is *nothing better*. (Pol., 1,2)

If anyone follows a *schismatic*, he will not inherit the kingdom of God. (Ph., 3,3)

2) Bishops:

Whoever does *anything without bishop* and presbytery and deacons does not have a *clean conscience*. (Tr., 7,2)

You must all *follow the bishop*, as Jesus Christ followed the Father . . . (Sm., 8,1)

Cling inseparably to Jesus Christ and *to the bishop . . .* (Tr., 7,1)

Let everyone respect the deacons as Jesus Christ, just as they should respect the *bishop, who is a model of the Father*, and the presbyters as God's council and as the band of the apostles. *Without these no group can be called a church.* (Tr., 3,1)

It is good to *acknowledge God and the bishop.* The one who honors the bishop has been honored by God; the one who does anything without the bishop's knowledge serves the devil. (Sm., 9,1)

It is obvious, therefore, that *we must regard the bishop as the Lord himself.* (Eph., 6,1)

3) Real Presence:

I want the bread of God, which is the *flesh of Christ.* (Rom., 7,3)

Participate in *one Eucharist* (for there is *one flesh* of our Lord Jesus Christ, and one cup which leads to unity through his blood. . .). (Ph., 4,1)

They abstain from the Eucharist and prayer, because they refuse to acknowledge that *the Eucharist is the flesh of our Savior Jesus Christ.* (Sm., 6,2).

4) Vicarious Atonement (a species of penance):

I am a humble *sacrifice* for you. (Eph., 8,1)

Grant me nothing more than to be *poured out as an offering to God* while there is still an altar ready. (Rom., 2,2)

. . . I might prove to be a *sacrifice* to God. (Rom., 4,2)

May my spirit be a *ransom* on your behalf. (Sm., 10,2)

May I be a *ransom* on your behalf in every respect. (Pol., 2,3)

5) Justification:

Those who profess to be Christ's will be recognized by their *actions*. For the Work is not a matter of what one *promises* now, but of *perseveringo* the end in the power of faith (Eph., 14,2)

6) Infallibility:

The Lord accepted the ointment upon his head for this reason: that he might breath *incorruptibility upon the church*. (Eph., 17,1)

St. Irenaeus (c.130-c.200)

1) *Sola Scriptura* / Tradition:

The Church . . . has received from the Apostles and from their disciples the faith. (*Against the Herestics*, 1, 10, 1)

The Church, having received this preaching and this faith . . . guarded it . . . She likewise believes these things . . . and harmoniously she proclaims them and teaches them and hands them down, as if she possessed but one mouth . . . the authority of the tradition is one and the same. (*Ibid.*, 1, 10, 2)

Every Church throughout the whole world has received this tradition from the Apostles. (*Ibid.*, 2, 9, 1)

Polycarp . . . was instructed . . . by the Apostles, and conversed with many who had seen Christ . . . He always taught those things which he had learned from the Apostles, and which the Church had handed down, and which are true. (*Ibid.*, 3, 3, 4)

The true gnosis is the doctrine of the Apostles, and the ancient organization of the Church throughout the whole world . . . and the very complete tradition of the Scriptures. (*Ibid.*, 4, 33, 8)

2) Real Presence:

The bread over which thanks have been given *is the Body* of (the) Lord, and the cup *His Blood.* (*Ibid.*, 4, 18, 4 / cf. 4, 18, 5; 4, 33, 2)

3) Justification:

[Paul], an able wrestler, urges us on in the struggle for immortality, so that we may receive a crown, and so that we may regard as a precious crown that which we acquire by our own struggle, and which does not grow on us spontaneously. And because it comes to us in a struggle, it is therefore the more precious. (*Ibid.*, 4, 37, 7)

4) Penance:

Ludwig Ott cites his mention of backsliders re-accepted after public confession and penance (*Ibid.*, 1, 6, 3; 1, 13, 5; 4, 40, 1).

5) The Blessed Virgin Mary:

> "Mary . . . by obeying, became the cause of salvation both for herself and the whole human race . . . What the virgin Eve had tied up by unbelief, this the virgin Mary loosened by faith." {*Ibid.*, 3,21,10}

6) The Preeminence of the Church of Rome (i.e., Catholicism):

> . . . Peter and Paul were evangelizing in Rome and laying the foundation of the Church . . . the greatest and most ancient Church known to all, founded and organized at Rome by the two most glorious Apostles, Peter and Paul, that Church which has the tradition and the faith which comes down to us after having been announced to men by the Apostles. For with this Church, because of its superior origin, all Churches must agree, that is, all the faithful in the whole world; and it is in her that the faithful everywhere have maintained the Apostolic tradition.

> The blessed Apostles, having founded and built up the Church, they handed over the office of the episcopate to Linus. Paul makes mention of this Linus in the Epistle to Timothy [2 Tim 4:21]. To him succeeded Anencletus; and after him, in the third place from the Apostles, Clement was chosen for the episcopate . . .

> In the time of Clement, no small dissension having arisen among the brethren in Corinth, the Church in Rome sent a very strong letter to the Corinthians, exhorting them to peace and renewing their faith. (*Ibid.*, 3, 1, 1; 3, 3, 2-3)

St. Athanasius (c.296-373)

1) Real Presence:

> After the great and wonderful prayers have been completed, then the bread is become the Body, and the

wine the Blood, of our Lord Jesus Christ. (*Sermon to the Newly Baptized*)

2) Justification (Arminianism):

Since we are sons and gods because of the Word in us, so also, because of the Spirit's being in us, - the Spirit who is in the Word which is in the Father, - we shall be in the Son and in the Father . . .

Therefore, when someone falls from the Spirit through any wickedness - that grace indeed remains irrevocably with those who are willing to repent after such a fall. Otherwise, the one who has fallen is no longer in God, because that Holy Spirit and Advocate who is in God has deserted him. (*Discourses Against the Arians*, 3, 25)

3) The Papacy:

[St. Athanasius repeatedly aligned himself with the Roman See in his struggles for orthodoxy and against heretical rulers in the East]

I rest my case. Is this a "fine" enough "brush" for you? St. Ignatius and St. Irenaeus each fail six of your litmus tests for bona fide Christianity, and St. Athanasius three. All this was found in my limited patristic resources (Lightfoot and Jurgens . . .). This enterprise is so patently unnecessary as to be almost absurd -- so self-evident is it that the fathers were Catholic. When will this ridiculous game of desperate Protestant pretense cease? I don't look at all kindly on historical revisionism, especially in the cause of schism. I'll be looking forward eagerly to your Protestant interpretation of the above data. Good luck! You'll need it. . . .

I suppose Newman was dishonest with himself and others, too over the issue of papal infallibility? Not quite, James. He was what is called an "inopportunist" before the definition -- one who thought that the time was not right for it. Primarily, he was opposed to the ultramontane faction. The definition was actually a triumph of the center or the moderate viewpoint, so to speak, since it limited infallibility quite a bit and gave it very specific criteria. Newman had full liberty as a Catholic to question the possible future dogma before it was defined, and in so doing, showed great courage, concern for the well-being of the Church, and integrity. In fact, I believe (I'd have to verify this) he questioned only a more *sweeping* definition, as proposed by the ultramontanes.

He was just as consistent and honest when he submitted (what you call a "collapse" -- I used to make the same argument, by the way, after Salmon) to the definition afterwards because this is how Catholicism operates. Those are the rules of the game, and those who can't abide by them (such as Dollinger and millions of liberals today) ought to get out of the game and play another one where they can avoid being disingenuous, to put it mildly. What Newman did was no different than opposing a proposal for a change in a civil statute but then agreeing to obey it if it becomes law.

I suppose one can never make a square peg fit into a round circle, and it will always be well-nigh impossible for the "free" Protestant, with his "Christian liberty" to grasp the idea of submission to Church authority. This act is regarded as a crutch and wimpish intellectual suicide, when in actuality it is simply the common-sense realization of one's own clear limitations and the simultaneous acknowledgment of a much greater, corporate, divinely instituted, Spirit-led Church.

I've never understood how Protestants can (often slavishly) follow either their own fancies or those of their pastor, oftentimes thoroughly ignorant of, and divorced from Church history, yet excoriate Catholics for showing the same deference to the pope and the whole grand tradition of the Church. Our view is by no means less plausible, even on the face of it. . . .

The validity of ecumenical councils is determined by their approval (in entirety or in part) by the pope, not my own particular preferences. Otherwise we do indeed have a certain chaos and indeterminism, as you note (the Orthodox have this very difficulty).

I have a simple suggestion for you to figure out what Catholics are bound to believe: pick up the new *Catechism*. Whatever you find in there is -- you can rest assured -- Catholic teaching. As for the various levels of doctrinal certainty, read Ludwig Ott's *Fundamentals of Catholic Dogma*. When he describes a doctrine as *de fide*, it has been infallibly defined [at the highest level], usually by a council, sometimes by a pope. "How truly wonderful" indeed.

By the way, is TULIP infallible? On what grounds? And if it is, along with so many other Protestant dogmas (such as your "epistemological leaps which I listed above), how is your philosophical stance any less "problematic" than ours? If TULIP isn't infallible, then why did I flunk Protestantism 0101 for not espousing it? Hmmm? . . .

If Protestantism isn't man-centered, why do congregations all too frequently have one heaven of a time coping when one man -- the pastor -- leaves? At three of the churches with which I had ties: a Lutheran, an Assembly of God, and a non-denominational church, there occurred severe "succession crises" -- twice at the latter (I took no part whatsoever in any of these civil wars, in case you're wondering).

Now, why would this be, unless they were man-centered? What's the big deal about *one man* moving out and another moving in? All of these instances were typified by great animosity, lack of commitment among many members towards the church (with them leaving), and petty, backbiting politics. And you guys talk about us and our "sacerdotalism," etc.

Also, the mentality of selecting a church based on ear-tickling doctrines (which is so easy to do in Protestantism -- the spectrum runs the gamut) -- is also man-centered. Pragmatism, experientialism, worldliness, antinomianism, "cheap grace," materialism, narcissism, public relations, church growth rather than individual growth in spiritual maturity -- all these trends are strong.

What would you expect, though, from an outlook that made individualism supreme, even over against truth, when they conflict? All Catholic doctrines which you think detract from Christ do not at all, rightly understood. You are again the unconscious victim of the "dichotomous mentality" that Louis Bouyer talks about with such keen insight. . . .

I noted above that I don't have the (technical) materials to delve into this obsession you have with Lateran IV and persecution of heretics. But even if I did, I would not answer until you dealt with the same type of persecution within Protestantism, and what it does to *your* lofty claims of spiritual superiority to us (see enclosed tract on that). You've absolutely ignored this thus far (do I detect a pattern here? Might it be called . . . evasion?).

As usual, the Protestant has to create a double standard when comparing the rival claims. It's okay to talk about Catholic historical shortcomings, but not Protestant ones, and conversely, it's alright to extoll the virtues of Protestantism (and there are many), but we must not note anything good about "Romanism." That's too dangerous. I agree, you don't claim *infallibility*, but you *do* claim *superiority*. That being the case, there is good reason to be suspicious of super-pious claims from the Deformers, when one learns about the horrible crimes committed and/or sanctioned by *them*.

At last! Something with which we can agree and cooperate in opposing: various Jehovah's Witnesses heretical doctrines of the Godhead. What a breath of fresh air. God's omnipresence is denied in *Aid to Bible Understanding*, 1971, p. 665:

> The true God is not omnipresent, for he is spoken of as having a location. His throne is in Heaven.

Dud [Judge] Rutherford even went so far as to state that:

> . . . the Pleiades is the place of the eternal throne of God. {*Reconciliation*, 1928, p.14}

As for "Jehovah's" body:

> God is a person with a spiritual body . . . They will then see God . . . and also be like him (1 Jn 3:2). This, too,

shows that God is a person, and that he has a body. (*You Can Live Forever in Paradise on Earth*, 1982, pp. 36-37)

The bodies of spiritual persons (God, Christ, the angels) are glorious. (*Aid . . .*, 1971, p. 247)

They deny God's omniscience as well: *Aid*, p. 595; *Watchtower*, 7-15-84, pp. 4-5. But they'll contradict themselves elsewhere, too, as I'm sure you're well aware.

"I'm not going to be referring people to a source they can't even read." Well now you *can* read it! You had to wait all of a month or so (I know how excited you are to receive my arguments, which are fatal to your position). Your comments on the "98 pages" are the hysterically funny ones, if you ask me. If you'll go back to my p. 11 you'll find that I make a simple, unadorned statement of fact, i.e., that I have written extensively on the papacy, and that this will provide my answer to your arguments on that subject.

There is neither pride, nor any implication that thereby the debate is "finished," as you comically reply. I merely make reference to my paper. Eight lines are obviously not "all [I] can come up with." Get real! This is the whole point: that if you want to delve into the papacy and infallibility (which is probable), you can read my paper (the longest in my book). Did you think I would keep it from you?! I'm trying to save space (and my eyes and fingers) by referring to completed works.

You, on the other hand - it must regrettably be pointed out - constantly drone on about all the people you've debated and how they were all beaten, etc., and how much you know about *sola Scriptura* ("a recognized expert") as, e.g., in your raving paragraph on p. 8.

It could only be your apparent unfounded *assumption* that practically every critical comment I make is motivated by conceit, ignorance, or an intention of sophistry, that makes you construct an elaborate scenario of *my* mindset out of a reference (much like a footnote) to an existing paper. I belabor this minor point because I think it illustrates well the difference in how you regard me versus how I view you. I think you're sincerely misinformed and wrong about Catholicism, with a considerable bias against it which often blinds you, and that you have many (I believe unconsciously held) contradictory views.

I make no negative judgments as to your motivations, intelligence (which I have praised several times), honesty (excepting intellectual dishonesty, which I consider, again, largely unconscious anyway), or character. If it ever appears that I do, please be assured this is *not my intention* and interpret overly harsh words in light of this statement of belief and purpose. I try my utmost to critique your *ideas*, not *you* (and these observations can be quite scathing, as you know).

You, on the other hand, indisputably question my character and competence, in terms of intellectual ability, deliberate (I believe this is your view) misrepresentation of your opinions, a supposed marked arrogance, a false charge of cowardice, and many other personal descriptions and slander which have no place in a reasoned debate. As I dealt with these elements early on I will leave it at that and plead for more detached, "scholarly" objectivity from you in the future.

You go on to assert that I am hypocritical since I supposedly avoided your argument but accuse you of the same tactic. You are again making a false analogy. I referred you to the longest chapter of my book, which you now possess on paper. This is no avoidance whatsoever; quite the contrary. If anything, it is overkill! You, conversely, did indeed "blithely dismiss my points 7 and 8" of my first letter. True, for #7 you (like me) referred me to your book for an answer, but I replied that the specific question I raised was not dealt with there (the inconsistent Protestant appeal to councils).

Since you have not answered #7 to the slightest degree in this letter, it remains unanswered, like so many other of my challenges to you. #8 was conveniently dismissed as irrelevant with, as I noted, a 14-word sentence. I clarified my intent in my last letter, but to no avail. It, too, awaits a *real* answer, and I submit that some kind of reply, however short, would be a requirement of both courtesy and a healthy, self-confident intellect (which you do possess).

You think that my query is answered by an attack on Catholic popular morals and the bad popes, and a mention of Packer's *A Quest for Godliness*, as if any of this has the slightest relevance to the original question #8. To parody you, I *do* think you have no answer, and that is indeed to *my* advantage in this debate, since it confirms my opinion on this matter. Yet you accuse *me* of hypocrisy. How many examples of this sort of thing do I have to point out to you? They are the primary reason why this letter is 36 pages! (I pray that I am near the end. I'm trying -- I really am).

If you have a good patristic library and know Greek and history, all the more pathetic are your claims [about] the fathers . . . My examples of the three fathers you brought up above are a case-in-point. I literally can't wait to see what you do with that information.

I don't know Greek, so what am I to do with your lengthy Greek quote? Stay up all night with my *Englishman's Greek Concordance* deciphering its literal meaning? Maybe I'll have my friend, who teaches Latin, transcribe my next letter, so you can do some similar work. Fair is fair, after all. Uh oh! St. Clement used the term *elect*?! Really?! Egads! Now, I'll have to rethink my whole position! This is a classic case of your Protestantism (and Calvinism in this case) blinding you to objective truth.

You think that Catholics must somehow avoid and rationalize away the very word "elect" in order to prevent grave danger to our doctrine. This is sheer nonsense and foolishness, and ought to embarrass you. obviously -- *eklektos* being a prominent NT word -- it has been dealt with by Catholic scholars down through the ages, believe it or not. We don't have to ignore biblical words and entire biblical sub-strata, as Protestants constantly do.

The cogent point here is whether or not *free will* is wiped out by the concept of divine election, since that's the primary bone of contention, as Luther himself states. I think it is *not*, and St. Augustine agrees with *me* on that point, not you and Calvinism (I'm eagerly awaiting your reply to those quotes above, too). "St. Paul and St. Augustine and Melanchthon and Wesley and C. S. Lewis I know, but who is this White guy?"

. . . St. Ignatius is referring to the desertion of God, not the bishop (the parallels to Eph 6:10-18 are pretty unmistakable, I think). Jurgens uses the Divine pronoun in 6:2: "Be pleasing to *Him* whose soldiers you are . . ." Now, I think my original point was clear enough. But that's only my opinion. Maybe it wasn't. Since the context is the use of military metaphor, as in St. Paul, desertion, it would seem to me, is a metaphor here for falling away from the faith.

Since Calvinists presuppose the impossibility of this, they can only postulate that such a soldier was never really in the ranks to begin with (i.e., never among the elect). But this is clearly nonsensical and does violence to the metaphor. A soldier is a soldier. The notion of military desertion assumes that the soldier had to desert from something.

Likewise with the many scriptural admonitions warning against "falling away," etc. This is why I said, "so much for Calvinism," since St. Ignatius' word-picture seems to me to run counter to U, I, and P of TULIP. I think this is as sensible an interpretation as any. . . .

I didn't make "blanket accusations against Protestant apologists" but against "anti-Catholic debaters," which is quite different and a vastly smaller fraternity. . . . I haven't made a study of the same (as you recall, I won't even read these books), but have noted this tendency in the normal course of my studies in apologetics and reading of *This Rock*, etc.

I went over the "anti-Catholic" terminology bit already. If the "Catholic" debaters are separatists, then they are "anti-Protestant" in the same sense in which I use "anti-Catholic." If they are true and consistent Catholics (who accept Vatican II, including its *Decree on Ecumenism*), they are not "anti-Protestant," any more than ecumenical Protestants are "anti-Catholic." . . .

I disagree with you about the "Lord's Prayer" incident. I don't accept your first reason. I think, rather, that communion requires, and is the sign of, unity, and don't think any pretense is involved here. But then, again I am an ecumenist and you're not. I would hesitate only in praying with someone who was invoking an entirely different God or some lesser entity, as in eastern religion. I guess that's how you see Catholics, so, given this premise, I suppose you couldn't pray with them. Your third objection is legalistic and proves too much (do you object to invocations at graduations and in the Senate, and grace at family reunions, too?). But I'll grant you the consistency of your convictions, even though, at bottom, I find the premises and attitude reprehensible, as I do anti-Catholicism in general.

I don't know what to make of your interpretation of the Madrid debate. Perhaps there was a subjective misinterpretation on his part as to your willingness to shake hands. I even considered that possibility when reading the account. This is a plausible enough scenario, all things being equal. But knowing Pat a little bit, and your reasoning and general negative attitude towards Catholic apologists pretty well by now, I would have to defer to his account if all the evidence I have is your word versus his.

One thing I'm absolutely sure of: he is not the compulsive liar and buffoon you make him out to be, with your "20 pages of small-print, triple-column text" (to refute his errors) remark concerning his article. This is a very low blow, and, having experienced your venom towards myself, I would not be at all surprised if much of your objection consists of *non sequiturs* there as well.

Sure, I'll listen to your debate, but I fully expect to find exactly what was described by Madrid and Akin because I've observed how you often ignore or irrationally misunderstand my challenges and how Protestants in general have a massive blind spot with regard to *sola Scriptura*, and, indeed, almost all of their serious deficiencies (a fish doesn't know it's in water, either). I also watched Dave Hunt make a fool of himself in "debate." He wrote to me and said he *didn't have to quote the fathers* to show what the early Church was like, but only the Bible!!!!!

I will ignore your cheap shots at my honesty (twice), courage, and scholarly abilities. I told you who Gary Michuta is, so your remarks about him are plain silly. Why should you *care* what Catholic you debate if we're all idiots, idolaters, Pelagians, and fools, anyway?

116

You also completely ignored my arguments about Wycliffe and Hus. I'll accept in good faith your word on p.15: "There is more I'd like to get to . . ." and assume that you do have some sort of answer to this contention of mine as well as the twenty or so other unanswered ones to be dealt with, and will respond in due course.

In Christ and His Church, with Scripture and Tradition, Faith that Works, Grace and Sacraments, Mary and the Saints, Penance and Purgatory, Pope and Bishops, Peace and Truth, Love and Mercy,

Dave Armstrong

* * * * *

11-10-95

Dave Armstrong

"Catholic Apologist and Free-Lance Writer"

Dear Mr. Armstrong:

I am in receipt of yet another of your letters [I couldn't locate these in my files, but as I recall I did become overly agitated by White's continual refusal to respond] designed to distract and goad me into investing time in answering your letter of 5-15-95. I confess, you have me. I have never figured out how to answer letters that are filled with whining, crying, complaining, and general substanceless meandering. And sadly, I can't suggest anyone else who would be willing to invest their time in responding to such materials, either. Most folks I know are too busy doing constructive things with their lives. Personally, I'm busy teaching for Golden Gate and Grand Canyon, writing a book on Roman Catholicism for one of the largest Christian publishers in the U.S., and producing chapters like the one I am attaching for you that will appear in the upcoming Soli Deo Gloria publication on *sola scriptura*, along with chapters by John

MacArthur, John Gerstner, and R.C. Sproul. My travels will soon be taking me to British Columbia, and hopefully, to New York to debate Gerry Matatics yet once again, sometime early next year. So, Dave, I'm sorry to have to inform you that I have far more pressing issues to address than your letter and its extensive flights in illogic and personal attack. I hope you enjoy the chapter.

Sincerely,

James White

Chapter Two

Dialogue on the Alleged "Perspicuous Apostolic Message" as a Proof of the Quasi-Protestantism of the Early Church
[May-June 1996]

This took place on Mr. White's e-mail "*sola Scriptura* list*" (by this time I was online, but didn't yet have a website), that he actually invited me to. It included Protestants, Catholics, and even a few Orthodox. Here we clearly observe White's trademark evasiveness when I ask him "hard questions."

It's a pattern and tactic that he has perpetually followed all through the years with me. His other overwhelming tendency is rank insults. But there were still relatively few of those at this early stage of the game: only relentless evasion and obfuscation.

* * * * *

*There would be no criticism if the Roman Catholic side was not using the argument "*sola scriptura *doesn't work because* sola scriptura *hasn't brought about monolithic theological agreement on all issues." Dave Armstrong has made that argument in posts here,*

Maybe you have me confused with one of the other two Daves in the group, since, to my recollection, I have never made such an argument. What I said was that *perspicuity* fails as a thought-system because it presupposes possible (and actual) agreement among Protestants, at least on the so-called "central" issues, based on recourse to the Bible alone. This is clearly false, and a pipe-dream. My point is: "what criteria of falsifiability will suffice to challenge the Protestant notion of perspicuity, given the fact of 24,000 sects?" In the opinion of Catholics, this sad state of affairs is more than enough to put the lie to perspicuity, as formulated by Luther, Calvin, and current-day evangelical scholars such as R. C. Sproul.

Now don't try to tell us that "this is not how perspicuity is defined," etc. I've heard it 1000 times if I've heard it once that Protestants agree on the central issues, and that this "fact" supposedly salvages perspicuity and *sola Scriptura*. But I can't find any Protestant willing to face this ridiculous division squarely.

I believe it is vitally important to believe in what the Apostles taught. Which, of course, is exactly why I cannot embrace the teachings of Rome. In fact, it is fidelity to the apostolic *message that is the strongest argument against the innovations of Rome over time, Dave.*

Why not boldly tell us, then, James, precisely *what* "the Apostles taught"? In particular, I am curious as to their teaching in those areas where Protestants can't bring themselves to agree with each other; for example:

- 1.TULIP
- 2. Baptism
- 3. The Eucharist
- 4. Church Government
- 5. Regeneration
- 6. Sanctification
- 7. The Place of Tradition
- 8. Women Clergy
- 9. Divorce
- 10. Feminism
- 11. Abortion

I've heard recently that even John Stott and F. F. Bruce have questioned the existence of eternal hellfire. And they're supposed to be "evangelicals"?! How can you have "fidelity" to an "apostolic message" if you can't even define what it *is*? And if you either don't know, or are reluctant to spell it out here, then you illustrate my point better than I could myself: either your case collapses due to internal inconsistency, or because of the chaos of Protestant sectarianism, which makes any such delineation of "orthodoxy" impossible according to your own first principles; or if theoretically possible, certainly unenforceable.

I think this is at least as compelling as the "infinite regress" scenario, with regard to infallibility, which would wipe out all authority and/or certainty, whether from a Protestant or Catholic (or Orthodox) perspective. After all, one must exercise *some* faith, somewhere along the line, as I think all here would agree. When Catholics accept infallibility of popes and councils, this is an implicit faith in our Lord, Whom we believe protects same from error.

Absent some response to this, Protestants are simply engaging in fantasy, pipe-dreams, and games, in violation of biblical, divine injunctions such as, ". . . teaching them to obey *everything* I have commanded you" (Matthew 28:20) -- not just the mythical "central," "primary," "essential" doctrines, and "who cares whether we agree on the peripherals." Get real (and biblical)! Eagerly awaiting your response (nothing fancy required, just a laundry list) to my -- as of yet - unanswered challenge.

That's pretty easy, Dave. I have 27 books filled with their teaching. Where shall we start? I guess we could start with the apostolic teaching that we are justified by faith and so have peace with God (Romans 5:1). That's a wonderful thing to know, isn't it?

It certainly is. And we agree in large part. But when you guys corrupt the traditional understanding into *sola fide*, we must part ways. Why, though, if *sola fide* is true, did "scarcely anyone" teach it from Paul to Luther, according to Norman Geisler, in his latest book *Roman Catholics and Evangelicals* (p. 502)? Very strange, and too bizarre and implausible for me.

The Apostles also taught that Jesus Christ was and is fully deity (Colossians 2:9), and that's really important, too!

Absolutely. But you guys got this doctrine from us, so big wow!

Are you saying that the Bible is insufficient *to answer these questions? That God's Word is so unclear, so confused, so ambiguous, that these issues* cannot *be determined by a careful and honest examination of the Bible?*

It's irrelevant what *I* think, because I'm asking *you*. But let's assume for the sake of argument that it *is* clear, sufficient, and perspicuous. Okay, now, *please tell me what it teaches* on these issues! Does anyone not understand my argumentation here? Is it that complicated? This is the essence of my whole argument in this vein. If we grant your perspicuity, then tell us these doctrines that are so clear. Yet you guys want to either run or cry foul when we hold you to your own principles!

Why not throw in the Trinity, the deity of Christ, and the person of the Holy Spirit, as most do when they decide to start going after the Bible?

We agree on these three doctrines, so they are irrelevant to the discussion. I'm asking for clarification on the issues which divide

Protestants, for we regard this division as a disproof of perspicuity. No one's "going after the Bible." I for one have a whole wall full of 25+ Bible versions, and all sorts of Bible reference works. I don't need to defend my love for the Bible (nor does the Catholic Church, for that matter). I'm saying: be true to your own principles, and don't be ashamed of them. Either demonstrate this abstract, ethereal notion of perspicuity concretely and practically, or cease using it if it has no content, and if it is only useful as a content-less slogan to bash Catholics with.

People who call themselves Protestants disagree on every point above; people who call themselves Roman Catholics disagree on every point above, too. So what?

This is your typical evasion, which I severely critiqued in a related post. I don't care about "people who call themselves [X, Y, Z]." One can only go by the official teachings of any given group. You don't go seek out a backslidden Mormon in a bar in Salt Lake City to determine the beliefs of Mormons! You go to *Pearl of Great Price, Doctrines and Covenants,* and *The Book of Mormon.* This is utterly obvious. Yet when it comes to us, you want to preserve your "argument from Catholic liberals," since it is apparently the only "reply" you have to a critique of your views. Is it a proper answer if an atheist, asked why he doesn't believe in God, says, "Well you theists can't agree whether God is a singular Being or a Trinity, so there!"? We are critiquing *your* position. Besides, we have already answered your tired objections on this point many times (myself at least five times, and David Palm, a few more). But you guys keep wanting to avoid my question as to the precise nature of this "apostolic message" to which you refer [anti-Catholic apologist Eric Svendsen also attempted some non-"replies"]. Again, I'm just holding you to your own words. If you would rather admit that your own phrases have neither definition nor doctrinal or rational content, that would be one way (albeit not a very impressive one) out of your felt dilemma.

First, the apostolic message is far more narrow than you'd like to make it. The apostles did not address every single issue there is to address. They did not address the issue of genetic engineering, for example. Nor did they discuss nuclear energy. Does that make the Bible "insufficient"?

Another fruitless exercise in evasion: "if you don't have an answer, then hopelessly confuse the issue by introducing *non sequiturs.*" This is no answer at all. Are you going to seriously maintain (with a straight face) that the Apostles (in the Bible) did not address issues on my list such as: baptism, the Eucharist, church government, regeneration, sanctification, tradition, or the spiritual gifts? How ridiculous! Why don't you select just five of this present list of items out of my entire list of 18 in which Protestants differ, and tell me what the Apostles taught, so I can know what you know?

Only if you make "sufficient" a standard that is absurd and beyond reason.

What's absurd? I'm simply asking you to define what you mean by "apostolic message." How is that at all "beyond reason"? Pure obfuscation . . .

Imparting exhaustive knowledge of all things is not one of the tasks of the Bible.

More obscurantism, designed to avoid (unsuccessfully) the horns of my dilemma.

I hope all on the list realize what is being said here. A person with the entire NT in his hand cannot know what the apostolic message was unless he likewise has Roman "tradition" alongside! Imagine it! Those poor Roman Christians. From about A.D. 55 until around A.D. 140 they could not have demonstrated fidelity to the apostolic message! Why not? Because they didn't have access to Roman Catholic tradition (there was no monarchial episcopate in Rome until the latter period, and hence no "Pope"). Does that make any sense? Of course not.

All the more reason for you to tell us what this mysterious "apostolic message" is. According to this curious illogic, one can "*know*" what the message is, without the Catholic Church, but they can't tell *me* what it is, what it consists of!

I am (hauntingly) reminded of my JW [Jehovah's Witnesses] friends who consistently point to the monolithic theology of the Watchtower Society as evidence of their "truthfulness."

Nice try. Here is a prime example of sophistry. Note how, again, this has nothing to do with the discussion at hand. Rather than answer a simple question of mine, directly related to his own statement, he prefers to compare the Catholic Church to an Arian heresy (which happens to be my own area of expertise, by the way). Even so, if James will answer my question, I'll be happy to demonstrate how Catholicism is infinitely more credible than JW's.

> When Catholics accept infallibility of popes and councils, this is an implicit faith in our Lord, Whom we believe protects same from error.

I wish it were faith in Christ the Lord;

It is, James. Did you not read my last sentence? Perhaps, like John MacArthur, you would like to contend that us poor, ignorant Catholics worship a different Christ, too?

Christ is the way, truth, and life, and hence fidelity to Him would cause one to put truth and consistency in the forefront of the examination.

What does this have to do with anything? Consistency is primarily what I'm calling for, and I'm asking you what the truth is, but you don't want to tell me! There are delicious ironies here to savor!

Yet, any honest examination of councils and Popes demonstrates that they have often contradicted each other. But, *the committed Roman Catholic finds a way around these contradictions, not because they are not really contradictions, but because of the* pre-existing *commitment to the Papacy and the related institutions.*

Straying. What is this, a replay of the Diet of Worms or something? I was chided for entering in articles which were *on* the general subject, so how can I answer here broad swipes at my Church such as these?

I get the real feeling, Dave, that you well know that your questions have been *and* will be *answered,*

If they have, I've missed it. Please, somebody send me that post. If they "will" be answered, when, and by whom, I wonder? But I don't "know" one way or the other, despite your "real feeling."

but that isn't going to stop you from using such language in the future in another forum, to be sure.

No, you're right, not till I get an answer. Sure, the language was exaggerated, but such excesses result from the frustration of repeatedly not receiving a simple answer to a simple-enough question.

You may wish to say that you "know" "everything" Jesus taught His disciples. Do you really, Dave?

No. Do you wish to say this?

Are you prepared to defend the thesis that Jesus taught the disciples the Immaculate Conception, predicted the Bodily Assumption, and that Peter really did believe in Papal

126

Infallibility? I challenge any Roman Catholic apologist on this list: you can't defend those doctrines from the Fathers. Those doctrines are not a part of the patristic literature. I'll be glad to demonstrate that.

Answer my question, and we Catholics will be glad to deal with yours, but I would say that it would be more profitable to do that in a whole 'nother discussion group, so as not to cloud the issues which will take a considerable amount of time to work through as it is.

[this list *was* supposed to be devoted to *sola Scriptura* and related issues of Tradition, after all, so the reader will note that I sought to stay on topic, while James wished to go all over the ballpark, in his evasions]

> Eagerly awaiting your response (nothing fancy required, just a laundry list) to my -- as of yet -- unanswered challenge,

What challenge is that, Dave?

Please read the first sentence above, after the introductory line. That explains it! You didn't know what I was asking for! Now that you know it, surely there is an answer, no? Just a list of the true apostolic teachings on baptism, etc. . . .

> Why don't you select just five of this present list of items out of my entire list of 18 in which Protestants differ, and tell me what the Apostles taught, so I can know what you know?

Your argument won't get you anywhere, Dave (and your style is certainly not going to win you any points with the more serious of our readers, either).

Is that why no one is answering? My style? Maybe I'll try a boring, staid approach, then.

You well know what the Bible teaches on these topics.

James, James! This is the whole point! *We* know, but *you* guys can't figure it out. Hence your reluctance to answer (I can think of no better reason). You claim busy-ness, which plagues us all, but you still have time to write this and evade my question again. A short answer to my question surely wouldn't put you out.

Problem is, you don't accept that.

How silly is this? I "don't accept" what the Bible teaches on these points, but you don't have the courtesy to explain to me just what it *is* that it teaches on them. Such a view is below contempt, and should cause you to blush with shame.

Instead, you accept another authority that tells you something different.

Sheer goofiness. Different than *what*? Again, if I don't have your answer, what do you expect me to believe? If this isn't *The Emperor's Clothes*, I don't know what is.

Tell us all again, Dave: are you saying the Bible is insufficient to answer these questions? Are you saying we can't know what the Bible teaches about tradition, for example? That a serious exegesis of relevant texts can't provide us with any level of certainty or knowledge? Is that what you really want to say to this group, Dave?

Quadruple "no" (that's no no no no). Now, how 'bout your equally forthright answer to me?

We all have our traditions. In point of fact, all of our traditions are fallible outside of Scripture. Those of us who recognize the fallibility of our traditions will test those traditions by Scripture. I know that's what I do, anyway. And, thankfully, the Scriptures are more than capable of providing the means of testing those traditions.

Yes, but since you guys can't agree with the interpretation of Scripture, of what practical use is an infallible Bible? If the interpretation is fallible and contradictory, then -- practically speaking -- the Bible in effect is no more infallible than its differing interpretations. But, if you're a Protestant, this is apparently of no consequence. Relativism is smuggled in under the aegis of private judgment and so-called "tolerance." This is all old news, but maybe if we repeat it enough times it will start sinking in.

But the simple fact of the matter is that the Catholic Church of 400 AD is not the Roman Catholic Church of 1996.

Correct. There is a 1596-year difference, and living bodies grow quite a bit in that great time-span. But this does not make them different organisms. The city of Jerusalem is a lot different now than in 400, but it is still Jerusalem, is it not? I'm a lot different than I was in 1966, but I'm still me! This aspect involves development of doctrine. One thing we know for sure: this "Catholic Church" of 400 (which was also very much centered at Rome) is *certainly* not organically connected to the current-day chaos of Protestant sectarianism.

Is it really true that there are some on this list who believe that without outside "tradition" or revelation, that we cannot, in fact, demonstrate the deity of Jesus Christ?

Not likely, James. If you can find even one, I'll eat my (free) copy of *The Fatal Flaw* [one of James' anti-Catholic books]. That said, I would point out, nevertheless, that, e.g., proponents of the heresies of Monophysitism (i.e., that Christ had one Nature, not two) and Monothelitism (i.e., that Christ had one will, not two) in particular, argued from Scripture alone and thought that Rome and the other orthodox churches were adding traditions of men to Scripture. So, when you get down to fine points, there is indeed a need for some authoritative pronouncements, as Church history itself clearly and unarguably affirms. Or is it your position that the pronouncements of Nicaea, Constantinople I, Ephesus and

Chalcedon on matters of the Trinity were altogether irrelevant and unnecessary? Something may indeed be quite clear (which I maintain is the case for many, many doctrines -- it is the premise of my book, *A Biblical Defense of Catholicism*, for Pete's sake), but there will arise people who manage to distort it, and so a conciliar definition and clarification becomes necessary in a *practical*, very "human" sense.

Surely we've all tangled with a [Jehovah's] Witness or two over the years. Am I to understand it that in the final analysis those who deny sola scriptura *ended such conversations with the anathema of the infallible interpreter? Was the final argument "It means this because the bishop of Rome says so?"*

Of course not. The response would be (at least in my case), if any appeal to tradition be made, rather: "*All* of the predominant Christian traditions for 2000 years have agreed that Jesus is the God-Man, whereas your belief originates from a late heresy called Arianism." Personally, for 15 years now I've followed in my own evangelism and apologetics a guideline from Paul: "be all things to all people." In this instance, your polemical caricature of how a Catholic would approach such a situation is absurd, and no one I know would ever use it. But historically speaking, yes, orthodoxy was -- in the final analysis -- determined by the Roman position, again and again, and again. I detail this in my brief history of early heresies in my chapter on the papacy, lest anyone doubt this, and many non-Catholic scholars such as Jaroslav Pelikan freely concur with this judgment.

We see the same dynamic, e.g., with regard to eastern schisms. There were five major ones prior to 1054 (over Arianism, St. John Chrysostom, the Acacian schism, Monothelitism, and Iconoclasm), and *in every case*, Rome was on the right side, according to today's Eastern Orthodoxy. Note that these are simple, unadorned facts of history -- they leave little room for differing interpretation, but they sure cast doubt on the tendency of certain members of a Church with such a history declaring it the historical repository of "orthodoxy" over against the Catholic Church.

When it comes to doctrines such as baptism, all of a sudden the Protestant must appeal to tradition, but not universal Christian tradition (prior to 1517). Rather, he resorts to a mere denominational tradition. Thus James White must appeal to a late tradition of non-regenerative adult baptism, which originated 15 centuries after Christ. He freely admits (for once) that practically all the fathers erred on this doctrine, whereas the Anabaptists and himself got it right. And so, accordingly, he goes to the Scripture and finds his "proof texts."

But even his master Calvin disagrees with him (about *when* baptism should occur), and also people in this group. So Calvin and Wesley and Luther have their proof texts which they believe contradict James White's. And so on and on it goes. Protestants have five camps on baptism. So instead of "Rome saying so," now it is because Calvin, or Zwingli, or James White "said so." Or, well, I almost forgot: "*The Bible* says so!" Given the sterling record of orthodoxy of Rome, I would say that such an appeal (if made at all) carries far more weight than the appeal to a single, self-proclaimed, self-anointed "reformer" such as John Calvin.

No offense intended, but in reality, it seems to me that when a convinced Roman Catholic encounters another system that, like Rome, claims special authority (like the Watchtower Bible and Tract Society), do we not here have an impasse?

Have you not read my extensive analysis of how these heresies and Rome are fundamentally different? Now granted you disagree with it, but that's different from foolish proclamations such as the above, which attempt to bamboozle people into thinking that I espouse a position which I in fact argued strenuously against in this very group. How quickly also you forget my quadruple "no" to your query recently, and my reply that I had produced 40 proofs for the Personhood of the Holy Spirit (everyone here is my witness), and that it was a "clear" doctrine in the Bible. But no matter: just blithely go on misrepresenting another's position.

The Roman Catholic, in the final analysis, says that John 20:28 says X because Rome says so (indeed, has Rome ever really said what John 20:28 means infallibly? I mean, Rome teaches the deity of Christ clearly enough, but what about the specific passages themselves?).

This is ludicrous. You assume falsely once again that because we believe Scripture does not function as a perspicuous authority apart from some human ecclesiastical authority, therefore *every* individual passage is an utter "mystery, riddle, and enigma" (to borrow from Churchill's description of Russia). Of course, this doesn't follow, and is another straw man - not very useful for the purposes of constructive dialogue. Besides, wouldn't your time be more profitably spent in rejoicing that we teach a doctrine of such paramount importance as the deity of Christ, instead of such minutiae?

The JW says John 20:28 can't say X, but must say Y, again, because Brooklyn says so. Both have ultimate commitments to ultimate authorities, and in the final analysis, how can any progress be made?

The hidden false assumption here is that the Protestant has no such "ultimate authority." But of course he does, and must. It is either he himself, or some aspect of a denominational tradition, which contradicts other such traditions (some of which must necessarily be man-made whenever they're contradictory). Sorry, but I don't see how such a system is at all superior to ours.

Now, on the other hand, is it not part of the appeal of Rome to point to conversations such as this, and the struggle to refute the "heretics" like the JW's, and say, "See, you can only have arguments about probabilities with Protestantism. We give you final certainty through the Church." I think all Protestants need to recognize the draw this has for people.

So please tell me, James: was my conversion due to a sincerely-held, reasoned, faith-based, morally-influenced, historically informed, biblically justified conclusion (regardless of your obvious disagreement), or simply psychological and emotional, irrationalist, subjective criteria? And are not such speculations instances of "judging the heart?"

The scandal of the plowman is not universally attractive.

I'm happy to see you admit it is a scandal.

The draw of the "infallible fuzzies" is very, very strong, and we must be well aware of this reality in thinking about the reasons why individuals convert to Roman Catholicism (or any of the other systems that likewise offer such promises of infallible certitude).

Again, do you deny that my conversion (and that of the many other converts such as David Palm, James Akin, Scott Hahn, Richard John Neuhaus, Howard, Muggeridge et al) is sincere and based on conviction and reflection? If so, how is this different from what Marxists, skeptics, atheists, various philosophers, etc. think of *all* Christian conversion? I have no problem granting sincerity and conviction to all here (after all, I once was an evangelical, and I fully remember my motivations and grounds for my beliefs). Some of us, James, think that certainty is an admirable goal in matters spiritual, moral, and theological. You despise Rome, we don't. We see it quite differently. Why must you stoop to crack psycho-babble-type "analysis" in order to explain our inexplicable odysseys?

The answer, of course, is not to come up with ways of offering what does not, in fact, exist. The answer lies in remaining true to the Word, explaining the issues clearly,

Theological certainty does not exist? So Christianity is indeed reduced to philosophy. That is a slap in God's face, as far as I'm concerned (although I'm sure you don't mean it in that way). The

God I serve is able, through His Holy Spirit, to impart truth to us, as the Bible teaches. "True to the Word"? You seek to be, so do I (believe it or not), so does Orthodox tradition. Now what do we do? "True to the Word," yet so many disagreements over that very Word of "truth." How do we resolve this dilemma? Throw up our hands in despair? Or admit that Catholics might be on to something?

and recognizing that in the final analysis, issues such as conversion to or from a position is primarily a spiritual matter. I can't stop someone from converting with all the arguments and facts in the world.

Yes, as I suspected. Conversion (i.e., if to Catholicism) is an irrational decision. So in my case, all my reading of Newman, Merton, Bouyer, Ratzinger, Gibbons, Howard, Luther, Calvin, Adam, Chesterton, etc. was all just "surface material," irrelevant to my final decision, which was in reality predetermined by an obsession with "smells and bells," a fondness for an infallible "crutch," a prior hatred of contraception, hero-worship of Catholic pro-life rescuers, an infatuation with statuary and idolatry, an absurd affection for genuflection, etc. *ad infinitum*? Right.

But, I'm still called upon to present those arguments and facts, trusting that the Lord's will be done.

And so are we. Let the better argument prevail. May God our Father open all our eyes to our own blind spots. May the Lord who gave us eyes and minds cause us to use them in order to see and know all of His truth, in its magnificent fullness and glory. And may there be unity in His Body, whether or not the institutional ruptures remain, as in all likelihood, they will, until He comes again. Amen.

Chapter Three

"Live Chat" Dialogue on Patristic Consensus (Particularly, Mariology) + Analysis of Mr. White's Applied Techniques of Sophistry
[29 December 2000-January 2001 / 2 December 2007]

The following live, absolutely spontaneous exchange (with an "audience") occurred in the chat room of the website of Reformed Baptist anti-Catholic apologist James White, on 29 December 2000. Just before this happened, I had been engaged in a meticulously pre-planned "live chat" dialogue with a Reformed apologist and underling of White's, that was set up in his chat venue. This person gave up about a third of the way through the prearranged format.

At that point, with things looking rather grim and disappointing for the "Reformed" side, White jumped in and asked to dialogue with me. If it weren't for the unusual circumstances, it probably wouldn't have occurred at all. White felt he had to be the impromptu champion for the anti-Catholics. And indeed it never happened again, and never had before, as White later turned down multiple requests of mine for a further live chat (even though I gave him huge handicaps: knowing how reticent he was to do it).

I was unable to cut-and-paste excerpts from my website while I was in the room (nor did I wish to: I wanted informality and discussion as it would occur in someone's living room, over tea and crumpets). The dialogue is unedited, excepting chronological changes to make it clear what question a reply was responding to, comments about time limits and rules, and inadvertent factual error (e.g., White cited Ignatius when he meant Irenaeus).

Shortly afterward, I added commentary and links separately from the actual chat: footnoted to the dialogue text, so that later elaboration will be easily distinguishable. Almost seven years later I wrote an analysis of what I felt were sophistical techniques employed by White during this exchange (these comments will be bracketed below). I had maintained for many years that White is habitually guilty of this shortcoming in his debates (real or alleged). The analysis allowed me to demonstrate exactly why I have that opinion, by utilizing real examples.

* * * * *

Mr. Armstrong, care to dialogue a bit?

". . . no, no more than it was for the fathers who appealed to apostolic tradition."

Remember that statement Dave?

Yes.

Dave: The earliest reference in all patristic writing to something "passed down from the Apostles" that is not in Scripture is Irenaeus' insistence that those who knew the Apostles confirmed that John 8 teaches that Jesus was more than 50 years of age at his death. Rome has rejected this idea. [Footnote 1] If "tradition" can be corrupted in its first instance, upon what basis do you affirm the idea that such doctrines as the Bodily Assumption, without witness for over 500 years, is truly apostolic? [Footnote 2]

Who claims that this is the first instance of tradition passed down? Now we are in areas that require research to answer, so I can hardly do that on the spot.

Well, if you can find an explicit statement that is earlier, I'd like to see it. To my knowledge, it is the earliest example.

I doubt that.....the principle is explicitly biblical in the first place. If indeed the notion [tradition passed down] is in the Bible, then that is the earliest instance, not Irenaeus.

I'm sorry, I must have been unclear: I was referring to a statement by an early Church Father concerning an alleged extra-biblical tradition passed down from the Apostles. And I believe Irenaeus' claim is the earliest....but that point aside....

Okay, that may be (I don't know).

I assume, then, you are not familiar with this particular issue? Okay, then let us use another example. Basil said that it was an apostolic tradition to baptize three times, facing east, forward. Upon what basis do you reject his testimony, if you do?

[I could hardly answer on the spot, completely unprepared, not even knowing this exchange was going to take place. I had prepared myself to debate someone else. But note how White uses the "rapid-fire" approach. It's the illusion of appearance of strength via mere method: one of the oldest tricks of sophistry in the book. This is the second thing he quickly introduces. Then he introduces a third: whether Mary sinned]

Patristic consensus over what period of time? For example, the "patristic consensus" through the end of the fourth century was that Mary had committed acts of sin. That is no longer the "view" taken by Rome.

[the second sentence above is sheer nonsense, as I proceed to show, even on the spot, because it is so outrageously false]

The patristic period is generally considered to go up to John Damascene, no?

That all depends. :-)

[I don't know what Mr. White thinks it "depends" on. According to *The Oxford Dictionary of the Christian Church* (p. 504): "the patristic period is generally held to be closed with St. Isidore of Seville in the West and St. John of Damascus in the East." White likes historian Philip Schaff, who described John Damascene as the "last of the Greek Fathers" (*History of the Christian Church*, Vol. IV: Chapter 14, section 144, p. 626). So why does he question (and "smile" about) this assumption of mine?]

No; some fathers thought she sinned, but I don't believe they were the majority, by any means.

Would it follow, then, that you believe the "patristic consensus" up through John Damascene supports such doctrines as the Immaculate Conception and the Bodily Assumption?

[Note the sophistical topic-switching again. This is quite clever, albeit cynically transparent to anyone who understands rhetoric and debate. Having already introduced his third topic in about as many minutes: the actual sin of Mary and what Church fathers held on that, and having introduced a false summary of patristic views on that score, he now shifts to the Immaculate Conception and the Assumption: the first being a greatly advanced development of the sinlessness of Mary and the second being another doctrine altogether. I'm now supposed to discuss -- without notes and preparation -- *five* relatively complex topics at once?]

Can you name five or ten who thought that?

[I was still referring to the previous "sins of Mary" question. Mr. White would fire out a new question (like having 15 peas in a pea shooter) before I barely answered his last one. Anyone can see the foolishness of such a juvenile method of supposedly "seeking truth"]

Yes. Origen, Chrysostom, Cyril of Alexandria, Basil. Big names. :-) Even Anselm held Mary was born with original sin.

How about western fathers? Those are all eastern guys. :-)

[note the manifest sophistry here, as I will keep pointing out in the exchange itself. Mr. White's original (non-factual) claim was: "the 'patristic consensus' through the end of the fourth century was that Mary had committed acts of sin." Starting on this false premise, when asked to name names, he cites (correctly) four eastern fathers and no western ones. But patristic consensus includes *both* east and west. Therefore, if he can't come up with *western* fathers believing as he claims, his assertion *collapses*. It's as simple as that. Case closed. And Mr. White not only has to simply name one or two fathers to prove his point; he has to establish *"consensus"*, which is far more difficult to do. But he quotes four men from the east and then a westerner who isn't even in the patristic period. This is when the tide started to decisively turn in the debate, because I knew from the patristic knowledge in my head that Mr. White was out to sea and faltering even in his factuality, let alone any arguments he wished to ground upon these alleged "facts" that are actually falsehoods]

Anselm isn't. :-)

Anselm was not a father.

[Bingo!]

Let's hope not. :-) He was under orders.... just kidding.

[his humor was more successful than his arguments and pseudo-facts. I suggest that Mr. White would have far more success sticking to stand-up comic routines rather than attempting serious patristic argument]

All you're doing now is helping to support Roman primacy and orthodoxy. The east had a host of errors. They split from Rome five times, and were wrong in every case by [the criteria of] their *own* later "Orthodox" beliefs.

Hmm, so you are switching now to a Western "consensus"?

No, but your citing of only eastern fathers hardly suggests that this is overall "patristic consensus," does it?

[this is a ludicrous remark on White's part. I made the rather obvious point. White was the one claiming "patristic consensus." But he cites only eastern fathers; I call him on it, and then he makes this dumb remark that *I* am calling for (or "switching" to) a "western consensus." This shows that he was on the ropes and was trying all the more to exercise sophistry to extricate himself from his foot firmly entrenched in his mouth. I don't think he is even *conscious* that he is doing this. Sophistry has so long been the trick of his trade in debating Catholics that it just comes out like breathing or blinking without having to think about it at all. He always has to oppose the Catholic, no matter how silly and absurd his objection may be. This is an absolutely *classic* case of poor debating and arguing on his part]

I would dispute that, actually, but I'd like to stick to the issue I've raised here.

[Mr. White referring -- with a straight face, apparently, actually serious -- about sticking to the issue, after how he has behaved above, is about the equivalent of an alcoholic saying we shouldn't drink liquor . . .]

Is it your belief that these two dogmas are apostolic in origin?

First name me western fathers who thought Mary sinned, since you brought this up.

[this is my attempt to keep White on the subject and to force him to face and try to alleviate the difficulties I had raised for his position]

140

Actually, Augustine's influence regarding the universality of original sin had to be overcome for the Immaculate Conception to be contemplated and codified, sir. :-)

[lacking any good answer for my actual question, Mr. White obfuscates and engages in obscurantism (tried and true methods of the sophist) by changing the topic to *original sin* and Augustine's view, rather than *actual sin* of Mary, which was his *own* original claim as to "patristic consensus." This is very clever. But we can all see through it, especially when analyzed in this fashion. Mr. White loves "post-mortem" debate analysis. Well, now we have given him a bit of his own medicine]

But that's a separate issue. Did Augustine think Mary sinned?

[note how I brought it right back to my *actual question*, Chris Wallace-style, refusing to play Mr. White's game]

No, not in her personal life. But he did believe she contracted original sin, correct?

[the quick answer and then rapidly moving on to another separate question, so as to do some damage control . . .]

There is the distinction between actual sin and original sin in Mary's case.

Do you consider Tertullian a Western?

Yes.

Would you include Hilary? J. N. D. Kelly lists them both in that category. I think that makes six, does it not?

I'm not sure, but you started by discussing acts of sin, now you are switching to original sin.

Actually, for both Tertullian and Hilary, it would be acts of sin.

Okay, so you have two?

Yes, two.

[how, then, is this a "consensus"? I wrote a book compiling patristic beliefs, and listed sixty Church fathers who are widely cited as such, up through John Damascene. Mr. White has provided us with exactly six names of fathers who held that Mary sinned (and of the two westerners, one later became a Montanist heretic and the other spoke of it just once, and rather mildly), or about 10% of the fathers (or reasonable facsimile thereof). And he wants us to think this is a "consensus."]

May I ask how many you have that positively testify of the later Roman belief in the same time-period?

One second . . . consulting some papers.

[Mr. White didn't even allow me any time to look. He went right on to the next thing]

Be that as it may, does it not follow from these considerations that there is no positive consensus upon this issue? The only relevant answer to that would be to ask, "Who wrote on the specific question of Mary's sinlessness? Not many."

Was this in Tertullian's Montanist or semi-Montanist period? About how many fathers were there, in your estimation?

The Tertullian citation is De carne Chr. 7. [Footnote 3]

How many say she was without sin? That's what you are asking? Actual sin?

I think you can see my point, can you not, Mr. Armstrong? If these concepts were, in fact, passed down through the episcopate, how could such widely differing church leaders be ignorant of these things?

142

The same way Luther was ignorant about baptismal regeneration, and Calvin of adult baptism. :-) Neither got it right, according to you.

[meant to convey the blatant double standard in Mr. White's previous question. I could disprove his claim about the Mariology of the fathers, but he couldn't change the fact that both Luther and Calvin got major things wrong, by his own Baptist reckoning, some 700 years after the patristic period. In other words, anti-Catholics always want to carp on and on about supposed "late inventions" while ignoring the host of those introduced by their own founders]

Well, it would seem that if you wish to substantiate a dogma *of the Immaculate Conception, the task would be rather easy to demonstrate a* positive *witness to the belief in the patristic period, would it not?*

I think this can be done, but probably not to your satisfaction.

[one must understand that the sinlessness of Mary is the developmental kernel of the Immaculate Conception, which extends the divine grace given to her also to removal by God of original sin. No one is claiming that the immaculate conception is in the Fathers. But Mr. White, remember, denied even that denial of actual sin was the "consensus"]

Does it follow, then, that you parallel individual Reformational leaders with the early Fathers, the very ones entrusted with "apostolic tradition"? Or was that rhetorical?

I was making a point about noted leaders and teachers differing. We would expect that in the fathers to an extent, being human; nevertheless, there is still overall consensus.

Have you ever listened to my debate with Gerry Matatics on the subject of the Marian dogmas, Mr. Armstrong?

No. Did you win that one? :-)

It's on the web.....Gerry said I did, actually. :-) As did Karl Keating. Does that count? :-)

I can name names as to who believed in sinlessness, but I don't have it at my fingertips......

Be that as it may, during the course of the debate I repeatedly asked Gerry for a single early Father who believed as he believes, dogmatically, on Mary. I was specifically focused upon the two most recent dogmas, the Immaculate Conception and the Bodily Assumption.

Of course, if you are looking for a full-blown doctrine of Immaculate Conception, you won't find it.

[thus I make the point about doctrinal development. The trouble with this argument of Mr. White's is that he wants to discount Catholic Mariology because it developed relatively late, while at the same time he fully accepts Protestant novelties like *sola Scriptura* and *sola fide* and (widespread) denial of baptismal regeneration, which are virtually nonexistent in the fathers. He has no trouble accepting all those truly late doctrines, while objecting that ours develop, just like Christology, trinitarianism and the canon of Scripture also did]

How would you answer my challenge? Did any early Father believe as you believe on this topic?

The consensus, in terms of the kernels of the belief [i.e., its essence], is there overall. I would expect it to be the case that any individual would not completely understand later developments.

So many generations lived and died without holding to what is now dogmatically defined? [Footnote 4]

144

[Mr. White doesn't get it: that *all* doctrines develop. Since he does not, and tries to make hay out of nothing, for rhetorical and polemical purposes, I provided a parallel by bringing up a late-developing doctrine that *he* accepts: the New Testament canon]

Did any father of the first three centuries accept all 27 books of the New Testament and no others? [Footnote 5]

Three centuries.....you would not include Athanasius?

I think his correct list was in the 4th century [indeed, it was in 367, and he was born around 296], but at any rate, my point is established.

[Mr. White couldn't even name *one*, because there was no correct list before 367, and even with his mastery of sophistry, he couldn't change that fact or mask it. Thus, "many generations lived and died without holding to what is now dogmatically defined" -- by the Church -- about the New Testament canon. Mariology is unfairly subjected to a standard that White won't apply to his own belief in the New Testament canon, as received by Catholic tradition]

How many fathers of the same period denied baptismal regeneration or infant baptism?

[Mr. White knows he is on shaky ground here, too, when pressed about other Protestant parallels of "late-arriving doctrines" and so he obfuscates]

The issue there would be how many addressed the issue (many did not). But are you paralleling these things with what you just admitted were but "kernels"? [Footnote 6]

If even Scripture was unclear that early on, that makes mincemeat of your critique that a lack of explicit Marian dogma somehow disproves Catholic Mariology.

[BOOM! This was the clinching remark, as far as I was concerned then, and now. In my opinion, Mr. White lost this debate at this point, if not earlier]

I'll address that allegation in a moment. :-)

[He never did. Alas, technical computer problems soon whisked Mr. White away, safe from annoying and revealing cross-examination questioning. Ah, but what could have been. The "if only's" of history . . .]

By the way, would you like that specific Irenaeus reference to look up? Just in passing?

[who *cares*, by this point? A desperate return to an earlier futile argument . . .]

I can look it up...I have enough resources. The question of this dialogue is whether we are gonna address topics which require heavy research..... That is more appropriate for a paper. If I were answering all your questions in a paper I would have spent a good three hours already. A guy like Joe Gallegos could instantly address questions about particular fathers' beliefs....... but I'll still give you names who taught Mary's sinlessness, if you like.

[Mr. White seemed to require me throughout, to give rapid answers to his lightning-quick and ever-changing technical questions concerning particular patristic beliefs. That was not possible (I wouldn't be able to type fast enough even if I had all the answers in my head), but I believe I managed to "de-fang" him by the use of analogy, which has been fleshed out to full and devastating effect in my footnotes]

I was thinking of the others looking on. :-) *It is chapter 22, section 5, of Irenaeus' work,* Against Heresies, *Book 2, I believe....*

So where do we go from here?

Anyway....You seem to think that if there is disagreement on any issue, this means the Scripture is unclear, correct?

[another topic introduced; Mr. White deftly avoids the devastating implications of my previous progression of analogical argument. The man knows when he is bested in dispute; he proves it by his change-the-subject tactics. On the other hand, when he senses he is prevailing in a line of argument, he keeps honing in for the kill. Anyone can see which tack he took with me. He was on the ropes, faltering, failing, floundering away . . .]

No; rather massive disagreement on many issues seems to me to fly in the face of this alleged perspicuity. I think Scripture is clear, by and large, actually, but human fallibility will lead to "hermeneutic relativism," thus requiring authoritative interpreters.

What do you do with Peter's words? 2 Pet 3:15-16:

> and regard the patience of our Lord as salvation; just as also our beloved brother Paul, according to the wisdom given him, wrote to you, as also in all his letters, speaking in them of these things, in which are some things hard to understand, which the untaught and unstable distort, as they do also the rest of the Scriptures, to their own destruction. (NAS)

A good description of many Protestants! How does this bolster perspicuity?

If the untaught and unstable distort the Scriptures, then what can the taught and stable do, of necessity?

It doesn't follow logically that if the unstable distort the Scripture, that the stable will always get it right, does it?

()()() James is Away. Lord willing, he will return. :) ()()()

[what a shame that he could neither stick around nor stick to any given subject, to reach any sort of conclusion. I think it is unarguable that he used many techniques of sophistry, obfuscation, and obscurantism in this pathetic exchange. I should have made an analysis like this years ago . I'm really glad I eventually did so, so as to give concrete demonstration of the shortcomings in Mr. White's debate method that so many Catholics have observed and become fed up with by now]

FOOTNOTES

1. *Early Patristic "Extra-Biblical" Citations* Without too much trouble, I managed to find what I believe to be an earlier reference, in this instance, to what the writer describes as "Scripture" (I assume he would hold that the Bible was "passed down from the Apostles" and that Mr. White would grant the point). The writer is St. Clement of Rome, in his Letter to the Corinthians (aka First Clement), dated 95-96 A.D. In 23:3, he writes:

Let this Scripture be far from us where he says . . . .

Then he proceeds to cite a passage which is *not* in present-day Scripture (it is also cited in 2 Clement 11:2-4 -- not considered to have been written by St. Clement, but perhaps the oldest Christian sermon extant: c. 100 A. D. --, where it is described as "the prophetic word"). The famous Protestant scholar J. B. Lightfoot speculated that it was from the lost book of Eldad and Modat mentioned by Hermas (Vis. 2.3.4).

Now how is it that a prominent Church father in the first century can be so ignorant as to the contents of "Scripture," when James White and Protestants must believe Scripture to be apostolic in order for it to be inspired and the rule of faith, over against both tradition and Church?

But Mr. White's argument suffers from an additional fallacy, viz., what shall we consider to be "scriptural" or conversely, "extra-biblical" in the first place? How do we ultimately determine that? This inevitably becomes at least partially a subjective affair. In addition to not properly knowing what Scripture is, St. Clement also urges his readers to conform to the glorious and holy rule of our tradition (7:2).

Mr. White, of course, rejects any "tradition" as a rule of faith; Scripture Alone is the rule of faith, according to Protestants. So St. Clement, by White's criterion, is referring to an "extra-biblical" notion. In point of fact, however, sacred tradition (even oral tradition) is indeed an altogether biblical and Pauline concept (1 Cor 11:2; 2 Thess 2:15; 3:6; 2 Tim 1:13-14; 2:2; 2 Pet 2:21; Jude 3).

Furthermore, moving on about a dozen years later to the epistles of St. Ignatius of Antioch, dated c. 105-110 A. D., we find a host of doctrines which Mr. White would consider "extra-biblical." Again, it is a matter of definition as to what is biblical, and what should be considered "orthodox" in Christianity.

Any citation, in fact, of a book as Scripture, *whether it was or not*, is an "extra-biblical tradition" since the biblical books (as decided by the Church and tradition) never list the books. Mr. White surely should have known this. But he wants to pass off this nonsense that Irenaeus thinking Jesus lived to fifty is the "earliest reference in all patristic writing to something 'passed down from the Apostles' that is not in Scripture." It's not so. The tradition of the biblical canon itself disproves it.

Furthermore, Clement teaches apostolic succession in 42:1-4 and 44:1-4 ("Our apostles . . . gave the offices a permanent character; that is, if they should die, other approved men should succeed to their ministry . . ."), a notion that White rejects and regards as unbiblical.

Finally, according to the eminent 19th-century Protestant patristics scholar Brooke Foss Westcott, there is some indication in Justin Martyr (100-165) of acceptance of an apostolic tradition, including an oral component. After an exhaustive, remarkable 75-page exposition of Justin's understanding of the canon of the New Testament. Westcott concludes:

There are indeed traces of the recognition of an authoritative Apostolic doctrine in Justin, but it cannot be affirmed from the form of his language that he looked upon this as contained in a written New Testament.

(*A General Survey of the History of the Canon of the New Testament*, Grand Rapids, Michigan: Baker Book House, 1980, from the 1889 sixth edition, 172)

2. *Development of the Doctrine of Mary's Assumption* This is a false analogy, because by Mr. White's criteria of "orthodoxy," "tradition" could not possibly have been first corrupted by St. Irenaeus. But be that as it may, I have dealt with the question of the slowly developing tradition of Mary's Assumption elsewhere. White's rapid-fire questioning and constant switching of topics and subtle changing even of terms within topics hardly allowed me to deal adequately with such a complex subject

3. *The Fathers on Mary's Sinlessness* Sure enough, *The Flesh of Christ* (dated 208-212 A.D.) is from Tertullian's semi-Montanist period. Protestants often fail to note the different theological periods with regard to citing Tertullian. Many will conveniently ignore this if a Tertullian quote suits their purpose (or else some are ignorant of the dating and/or of his later heresy altogether). Whichever the case with Mr. White, he failed to answer my question during the dialogue, thus illustrating another reason why these clarifying notes are important and useful. What I suspected turned out to be true. Whether Mr. White knew this beforehand or not, we don't know, as he didn't say.

As for Hilary of Poitier's views concerning the Blessed Virgin, in the book *Mary and the Fathers of the Church*, by Luigi Gambero (San Francisco: Ignatius Press, 1999, p. 186) the author (a priest with background in philosophy and also author of a four-volume work on Marian thought) wrote:

Hilary always considered it normal for Mary to have had some small imperfections . . . Our author does not mention any specific defect or imperfection in Mary's conduct but seems to hold that some such flaw exists, if even Mary must face the judgment of God. However, this is an isolated observation [Tractatus super Psalmum 118,12; PL 9,523], to which Hilary does not return.

Thus, Mr. White offers one western father (who held a quite "mild" opinion on the subject -- not exactly a spectacular, bold dissent), and another in his heretical period, plus four eastern fathers (which I was already generally aware of -- one always finds exceptions to the rule). This is what he considers a "patristic consensus." I consider it a pathetic argument. Catholic scholar Ludwig Ott (*Fundamentals of Catholic Dogma*) states that the western patristic consensus was "unanimous." Thus, Mr. White is trapped by the facts of history, not any rhetorical brilliance on my part.

As for Church fathers who refer to the Blessed Virgin Mary as the *New Eve* (Eve was originally sinless or immaculate), *Second Eve, sinless, spotless, pure, without stain, immaculate, the Ark of the Covenant*, or (negatively) who never attributed any actual sin to her, we find the following: Hippolytus, Justin Martyr, Irenaeus, Gregory Nazianzen, Gregory Nyssa, Cyril of Jerusalem, Epiphanius, Athanasius, Jerome, Eusebius, Ephraim, Ambrose, Augustine, Proclus, Theodotus, Peter Chrysologus, Andrew of Crete, Fulgentius, Leo the Great, Gregory the Great, Germanus, and John Damascene.

That adds up to at least 22 fathers in the affirmative, compared to five who attributed sin to Mary (not counting the Montanist heretic Tertullian). This is more than enough to achieve a "consensus," as even the phrase "unanimous consent of the fathers" never literally meant *all* of them.

The sinlessness of Mary is stated by many fathers. It is implicit in the "second Eve" motif. These things began to be developed so early that good Protestant historian Philip Schaff states that the "development of the orthodox Mariology and Mariolatry originated as early as the second century" (*History of the Christian Church*, Vol. III, 414). If the fathers hadn't been spewing all this abominable "Catholic stuff" then obviously Schaff wouldn't describe it as "Mariolatry." This proves that

Schaff thought it was indeed there. And the Mariology includes sinlessness. It's easy to document, contra Mr. White:

Eusebius, the great Church historian . . . calls her panagia, "all-holy". (PG, 24, 1033B)

St. Athanasius: . . . pure and unstained Virgin . . . (*On the Incarnation of the Word*, 8)

O noble Virgin, truly you are greater than any other greatness. For who is your equal in greatness, O dwelling place of God the Word? To whom among all creatures shall I compare you, O Virgin? You are greater than them all O Covenant, clothed with purity instead of gold! You are the Ark in which is found the golden vessel containing the true manna, that is, the flesh in which divinity resides. (*Homily of the Papyrus of Turin*, 71, 216)

St. Ephraem: Thou and thy mother are the only ones who are totally beautiful in every respect; for in thee, O Lord, there is no spot, and in thy Mother no stain. (*Nisibene Hymns*, 27, v. 8)

St. Gregory Nazianzen: He was conceived by the Virgin, who had first been purified by the Spirit in soul and body; for, as it was fitting that childbearing should receive its share of honor, so it was necessary that virginity should receive even greater honor. (Sermon 38, 13)

St. Gregory of Nyssa: It was, to divulge by the manner of His Incarnation this great secret; that purity is the only complete indication of the presence of God and of His coming, and that no one can in reality secure this for himself, unless he has altogether estranged himself from the passions of the flesh. What happened in the stainless Mary when the fulness of the Godhead which was in Christ shone out through her, that happens in every soul that leads by rule the virgin life. (*On Virginity*, 2; NPNF 2, Vol. V, 344)

[T]he power of the Most High, through the Holy Spirit, overshadowed the human nature and was formed therein; that is to say, the portion of flesh was formed in the immaculate Virgin. (*Against Apollinaris*, 6)

St. Ambrose: . . . Mary, a Virgin not only undefiled but a Virgin whom grace has made inviolate, free of every stain of sin. (Commentary on Psalm 118, 22, 30)

St. Jerome: 'There shall come forth a rod out of the stem of Jesse, and a flower shall grow out of his roots.' The rod is the mother of the Lord--simple, pure, unsullied; drawing no germ of life from without but fruitful in singleness like God Himself... Set before you the blessed Mary, whose surpassing purity made her meet to be the mother of the Lord. (Letter XXII. To Eustochium, 19, 38; NPNF 2, Vol. VI, 29, 39)

St. Augustine: We must except the holy Virgin Mary, concerning whom I wish to raise no question when it touches the subject of sins, out of honour to the Lord; for from Him we know what abundance of grace for overcoming sin in every particular was conferred upon her who had the merit to conceive and bear Him who undoubtedly had no sin. Well, then, if, with this exception of the Virgin, we could only assemble together all the forementioned holy men and women, and ask them whether they lived without sin whilst they were in this life, what can we suppose would be their answer? (*A Treatise on Nature and Grace*, chapter 42 [XXXVI]; NPNF 1, Vol. V)

St. Cyril of Alexandria: Hail, Mary Theotokos, Virgin-Mother, lightbearer, uncorrupt vessel . . . Hail Mary, you are the most precious creature in the whole world; hail,

Mary, uncorrupt dove; hail, Mary, inextinguishable lamp; for from you was born the Sun of justice . . . (Homily 11 at the Ecumenical Council of Ephesus)

Theodotus: Innocent virgin, spotless, without defect, untouched, unstained, holy in body and in soul, like a lily-flower sprung among thorns, unschooled in the wickedness of Eve . . . clothed with divine grace as with a cloak . . . (Homily 6, 11)

St. Leo the Great: For the uncorrupt nature of Him that was born had to guard the primal virginity of the Mother, and the infused power of the Divine Spirit had to preserve in spotlessness and holiness that sanctuary which He had chosen for Himself . . . (Sermon XXII: On the Feast of the Nativity, Part II; NPNF 2, Vol. XII)

St. Gregory the Great: The most blessed and ever Virgin Mary, Mother of God . . . has completely surpassed the height of every elect creature. (*In I Regum*, 1, 5)

St. Andrew of Crete: . . . alone wholly without stain . . . (Canon for the Conception of Anne)

St. John Damascene: O most blessed loins of Joachim from which came forth a spotless seed! O glorious womb of Anne in which a most holy offspring grew. (Homily I on the Nativity of Mary)

4. *Development of Doctrine in General* As is, unfortunately, so often the case with Protestants, Mr. White betrays a great lack of understanding of development of doctrine. The topic is too complex to fully delve into here, but here is a great quotation from Protestant apologist C. S. Lewis:

Change is not progress unless the core remains unchanged. A small oak grows into a big oak; if it became a beech, that would not be growth, but mere change . . .

There is a great difference between counting apples and arriving at the mathematical formulae of modern physics. But the multiplication table is used in both and does not grow out of date. In other words, whenever there is real progress in knowledge, there is some knowledge that is not superseded. Indeed, the very possibility of progress demands that there should be an unchanging element . . . I claim that the positive historical statements made by Christianity have the power, elsewhere found chiefly in formal principles, of receiving, without intrinsic change, the increasing complexity of meaning which increasing knowledge puts into them . . . Like mathematics, religion can grow from within, or decay . . . But, like mathematics, it remains simply itself, capable of being applied to any new theory.

(*God in the Dock*, edited by Walter Hooper, Grand Rapids, Michigan: Eerdmans, 1970, .44-47. Originally from "Dogma and the Universe," *The Guardian*, March 19, 1943, p. 96 / March 26, 1943, pp. 104, 107)

Furthermore, the "kernels" or essential elements of all the Catholic Marian beliefs can be found in Holy Scripture, to a much greater extent than most Protestants would ever imagine, and often fairly explicitly. If this is indeed the case, then these beliefs are quite apostolic and early: all deriving from the first century A. D. or earlier.

5. *Lack of Patristic Consensus on the New Testament Canon*
Mr. White thinks he has found a "patristic consensus" when a mere five Church fathers claim that Mary sinned. That supposedly shoots down Catholic Mariology in one fell swoop. Yet when I point out that *no* father from 0-300 A.D. accepted *all 27 books* of the New Testament *and no others*, as inspired and part of the Bible (*Bible Alone* being a crucial pillar of Protestantism -- one cannot have the Bible without knowing which books belong to it), he offers no reply -- and for very good reason, as there *is* none.

The canon of the New Testament is necessarily dependent on Church authority. Even the well-respected Calvinist R. C. Sproul admits that Protestants possess a "fallible collection of infallible books." The analogy is an exact parallel, and devastating: if five fathers disprove Catholic Mariology, then *not a single father* getting the New Testament right for 300 years refutes *sola Scriptura*. Mr. White had to (logically) either drop his fallacious argument, or his acceptance of *sola Scriptura*. Silence was a wise course in the midst of such a serious dilemma.

That being the case (and I think he knew it full well), he asked, rather, whether I included Athanasius in this period (the "first three centuries," as I stated). Well, no, since he lived from 296-373. He first listed our present 27 New Testament books as such in *367 A.D.* (which is more than 300 years beyond even the death of our Lord Jesus).

Disputes still persisted concerning several books after that, almost right up until 397, when the Canon was authoritatively closed at the Council of Carthage, so that the present-day "perspicuous" New Testament canon took longer to finalize than trinitarianism and the divinity of the Holy Spirit! But I guess a "consensus of one" in the year 367 is good enough for Mr. White, provided that it is harmonious with his own largely 16th-century-derived Baptist version of Christianity. This is all doctrinal development, pure and simple. But Protestants -- for some odd reason -- so often wish to ignore it when it touches upon their *own* peculiar doctrines.

How is it that Mr. White is so concerned about five fathers attributing fairly minor and very rare sin to the Blessed Virgin Mary, while in the "late" period from 250-325, the "perspicuous" biblical books of Hebrews, James, 2 Peter, 2 John, 3 John, Jude, and Revelation were still being widely disputed in the Church Universal? Is not that state of affairs far more fatal to Protestant claims concerning *Scripture Alone*, than minor dissent on Mary supposedly is to the Catholic position?

6. *Church Fathers' Unanimity on Baptismal Regeneration* Mr. White cleverly avoided the issue I was raising, in terms of the live chat, but he can't escape the logic of it, for the fathers taught

baptismal regeneration with virtually literal unanimity. White, of course, rejects both infant baptism (over against Calvin and the great majority of all Christians of all times) and baptismal regeneration (over against Luther and Wesley and Anglicanism, as well as Orthodoxy and Catholicism). It doesn't seem to trouble him that no one in the whole patristic period could "get it right," just as we saw was the case concerning the canon of the New Testament and the Real Presence of Christ in the Eucharist. On the other hand, his non-answer perhaps suggests that he *is* troubled -- down deep -- by all these "little" historical anomalies in his position, which I am discourteous and rash enough to point out.

Chapter Four

A Refutation of the Fallacies and Circular Reasoning of James White Regarding Authentic Tradition and *Sola Scriptura*
[27 December 2003]

Here I reply to Mr. White's Internet article, "A Response to David Palm's Article on Oral Tradition from *This Rock* Magazine, May, 1995," and also offer a critique of several erroneous statements and arguments from his book, *The Roman Catholic Controversy* (Bethany House, 1996), and another of his volumes devoted to "biblical authority": *Answers to Catholic Claims* (Crowne Publications, 1990).

* * * * *

It is then asserted that Jesus' refusal to overthrow the form of synagogue worship and teaching is tantamount to a recognition of extra-biblical binding revelation. The close observer will note a huge chasm here.

I don't think it is necessary to offer this argument in such strong terms. Binding *interpretation* of a revelation is not the same as a new revelation. What the passage [Matthew 23:2-3] clearly demonstrates, I think, is that there is authoritative tradition outside of the Bible, and even outside of the apostles, who were alive at the time this encounter took place, and soon to appear on the scene with great zeal, after Jesus' Resurrection. Jesus could easily have said that the Pharisees' authority was to shortly be superseded by the apostles but He did not, and Paul called himself a Pharisee and recognized the authority of the high priest.

The religious situation into which the Messiah came was hardly identical with the situation under Moses.

This is a *non sequitur*. The force of this particular argument does not rest upon whether "Moses' Seat" literally goes back to Moses. Rather, the salient point is whether it was a binding authority not based on solely the letter of the Old Testament. If so, *sola Scriptura* is in deep trouble.

Many things were different, and due to occupation, Roman rule, and many other factors, there were all sorts of things that were "extra-biblical" that were part and parcel of the Jewish life of the day. Are we to honestly believe that unless the Lord Jesus proved a revolutionary in rejecting every *non-biblical tradition and practice that this gives us wholesale license for the addition of such traditions today?*

Yes, but they are not "additions"; they were there from the beginning (in the Catholic view), and merely developed. The fact remains that Jesus accepted *this* particular "non-biblical tradition and practice." James White knows it, so he is playing the game of trying to minimize and de-emphasize this acceptance. It's a futile effort, and in so doing, he is already conceding four-fifths of the case (and trying to make out that he has not). Besides, Jesus was certainly a "radical" and a nonconformist through and through. Does White really think that He would have refrained from dissenting against *any* state of affairs or set of beliefs that He did not agree with? I see little reason to believe that He would do so, from the record we have. But White would have us believe that our Lord Jesus let a few of these "non-biblical tradition[s] and practice[s]" slip through the cracks, so to speak (even with regard to a class of people whom He vigorously condemns for hypocrisy on several occasions). This makes no sense at all, and it's special pleading.

Or should we not realize that in light of Jesus words in Matthew 15 that such traditions need to be tested by a higher authority (Scripture), and, if they do not violate the Word of God, *they can be followed and practiced?*

St. Paul said far worse of the Galatians than Jesus said of the Pharisees in Matthew 15 and elsewhere, yet he continued to regard them as brothers in Christ and as a "church". Why is it so unthinkable for Jesus to do the same with the Pharisees? In John 11:49-52, the Apostle John tells us that Caiaphas, the high priest "prophesied" and spoke truth (an act which can only be inspired by the Holy Spirit). Nicodemus and Joseph of Arimathea were righteous Pharisees. Jesus was even buried in the latter's tomb. As for the traditions needing to be harmonious with Scripture; *of course*, no one denies that. But the question at hand is whether there can be a legitimate tradition not found (i.e., not described or written about) in Scripture itself. Something can be *absent* from Scripture but nevertheless be in perfect *harmony* with it.

The acceptance of a tradition that is not contrary to Scripture is not grounds for the acceptance of others that are.

Catholics wholeheartedly agree; this is why we reject *sola Scriptura* and other Protestant novel doctrines that are not found in Holy Scripture.

And what is more, the acceptance of a tradition current at the time does not mean that the Lord Jesus accepted the claims *made by the Mishnah two hundred years later regarding the alleged basis of such traditions (i.e., those claims regarding Mosaic origin). . . . Let's note a few things: 1) The tractate indicates that the Torah was passed down to such individuals as Shammai and Hillel, yet, as students of NT backgrounds know, these two set up opposing schools with different understandings of tradition (should sound familiar!). Who was, in fact, the true recipient of this alleged oral tradition, then?*

I find this an extremely interesting argument, given the multiplicity of Protestant schools of thought, that endlessly conflict and contradict (thus making the existence of much falsehood and error in Protestant ranks logically certain and inevitable). White contends that because there were two schools of interpretation in later Judaism, therefore, the very notion of oral tradition itself is somehow suspect and must be discarded. Why, then, is he not similarly troubled and perplexed about the state of affairs in Protestantism? He firmly believes that there is one Christian truth, and that it is so clear in Scripture, but Protestants are unable to *find* it. And if one group *has* found it, how does the man on the street *determine* which group has done so?

Does this sad state of affairs make him skeptical of the inspired revelation of Scripture? Of course not. He believes it despite the multitude of competing interpretations and schools of thought. So why is it so inconceivable that there could also be such a thing as a *true tradition*, even though all do not hold it or acknowledge it? White (characteristically) doesn't apply the same standard to his own Protestant beliefs that he applies to Catholics.

In his book, *The Roman Catholic Controversy*, White states on page 91:

> The Bible is absolutely clear in the sense that the Westminster Confession states:
>
> > "Those things which are necessary to be known, believed and observed for salvation, are so clearly propounded and opened in some place of Scripture or other, that not only the learned, but the unlearned, in a due use of the ordinary means, may attain to a sufficient understanding of them."
>
> Does it follow, then, that there must be a unanimity of opinion on infant baptism? Does the above statement of the Confession even say that there will be a unanimity of opinion on the items that "are necessary to be known, believed and observed for salvation"? No, it does not.

And why not? Because people - sinful people, people with agendas, people who want to find something in the Bible that isn't really there - approach Scripture, and no matter how perfect it is, *people are fallible*.

One could have a field day with all the fallacies and errors in this facile analysis. I've noted many times in my apologetics that the "sin argument" concerning Protestant diversity of opinion is absurdly simplistic and remarkably judgmental, and casts doubt on major Protestant figures who couldn't agree. Luther disagreed with Calvin on whether baptism regenerates and on the Real Presence in the Eucharist, so who was right? Well, for White, Calvin was, because he agrees with him over against Luther.

But why did Luther get these "obvious" biblical teachings wrong? According to White, that is because he must have been a "sinful" person with an "agenda" that fatally clouded his approach to Scripture, and made him see things in it which weren't "really there." Trouble is, White has to also dissent from Calvin and side with the Anabaptists concerning adult baptism, so Calvin's sin kept him from seeing *that* clear truth of Scripture, and so on and so forth.

The whole thing reduces to absurdity and belittles great figures in Protestant history. We can simply regard each of these men as holding some false beliefs in all sincerity, and different interpretive traditions and ways of approaching Scripture and the Christian life. Catholics believe they were mistaken in many things, of course, but we don't have to run them down as unable to see the "clear" truths of Scripture due to some blindness in their character or thinking. Only the sort of fundamentalist Protestant view that White holds entails that sort of judgmentalism.

Secondly, regarding the Westminster Confession and its statement, "Those things which are necessary to be known, believed and observed for salvation, are so clearly propounded," for many Christians, including Luther and Lutherans, traditional Anglicans, and Methodists, and even later Protestant schools of thought such as the Churches of Christ, one of the things which is

163

necessary for salvation is baptism. Therefore, it would be clearly taught in Scripture (per the Westminster Confession). And so all these groups, and Catholics and Orthodox, believe it indeed *is* clearly taught in the Bible. But Protestants cannot agree on the correct teaching, and are split into five major camps. There is a reason why most Christians throughout history have accepted baptismal regeneration. It is clearly taught in Scripture:

> **Acts 2:38** And Peter said to them, "Repent, and be baptized every one of you in the name of Jesus Christ for the forgiveness of your sins; and you shall receive the gift of the Holy Spirit."

> **Acts 22:16** And now why do you wait? Rise and be baptized, and wash away your sins, calling on his name.

> **Titus 3:5** he saved us, not because of deeds done by us in righteousness, but in virtue of his own mercy, by the washing of regeneration and renewal in the Holy Spirit,

> **1 Peter 3:19-21** in which he went and preached to the spirits in prison, [20] who formerly did not obey, when God's patience waited in the days of Noah, during the building of the ark, in which a few, that is, eight persons, were saved through water. [21] Baptism, which corresponds to this, now saves you, not as a removal of dirt from the body but as an appeal to God for a clear conscience, through the resurrection of Jesus Christ,

According to James White, the people who see baptismal regeneration in these passages, are "sinful people, people with agendas, people who want to find something in the Bible that isn't really there." And presumably many of those Protestants who reject adult baptism or non-regenerative baptism think the same of White, since they accept the same principle of perspicuity of Scripture that he accepts. They must explain somehow why Protestants can't agree on such an important doctrine, given this "clearness" of Scripture. So they accuse others of blinding sinfulness, or they claim that baptism is merely a "secondary issue," upon which men can disagree, and that's fine and dandy, or else they start to question perspicuity itself. On page 92 of the same book, White writes:

> Are we to believe that the Bible is so unclear and self-contradictory that we cannot arrive at the truth through an honest, whole-hearted effort at examining its evidence? It seems that is what Rome is telling us. But because the Scriptures *can be misused*, it does not follow that they are *insufficient* to lead us to the truth . . . The reason that Rome tells us the Bible is insufficient, I believe, is so we will be convinced of Rome's ultimate authority and abandon the God-given standard of Scripture.

I don't have to believe this as a Catholic. I think Scripture is pretty clear (I've always found it to be so in my many biblical studies), but I also know from simple observation and knowledge of Church history that it isn't clear *enough* to bring men to agreement. White says that is because of sin and stupidity. Certainly those things are always potential factors. But I contend that the rampant disagreement is primarily because of a false rule of faith: *sola Scriptura*, a notion that excludes the binding authority of tradition and the Church, which entities produce the doctrinal unity that *sola Scriptura has* never, and *can* never produce.

"Rome" doesn't "tell us" what White thinks it tells us. What Catholics teach is that central authority and tradition is necessary for doctrinal unity; whether Scripture is "clear" or unclear. And we think Scripture itself teaches this (which is precisely why we believe it).

White thinks in dichotomous terms (a characteristic and widespread Protestant shortcoming), so for him, to accept binding Church authority is to somehow "abandon the God-given standard of Scripture," as if it were a zero-sum game where Scripture is the air in a glass and the Church is the water added to the glass: the more water ("Church") is added, the less Scripture there can be, so that a full glass of "the Church" leaves no room for the Bible at all as the "standard." Of course, none of this is Catholic teaching, nor does it logically follow from the notion of Church authority. It's a false dilemma and false dichotomy. But a certain Protestant mindset and mentality cannot grasp this. Thus, White states in another book:

> One will either subjugate tradition to Scripture (as the Reformers taught) or one will subjugate Scripture to tradition, and this is what we see in Roman Catholicism. The Pharisees, too, denied that they were in any way denigrating the authority of Scripture by their adherence to the "traditions of their fathers." But Jesus did not accept their claim. He knew better. He pointed out how their traditions destroyed the very purpose of God's law, allowing them to circumvent the clear teaching of the Word through the agency of their traditions . . . If Christ was right to condemn the Pharisees for their false traditions, then the traditions of Rome, too, must be condemned.
>
> (*Answers to Catholic Claims: A Discussion of Biblical Authority*, Southbridge, Massachusetts: Crowne Publications, Inc., 1990, 56)

What about the many false traditions in *Protestantism*? We *know* for a fact that many many such false traditions exist because there are competing views which *contradict* each other. That entails (as a matter of logical necessity) that someone is wrong, and dead-wrong. They can't all be right. There can't be five true doctrines of baptism simultaneously. Therefore, false "traditions of men" exist in Protestantism, and would be condemned by Jesus just as vigorously as supposed "false traditions" of Catholicism.

But do we ever hear White railing against *those*? Of course not. He doesn't write books and articles about Martin Luther's grave errors (from his own point of view) or about those of, say. St. Augustine. Instead, he accepts the view (or at least his behavior suggests this) that a lot of Christian doctrine is up for grabs and is "secondary." He winks at the diversity, just as all

Protestants must, faced with an opponent like the Catholic Church, which has at least preserved doctrinal unity (whether one agrees with the *content* of that unified doctrine or not).

. . . Next Mr. Palm says that since the Pharisees stood in this alleged line of succession, their teaching deserved to be respected. The problem is, however, that the Lord Jesus often did not respect their teaching. The issue in Matthew 23 was not respect for the teaching of the Pharisees, but respect for the authority of the person who sat in Moses' seat. The two are not necessarily co-extensive, . . .

It's very difficult to argue that Jesus did not refer to their teaching, seeing that He said, "practice and observe whatever they tell you." One would have to believe that this "whatever" included no *doctrine*. To make such an arbitrary distinction between "authority" and "teaching" is ludicrous (especially the more one knows about Jewish teaching methods and the history of Hebrew religion). If Jesus had said, rather: "practice and observe whatever *I* tell you," or, "practice and observe whatever the *apostles* tell you," White wouldn't have the slightest doubt about what was meant. He wouldn't try to limit the scope and extent of the authority.

and what is more, there is nothing in the passage that even begins to suggest that the Lord Jesus is making reference to the entire idea of extra-biblical tradition, authority, etc.

No? This is plainly false, by the following straightforward logic:

> 1. Jesus said of the Pharisees, "practice and observe whatever they tell you."

> 2. But Pharisees believed in an authoritative oral tradition, which included some content not included in the Bible (but not necessarily *contrary* to biblical teaching).

3. Therefore, Jesus was giving sanction to the teaching authority of oral "extra-biblical" tradition.

He is saying to obey the authorities in the synagogue service.

No He isn't; He is saying, "practice and observe whatever they tell you." That's not limited to the synagogue, much as White might wish it to be so, for his own purposes.

To read into this the acceptance of an entire concept of oral revelation passed down through some "magisterium" is to be way *beyond what is written.*

It doesn't have to be "oral revelation"; only authoritative oral teaching that goes beyond the letter of Scripture. That is enough to be blatantly contrary to *sola Scriptura*.

Mr. Palm then says, "Jesus here draws on oral Tradition to uphold the legitimacy of this teaching office in Israel." This is simply untrue. There is nothing in the passage that even makes reference to "oral Tradition."

"Moses' Seat" *was itself* such a tradition, which was not in the Bible. The very term comes from oral tradition. The words "oral tradition" don't have to be there; the *content* is. This is a remarkably silly statement from a man as educated as White. Even he agrees that the notion of "Moses' Seat" is not found in the Old Testament, and that it comes from Jewish tradition.

This can only be identified as wishful thinking, based upon an anachronistic insertion of later developments back into the text.

If you have no case, grotesquely exaggerate the flaws in the opponent's position (or manufacture some) and hope that your readers (or jurors, as the case may be) will be fooled . . .

. . . Mr. Palm's attempt to use the chair of Moses suffers from the same problem as his first attempt: it assumes what it seeks to

prove. It is circular, and does not provide anywhere near sufficient basis for its conclusions.

That is far more true of White's reply, as I think has been abundantly shown by now. Elsewhere in the article, he wrote:

It must be remembered that Jewish writers (including Matthew) felt much freer to engage in conflation and paraphrastic citation than we in our modern Western world . . . And why should we believe that Mr. Palm's leap into the undocumentable realm of "oral tradition" is any more solid than any of the suggestions that have been given for a Scriptural *source? If anything could be drawn at all from the phrase* h'rethen dia twn prophetwn, *it would be that this is indeed a conflated citation, drawn from the plurality of the prophets rather than from a single prophet.*

This exhibits White's peconceived notion that whatever is cited in some authoritative manner in the New Testament will somehow be shown to be from the Old Testament, even if this entails citing several passages together as one. Thus, he writes in one of his books:

> Did Jesus give place to the Jewish leaders' claim that they were the true inheritors of the traditions of Moses? Did He for a second acquiesce to their claim of "interpretive authority"? Surely not. He held those who claimed to "sit in the seat of Moses" accountable to the words of Scripture, despite their claim to be in sole possession of the "correct interpretation." . . . Jesus did not participate in their "veneration" of "tradition."
> . . . just as He rebuked the elders of the people of Israel for making the word of God null and void through their supposedly authoritative traditions, He would say the same thing today to the Roman Catholic people . . . For Him, the Word was final, it was not lacking in anything.

(*Answers to Catholic Claims,* 30-32)

But that assumption is strictly arbitrary, of course. White admits that the New Testament writers drew from many sources (he could hardly deny this even if he wanted to), but of course he has to deny that any were *authoritative*. With Matthew 23:1-3 it is different because Jesus is sanctioning Pharisaical authority in a blanket sense. In so doing, He necessarily is giving legitimacy to oral tradition, for this is what the Pharisees believed.

What is more, Mr. Palm slips into the common misrepresentation of sola scriptura that fills Roman Catholic apologetics works: the idea that sola scriptura, if it is true, must be normative during times of revelation.

Why would it *not* be? On what basis? The Bible says no more about this concept (exactly nothing) than it does about *sola Scriptura* itself. A false, novel principle is introduced with no biblical substantiation, then it is made the formal rule of faith of Protestantism, then it is argued that things were different during Bible times than they were now, with regard to the demands and nature of *sola Scriptura*. I just don't see any indication of that in Scripture.

If White *does* claim such scriptural support exists, he should, by all means, produce this biblical evidence. We all wait with baited breath. If he *cannot* do so, why does he believe this? He would have to do so on "extra-biblical" grounds, and to do that is to concede virtually his entire position, as any number of distinctive Catholic doctrines could be defended as also not *explicitly* biblical. But I maintain that there are no biblical proofs *whatsoever* for what White is contending (*sola Scriptura* and the idea that it only really starts *applying after the Bible is complete*). It's completely arbitrary, and yet another instance of begging the question and assuming what one is purporting to prove.

Sola scriptura refers to the functioning church, not to the church being founded and receiving revelation on a regular basis from living apostles.

I ask again, where is the support for this idea in Scripture itself?

There are no living apostles today, and revelation has ceased (even Rome agrees on this point). The issue now is, what is the infallible rule of faith? Does the Bible teach that that which is theopneustos ("God-breathed") is sufficient to function as the regula fidei? Yes, it does. That is the issue.

But *where*?! The Bible is sufficient for salvation and teaching, but it doesn't follow from those truths, that the Church and tradition are not binding and authoritative. *Sola Scriptura* is not so much false in what it *asserts* but in what it *fails* to assert, and what it positively *excludes*, contrary to Scripture.

In his book, *Answers to Catholic Claims: A Discussion of Biblical Authority*, White goes to even further extremes by coming to his conclusions for little reason other than his preconceived notions (more circular argumentation). Thus, he argues:

> But what of 2 Timothy 2:2? Does this not indicate the existence of an oral teaching that could be passed down separately from the written record? . . .
> . . . are we to believe that what Paul taught in the presence of many witnesses is *different* than what is contained in the pages of the New Testament? . . . Why should we limit what Timothy is to pass on to only those things that are *not* contained in the Bible, but instead make up some "traditions" that were to be entrusted to a particular class of individuals - those holding the "apostolic succession"? There is nothing to suggest that there was the slightest difference between what Paul had taught publicly and what he had written . . . Are we also to assume that there is *more* in the "oral teaching" than we have in the New Testament? Why? On what basis?

(*Answers*, 59-60)

White repeatedly engages in massive question-begging:

> But what of Acts 2:42? Does it not say that the early Church, long before the writing of *any* of the New

Testament, was devoted to the apostles' teaching? Yes, it does say that. But again, what does this have to do with the concept of the Bible being the sufficient rule of faith? We are not living in the time of the apostles, are we? New revelation is not being given right now, is it? . . . Then Acts speaks to us of a very unusual time, does it not? There is nothing in the fact that the early believers in Jerusalem devoted themselves to the Apostles' teaching that indicates that this teaching to which they devoted themselves is *other than what we have in the New Testament!* Is there anything that would suggest that what the Apostles taught these early believers was *different than* what they taught believers later by epistle? Do we not have accounts of the early sermons in the book of Acts that tell us what the Apostles were teaching then? Do we find the Apostles saying "what we tell you now we will pass down *only by mouth as a separate mode of revelation known as tradition*, and later we will write down some *other stuff* that will become sacred Scripture"? Certainly not. The fact that the early believers were devoted to the Apostles' teaching should only *strengthen* our desire to also be devoted to the Apostles' teaching - as it is found in the sacred Scriptures.

(*Answers*, 40-41)

There is absolutely no indication whatsoever that there is any difference in content between the message preached to the Thessalonians and the one contained in the written epistle. The Roman Catholic Church has no basis in this passage [2 Thessalonians 2:15] at all to assert that the *contents* of these "traditions" differs [sic] in the slightest from what is contained in the New Testament. Are we to assume that when Paul proclaimed the Gospel that he said something different than when he wrote his epistles? No, both Peter and Paul mean the same thing when they speak of *evangelizing.*

(Ibid., 61)

. . . for many Roman Catholic apologists, simply demonstrating that the apostles *spoke* something is enough to demonstrate that the written word is not sufficient. The underlying assumption is that what was *spoken* has to contain information that is not in what was *written* . . . We point out that there is no basis for asserting that the spoken teachings of the apostles differed in any way from the written record they left to us. There is no evidence of a belief in a second "mode" of revelation in the New Testament - no acknowledgment of a revelation outside of that given by the Spirit in the Scriptures.

(Ibid., 62)

White again engages in rhetorical irrelevancy by asking, "Do we find the Apostles saying 'what we tell you now we will pass down *only by mouth as a separate mode of revelation known as tradition,*' . . . ?" What this has to do with anything, I have not the slightest idea. But I guess it helps White to bolster his extremely weak case -- with holes large enough for a truck to drive through --, to pretend that Catholics believe in *sola traditio.*

The transitional period to which White refers ("We are not living in the time of the apostles, are we? New revelation is not being given right now, is it?", etc.), would actually be far longer than the lifetime of the apostles. It would extend all the way to the end of the 4th century, when the canon of the Bible was fixed (including the so-called "Apocrypha," which was included in Bibles all the way till the advent of Protestantism, when these books were "demoted" and first removed). So *sola Scriptura* could not be applied in the sense it is today, until almost 400 A. D., when Church authority and tradition set the limits of the canon. Does this not strike one as an exceptionally odd and weird point of view? The question of the canon itself is an extremely fascinating one and troublesome for *sola Scriptura*, but that is beyond our purview here.

One must also call attention to the fact that being separate from Scripture does not automatically mean "different from the *teaching* of Scripture." There need not be any conflict. Catholics believe that Scripture and Tradition are "twin fonts of the one divine wellspring." Sacred Tradition is not so much "different" from Scripture as it is "more." Thus, White sets up a false dilemma.

Arguing from the reasonable proposition that it is implausible that oral tradition would be "different" from Scripture, he falsely concludes that, therefore, no oral tradition exists, or if it does, it is irrelevant, and not binding in any way, shape, or form. He overlooks the possibility that oral tradition can supplement the Bible and offer authoritative interpretation of it (because he sees the two as somehow pitted against each other -- which itself is a false and unbiblical dichotomy).

But White does more than even this. He practically *equates* the "tradition" often spoken of in the New Testament with the New Testament itself:

> . . . A person with a Bible in his hands *has* the traditions of which Paul speaks.

(*Ibid.*, 58)

This is clearly absurd, and it is from plain common sense. James White admits that the Bible does not contain all knowledge, or even all *religious* knowledge, and cited John 21:25 to show this. There are many other such verses (e.g., Lk 24:15-16, 25-27; Jn 20:30; Acts 1:2-3). Jesus appeared for forty days after His Resurrection, in addition to all the days and nights He spent with the disciples teaching them. In one night He very well could have spoken more words than are in the entire New Testament. And He was with them for three years. St. Paul spent many years with Christians, and is described frequently as "arguing" or "disputing" with Gentiles and Jews. It is ludicrous and ridiculous to think that either Jesus or Paul were "Scripture machines" and that absolutely everything they taught (i.e., the ideas and doctrines) was later recorded in Scripture, and had to be, lest it be forgotten, and that nothing they taught was *not* in Scripture.

Consider, for example, just one passage: the account of Jesus' post-Resurrection appearance to the two disciples on the road to Emmaus (Lk 24:13-32). They talked for probably several hours, and the Bible informs us of one wonderfully tantalizing Scripture interpretation session from our Lord Himself (that every Bible student would give his right arm to have heard):

> And beginning with Moses and all the prophets, he interpreted to them in all the scriptures the things concerning himself. (Luke 24:27)

It's absurd to think that nothing in any of these gatherings was spoken which was not later recorded in Scripture: no idea, no doctrine or explanation of a doctrine or interpretation of various Scriptures (that the disciples and early Christians would have surely asked Jesus and Paul about). It is equally absurd to hold that no one could *remember* any of this, and that it could not become a Christian Tradition supplementary to and alongside Holy Scripture, and in perfect harmony with it. This would require a notion that all of this teaching was quickly forgotten and lost to posterity, and that only the Bible contained the truths which Christians need. Nothing else carried a similar authority. This scenario is implausible in the extreme; even laughably so. Yet White's empty axiom requires it.

On what basis does White assert these things? How does he know this? What proves it? When all is said and done, it will be seen that his assumption is based on nothing at all. It is an unproven axiom that he adopts simply because it fits into the schema of *sola Scriptura*. He assumes it without argument, and this premise is used in an overall *sola Scriptura* framework, but it is, of course, yet another circular argument: a vicious logical circle indeed. The "reasoning" (insofar as I can comprehend such incoherence) runs as follows:

> 1. When Paul refers to tradition he is referring to nothing more than what is in the Bible.

2. Therefore, there is no tradition to speak of, since it simply collapses or reduces as a category to "that which is in Scripture."

3. Therefore, the Catholic rule of faith (which includes so-called "unbiblical tradition") is unbiblical.

4. Whatever is unbiblical must be false.

5. Whatever is false must be rejected.

6. Therefore, the Protestant rule of faith, *sola Scriptura*, is true over against the Catholic "three-legged stool" of authority: tradition + Church + Bible.

The whole chain starts with a radically unproven premise. It proceeds to add error upon error and to build a house of cards, on sand. All indications from the Bible and from common sense; all plausiblity, suggests that #1 is false to begin with. But White thinks it is so true that he repeats it several times (often italicizing entire sentences), hoping that people who read it over and over will accept it and not notice that no *evidence* or biblical rationale whatsoever has been given, which would cause a reasonable person who accepts biblical inspiration to believe this.

If one sees the word "tradition" in the Bible, one must realize that it is merely a synonym for "Bible." When Jesus upholds the authority of the Pharisees, it means only that they can read the Bible in the synagogue, and cannot mean anything contrary to the preconceived axiom of *sola Scriptura*. When the New Testament writers cite "prophecies" that can't be found in the Old Testament, we will find them one day, and no one must rashly conclude that they are "extra-biblical." Etc., etc.

White's arguments regarding *sola Scriptura* are filled with fallacies and insufficiently supported contentions, begged questions and circular arguments. They collapse in a heap under even mild scrutiny, like a snowman on the equator.

Chapter Five

Rebuttal of James White's Critique of My Book, *The Catholic Verses*
[December 2004-January 2005]

The Catholic Verses: 95 Reduced to 91

Dave Armstrong lists four verses that "confound Protestants" under the subtitle of "The Binding Authority of Tradition, According to St. Paul," beginning on page 37 of The Catholic Verses. *They are:*

> **1 Corinthians 11:2** Now I praise you because you remember me in everything and hold firmly to the traditions, just as I delivered them to you.

> **1 Thessalonians 2:13** For this reason we also constantly thank God that when you received the word of God which you heard from us, you accepted it not as the word of men, but for what it really is, the word of God, which also performs its work in you who believe.

> **2 Thessalonians 2:15** So then, brethren, stand firm and hold to the traditions which you were taught, whether by word of mouth or by letter from us.

> **2 Thessalonians 3:6** Now we command you, brethren, in the name of our Lord Jesus Christ, that you keep away

from every brother who leads an unruly life and not according to the tradition which you received from us.

There is a tremendous amount of literature on the subject of "tradition" in the New Testament, and a very large portion of it would challenge the rather simplistic assumptions Mr. Armstrong presents in his discussion.

Summary statements are not arguments, nor are derogatory remarks about arguments (especially when the latter are not even adequately presented or cited).

He writes, "Catholics believe that there is such a thing as a binding, authoritative Sacred Tradition and that it is explicitly indicated in the Bible (notably in the above passages)." So, we here have Armstrong wedding himself to these passages as "explicitly" presenting Rome's full-blown (capital "S" capital "T") Sacred Tradition.

That's not my argument. Biblical tradition is not *absolutely* identical to "Rome's" defined Tridentine Tradition of 1500 years later, just as Chalcedonian trinitarianism is more complex than biblical trinitarianism of only 400 years earlier. Both are entirely *consistent* with the less-developed biblical theology.

But given the hesitation of many a Roman Catholic scholar, it is quite possible Mr. Armstrong has over-reached himself just a bit.

Correctly-understood, not at all.

The mere presence of the term "tradition" is hardly sufficient to establish the position enunciated by Armstrong.

White clearly doesn't know what my position *is*. That's rule #1 for any good refutation.

How a Protestant is "confounded" by these passages is difficult to determine, at least, if meaningful exegesis of the text is the standard.

Binding tradition not identical to Scripture is logically contrary to *sola Scriptura*, the Protestant rule of faith.

And the first thing to note about Armstrong's work at this point should have a rather familiar ring to it if you have been following the Dave Hunt series: there is no meaningful exegesis offered to substantiate these grand claims by Armstrong. *Examine pp. 38-40 for yourself, and you will find no discussion of grammar, lexicography, syntax, or anything else relevant to meaningful exegesis.*

I make no pretense of being a professional Bible scholar. My book is strictly popular apologetics. But even an amateur exegete like me can (like Balaam's ass) point out lousy, irrelevant "arguments" from "professional" exegetes like John Calvin (a primary purpose of the book). All I contended for here was the existence of binding tradition in Scripture (and the incoherence of Protestant alternatives). White hasn't disproven this *at all*.

Instead, Armstrong depends upon secondary sources, and even then, the conclusions offered by secondary sources. He quotes Thomas More, but then focuses upon John Calvin, evidently seeking, it seems to me, to prejudice the reader through the use of quotations using language that was common in the day but is considered harsh and even non-Christian today.

I cited Calvin's remarks in his *Commentaries* (presumably an "exegetical" work) for 1 Corinthians 11:2 and 2 Thessalonians 2:15. If he provided no cogent analysis, but only "harsh" language, that is his (and White's) problem, not mine.

Indeed, one can judge the character of the discussion by noting these telling words: "Be that as it may, it is scarcely possible to discuss that issue constructively, because (in my opinion) Protestants are so afraid that any serious discussion of Tradition will cast doubt on sola Scriptura *and lead to undesired 'Catholic' consequences." I'm sorry, but such rhetoric detracts from the work, at least for any serious minded reader.*

I simply gave my opinion from much firsthand experience, as an accompanying thought distinct from the argument itself.

Armstrong moves into a dialogue after this that again offers nothing in reference to exegesis of the texts themselves, and in fact has only a marginal connection to the issue of the meaning of "tradition" in the Pauline corpus. How one leaps from para,dosij *in Paul to Sacred Tradition as defined by modern Rome is left unanswered.*

How White moves from making no argument and not interacting with mine, to his triumphant conclusion is a mystery to me too. Note his fallacy in the last sentence: I never argued that the biblical *para,dosij* was the same as fully-developed Catholic Tradition. This is what is known as a "straw man" in logic.

Now what was particularly odd, I thought, is the fact that immediately *after this section Armstrong goes into his Matthew 23 discussion (pp. 43-53, arguably his most strenuous effort at what comes closest to what can be identified as textually-based exegesis),*

Why is that "odd"? The next section was about "oral and extrabiblical tradition."

which he had sent to me prior to the publication of the book.

. . . which Mr. White (as usual) never replied to. Instead, he offered personal insults and then silence.

He cites my comments from The Roman Catholic Controversy *in this section rather extensively. So, I wondered if he would attempt to respond to the exegesis of 2 Thessalonians 2:15 that I offered in the same work. I would expect that at least the substance of that section would* have *to be refuted for Armstrong to feel he had at all proven his case.*

Why does *White* in particular have to be refuted to prove my case? The book was mostly about historic Protestant exegesis. Most folks would think Calvin is a bit more important and influential historically than White, so I dealt with *him*. White dealt in depth with the issue of "Moses' Seat," so I cited him thusly, in *that* section.

But no effort at all is put forth to respond to the exegesis of the passage provided in The Roman Catholic Controversy. *The fact that this is a present command, that the tradition referred to had already been delivered, in fulness, to the entirety of the church at Thessalonica, is not noted.*

If I ever read one of White's books and get in the mood to refute it some day, then I will do exactly that. As it is, this is supposedly a critique of *my* book, and one doesn't do that simply by complaining that one's *own* book (one of many) was not refuted in some particular! Nice try at topic evasion, though . . . maybe next time we'll be blessed with White's reply regarding Moses' Seat (which argument I *did* thoroughly refute in my book).

(This observation would require the RC apologist to trace the content of his alleged oral tradition back to Thessalonica, and, as they well know, that cannot be done for the major elements of that alleged tradition as Rome has defined it).

As my argument does not at all *require* such a thing, this is a *non sequitur.*

The immediate context of the passage and its relevance directly to the gospel (and hence to the content of the "tradition" delivered by Paul) is likewise ignored. In essence, nothing presented in regards to the meaning of 2 Thess. 2:15 in context is addressed by Armstrong. It is hard to believe Armstrong has read

181

the comments on pp. 99-101 of The Roman Catholic Controversy *but he hasn't read pp. 95-98.*

I don't read White's books, so why is this surprising? If the man can't do a simple written dialogue properly, why waste my time? I dealt with Calvin's "exegesis," and White has totally ignored that, so he is simply not critiquing my book thus far.

Now, if the standard of being "confounded" involves presenting a compelling, exegetically sound, contextually derived interpretation of a passage resulting in a clear vindication of the Roman Catholic reading . . .

The book was not primarily exegetical; rather, it was designed to show the shortcomings and inadequacies of Protestant commentary when it comes to these passages. One can point out holes in an opposing position without (technically) engaging in the same thing (exegesis proper). If, for example, someone made a simple logical error in an extremely complicated theory in physics that I knew nothing whatsoever about, it would still be rational and acceptable for me to point it out. I made all this very clear in my Introduction, which can be read online. Once White figures out my goal and purpose in the book, perhaps his critiques will have some *relevance* and not descend into straw men and *non sequiturs*. As it is, he hasn't made a single extended argument against any particular argument of mine in this section.

(though, how Dave Armstrong, a private Catholic, could actually know the "official" Roman understanding of a passage without engaging in "private interpretation" is difficult to say anyway),

Off the subject . . . nor is this required of Catholics, anyway.

then we need to re-work the sub-title to "91 Bible Passages that Confound Protestants."

. . . and White's "response": "Four Straw Men That Purport to be Rational Replies."

Next we will look at Armstrong's handling of the passages he presents regarding Penance.

Great. Perhaps White can actually make a *counter-argument* next time. Let's hope and pray.

The Protestant Verses: Can Dave Armstrong Exegete This Passage?

I'd like to ask Dave Armstrong to provide a biblically solid, textually grounded, linguistically accurate, contextually sound interpretation of Romans 4:6-8:

> **Romans 4:6-8** 6 just as David also describes the blessedness of the man to whom God imputes righteousness apart from works: 7 "Blessed are those whose lawless deeds are forgiven, and whose sins are covered; 8 Blessed is the man to whom the LORD will not impute sin."

I scanned through The Catholic Verses *and couldn't find a reference to this passage (I may have missed it);*

Obviously, then, it has *nothing* to do with any argument in my book!

I looked at the Scripture index to A Biblical Defense of Catholicism *and it is not listed.*

That being *another* book, it obviously has nothing to do with a critique of my *present* book, either . . .

I tried googling Armstrong's blog and website, but got no hits on various ways of listing the passage. If Armstrong has already written something that fits this request, I will be glad to look at it upon referral. But, failing that, I would simply ask: "Who is the blessed man of Romans 4:6-8 in Roman Catholic theology?"

Why should I go off on White's rabbit trail, after he has systematically ignored my critiques of his material for almost ten years? If he actually tries to *interact* with some of mine, then he will find me much more willing to go off on tangents of his own choosing. But I won't bow to either (1) a double standard, or (2) diversion tactics to avoid dealing with the topic at hand (which he *himself* chose, in the present case, oddly enough).

I would assume Armstrong possesses a copy of The God Who Justifies

He assumes wrongly. I haven't read *any* of his books. The only ones I even *have* are those he sent me for free back in 1995 (thanks again, James!), and one (*The Roman Catholic Controversy*) that I found for a quarter at a used book sale (I'm willing to pay *that* much for anti-Catholic material; if it was a dollar, though, I would have thought twice). [*now* I do have a copy, and critique a chapter of it in chapter 12 below]

(though it is not referred to in his new book, which is especially interesting regarding the 24 page chapter on James 2:14-24 that Armstrong neglects in his book), [in *this* book it not only isn't neglected, but refuted point-by-point]

Again, White strangely assumes that I always have to deal with *his* arguments, when my purpose was mainly to examine historic Protestant commentary, from major figures in its history (or does White claim to be that?).

but should he not, allow me to reproduce the exegesis I offered of this section. I would be very interested in a response-in-kind from Mr. Armstrong. (Please forgive any formatting issues, the lack of italics, and of the footnotes that are in the original. Please refer to the published work for those details):

See my third response previous to this one. I am curious why White is suddenly so interested in my opinions, though, since he has always argued (and still in our previous round) that they have *no substance whatsoever.* [his entire citation was deleted, due to its being off-topic] My book is about how Protestants rationalize, special plead, avoid, obfuscate, etc. regarding biblical verses which (from our perspective) suggest some distinctive in Catholic theology.

White's aim above, on the other hand, is to exegete a passage that he considers a strong proof text for Protestantism. Apples and oranges. Perhaps a future book of mine can be devoted to showing how Protestant proof texts are utterly inadequate and able to be sufficiently refuted from a Catholic point of view and dismissed (sounds like a fun project to me).

But that time is not now, in the context of the ongoing critique of my book, and also given White's past utter contempt and ignoring of my arguments. I've always refused to play this game of topic-switching (with White and everyone else). I would do that even if we had the most cordial of relationships and he *had* answered my past writings and challenges to him. And that is because I maintain strong principles of how to go about a good dialogue properly and in an orderly, constructive fashion.

White, in fact, follows very similar principles himself. In a recent blog post ("Regarding Theological Dialogues") he stated that one must take one's time with serious theological topics, and not rush things. This is very good (nice to agree with White occasionally). Likewise, my principle and determination here is to not go off the previous topic in order to immediately treat some entirely different subject.

It has nothing whatsoever to do with the *worthiness and importance or value of the particular discussion itself.* In fact, I show much respect towards it by maintaining this principle, because I am saying that serious topics ought to be considered one at a time, carefully and deliberately. And that can't be done by rushing off on some rabbit trail, because the opponent thinks he has a slam dunk (while double dribbling and missing all his shots in the present "refutation / dialogue" that he seeks to avoid for the moment with a diversion). So, nice try . . .

Interesting Replies

DA has replied to my first comments on his book. They were...predictable. Armstrong says his book is not "primarily" exegetical. Quite true. It is not secondarily exegetical. It is not exegetical in a tertiary manner. It simply isn't exegetical at all.

It does contain *some* exegesis, but here's the *heart* of my purpose (from my Introduction):

> . . . only rarely do they seriously engage the biblical texts utilized by Catholics to support their positions . . . . critique of common Protestant attempts to ignore, explain away, rationalize, wish away, over-polemicize, minimize, de-emphasize, evade clear consequences of, or special plead with regard to "the Catholic Verses": 95 biblical passages . . . ultimate incoherence, inadequacy, inconsistency, or exegetical and theological implausibility of the Protestant interpretations . . . (pp. xii-xiv)

But, that's the whole point. The book pretends to "confound" Protestants with biblical passages, remember? I did not choose the title, Mr. Armstrong did.

Technically, *I* am not trying to "confound" anyone. It is the *Bible* that gives Protestants difficulty. I'm merely *documenting* exegetical bankruptcy, confusion, or irrationality.

And the only way to do that is to provide a meaningful interpretation of those passages.

That's logically distinct from critiquing *Protestant* exegesis. Biblical evidence for *Catholicism* is dealt with in my first two books.

And unless Mr. Armstrong is willing to just come out and say, "Hey, Rome tells me what these passages mean, I can't even begin to handle the biblical text myself," then some kind of argument is going to have be offered from the text itself.

That is a separate project. Catholic exegetes are no more bound to "official" interpretation of verses than Protestants. See my blog paper: "The Freedom of the Catholic Biblical Exegete."

And what I'm demonstrating is that when most "Dave Armstrong" level RC apologists . . .

Who *else* would be in this "level"?

quote a passage, they honestly have no idea what the passage is actually saying in its native context. They are eisegetically misusing the text, as I am documenting in regards to Armstrong. And that's the whole point of this exercise.

Why respond to silly, false accusations?

Armstrong also informs us that he doesn't read my books. That's okay. If he wishes to remain ignorant of the exegetical arguments presented against his position, I have no reason to encourage him to do otherwise.

This book is about *failed* Protestant *attempts to refute* Catholic biblical prooftexts. White has yet to deal with *those*.

It is just odd to me that someone would wish to put arguments into print that have already, and recently, been refuted. ignoratio elenchi.

White's arguments are not the sum and essence of Protestant exegesis. He has quite the inflated view of his own importance.

When I invited Armstrong to provide us with a meaningful, contextual examination of Romans 4:6-8, his response was classic: [cites my reply] . . . Well, okay. I guess we will be left to wonder if, in fact, Dave Armstrong can exegete that passage or not.

Wonder away. It is off-topic. Period.

Maybe someone else can ask and not get that kind of response.

When it is the *topic*, sure!

But again, I just state the obvious: the author of A Biblical Defense of Catholicism *and* The Catholic Verses *seems, anyway, by his initial responses, to be exceptionally unwilling to engage in exegesis of the text of Scripture. I don't know, maybe that strikes someone else as odd?*

White's continual dense inability (or unwillingness) to offer a logical and coherent critique is what amazes *me*.

The latest installments [of White's "reply"] are his "Quick Thought Regarding DA and Exegesis," where he expresses his confusion and clueless noncomprehension of the replies I have been giving. Here are some highlights:

. . . it seems to be pretty difficult to follow where he's going.

. . . [he] simply assumes the Roman interpretation, ignores the need to do any exegesis at all, and after all that, does not avail himself of counter-exegesis when it is only two pages away from passages he cites in his book . . .

I'm confused as well by the fact that when I mentioned looking for an exegesis of Romans 4:6-8 (which seemingly is not forthcoming: I'm sure I'm not the only one who would like to see Mr. Armstrong's exegesis of the text) in A Biblical Defense of Catholicism *he accused me of changing the topic; but now I am told to look there for the positive exegesis of these passages from the Roman Catholic side. Which is it? Sorta hard to figure out, isn't it? Indeed it is.*

To which I reply: read my explanations *again*. It'll come to you if you keep trying. Moving on, the next post White has blessed his readers with, is "Armstrong's Reading List," in response to my last post, where I had to prove that I had done some serious reading as a Protestant (!!!). This is an absolute classic gem of White's finely-honed art of personal attack, obfuscation, and sophistry. I shall cite it in its entirety:

Mr. Armstrong has provided a reading list on his blog.

No; I provided a list of books I had read, and which are in my library: heavily used for research (because White had ridiculously *denied* that I was well-read as a Protestant).

In essence, this means that instead of blaming ignorance for his very shallow misrepresentations of non-Catholic theology and exegesis, we must now assert knowing deception.

At this point, White has descended into virtual self-parody and high comedy. Having seen that his contention of my "ignorance" was blown out of the water by a simple citation of the books I have read and/or own, he faced a dilemma: the choice was (1) "admit that Armstrong actually *knows* something about Protestantism, so that I have been lying about him all these years," or (2) "deny that he is telling the truth about his reading and books." He chose (1) (well, the first clause, anyway), and decided to switch to the tactic of accusing me of "knowing deception," so as to "save face" (so he thinks).

So far, DA has been unable to provide even the slightest meaningful defense of his own published statements and their refutation.

No refutation has *occurred* (White has almost totally *ignored* the arguments in the book); what need of defense, then? So, mostly I have been clarifying simple logic and facts.

Which is really only marginally relevant to the real issue: hopefully, aside from demonstrating the exegetical bankruptcy of The Catholic Verses, . . .

Can *I* help it if White continually shows his inability to grasp the very *nature* and *purpose* of the book?

. . . answers are being given to all those observing and learning how to speak the truth to those who likewise would handle the Word from the vantage point of tradition rather than allowing it to speak for itself with its own voice.

Failing any logical argument, simply distort the other's belief and assert your own radically circular position . . .

Chapter Nine of The Catholic Verses *deals with the subject of Penance. Four passages are presented in this brief chapter, specifically:*

> **Philippians 3:10** that I may know Him and the power of His resurrection and the fellowship of His sufferings, being conformed to His death; (cf. Gal. 2:20)

> **Romans 8:17** and if children, heirs also, heirs of God and fellow heirs with Christ, if indeed we suffer with Him so that we may also be glorified with Him.

> **2 Corinthians 4:10** always carrying about in the body the dying of Jesus, so that the life of Jesus also may be manifested in our body.

> **Colossians 1:24** Now I rejoice in my sufferings for your sake, and in my flesh I do my share on behalf of His body, which is the church, in filling up what is lacking in Christ's afflictions.

The first two are grouped under the heading "Sharing in Christ's Sufferings" and the second under "Carrying Christ's Afflictions in Our Bodies." It is important for the reader to understand the relevance of the concept of suffering in Roman Catholic soteriology. But it is also difficult to explain or illustrate in a blog entry that is aiming for brevity as well. So here's a reading assignment for the serious reader. Go here [linked]*and read the first four chapters of this official Roman Magisterial document,* Indulgentiarum Doctrina, *the Apostolic Constitution on the Revision of Indulgences. Pay close attention to the language it uses regarding sin, punishment, suffering, penance, and grace. Now, if you are not in a position to read that much, allow me a few selected quotes:* [omitted, since off-topic]

Again, White illustrates his astounding inability (or deliberate unwillingness -- which would border on outright sophistry) to stay on the topic. I am not treating the subject of indulgences here (let alone magisterial documents on same). The specific topics are those that White noted above in my two sub-headings. I dealt with indulgences in my first book, *A Biblical Defense of Catholicism*, chapter 8, pp. 162-165, and also on pp. 152-155, including footnote #166, from Bertrand Conway.

My first book has been out for over three years (and he has a copy). If White was so eager to "refute" what I wrote about indulgences (including explicit biblical proofs right from St. Paul and Jesus), he has had ample opportunity. So why bring it up *now*, when it is extraneous to the subject matter of my current book? I also (it should be noted), dealt in a fair amount of depth with verses like those above, in my first book, in the long chapter on penance (pp. 147-165), whereas in the current work, I only briefly touched upon it with five pages. In fact, White's response on penance is more than twice as long as my entire short chapter (3359 words to 1615).

Sadly, this is a typical tactic of White's where I am concerned. He'll ignore massive writings that I have done on some subject (all the while mocking how many "substanceless" words I write). Then he'll select a brief treatment and act as if it were the *sum total* of my argument, and ridicule and dismiss it as absurdly inadequate (along with the obligatory potshots at my ability, intelligence, etc.).

He did this with my 35 minute-or-so presentation on *Catholic Answers Live*, concerning Bible and Tradition, devoting many of his webcasts to a mere introductory, ten-point talk, when I have written more on that topic (enough for several books) than any other. He wanted no part of those writings, but went right to the brief presentation. This "apologetic strategy" may fool some folks, but not the ones I am trying to reach (those with an open and fair mind, and willing to carefully consider both sides of a debate).

You get the "flavor," I hope. The concept of suffering is tied in with a synergistic, grace-prompted, but still free-will driven, concept of penance/merit/forgiveness.

Soteriology proper is a huge topic, beyond our purview. I refer readers to my first book: chapters on penance and purgatory (the latter is 27 pages).

Once again, in citing Phil. 3:10 and Rom. 8:17, Armstrong does not consider it necessary to actually handle the verses, establish context, meaning, anything exegetical.

This gets back to the nature and purpose of the book; already discussed.

They are simply cited, and then the assumption is made that Protestants have no place in their theology for "suffering."

This is exactly the *opposite* of what I contended, as even White's own citations of my words prove.

And his source for this (if you happen to be widely read in meaningful Protestant writing you are probably wondering, since you have read lots about suffering and its role in conforming us to the image of Christ) is...himself!

No, my "source" is long experience in Protestant circles and what many great Protestant authors have *themselves* noted (many examples provided below).

Evidently, Armstrong's audience does not include serious minded Protestants, for such writing immediately informs one that Mr. Armstrong's "Protestant" experience was anything but serious.

No need to respond to *ad hominem* attacks. I get plenty of laudatory letters from "serious minded Protestants."

Well, even if consulting secondary sources without providing primary exegesis would be sufficient, the point is that Armstrong has no concept of the depth of writing from non-Catholic sources on the meaning and purpose of suffering;

My providing of my list of Protestant authors read and books in my library quickly disposed of this lie (C. S. Lewis and Alvin Plantinga and Leibniz offer no depth on this subject?!). As a result, White was forced (by his own intransigence) to switch from calling me "ignorant" to now accusing me of "knowing deception." I fought shallow Protestant views of suffering as a Protestant as far back as 1982, when I refuted the "health-and-wealth / prosperity / hyper-faith" teachings, largely utilizing the wonderful critiques of a wise Protestant man and virtual father of the evangelical counter-cult movement, the late Dr. Walter Martin (*not* an anti-Catholic himself). I had been prevented from accepting such nonsense by the wonderful teaching of Pastor Richard Bieber, in whose church I first began seriously following Jesus. This godly pastor was the single most influential person in my early committed Christian life, besides my brother Gerry.

further, the Roman Catholic use of the term, especially in reference to penance, would require his proving that in the context of writing to the churches at Rome and Philippi Paul intended to communicate, through the term "suffering," the kind of thing Armstrong has in mind as a Roman Catholic, and once again, he does not even try *to make this connection. It is simply assumed.*

White again commits the fallacy (one of numerous ones in his "critique") of thinking that everything I try to utilize from

193

Scripture is intended as an explicit "proof" of full-blown, fully developed Catholic doctrine. This simply doesn't follow, nor is it true in fact.

Armstrong then says that outside of certain forms of Pentecostalism, "they will not deny that a Christian needs to, and can expect to, suffer." Expect to suffer? Surely. Walk as Christ walked and one will suffer the hatred of the world. But "need to" is a completely different animal, especially in the context of Rome's beliefs regarding the subject, as noted previously. I believe fully that God intends to conform me to the image of Christ, and a number of the experiences I will go through in that process will take the form of what can be properly identified as "suffering." But "need to" so as to expiate temporal punishment of sin? Need to so as to perfect my justification before God? Most assuredly not! This is the issue, and Armstrong leaves it untouched.

I wasn't *dealing* with all that. Again, I dealt with penance (and biblical evidences for same) at great length in my first book. This particular section was about (as White noted above) "Sharing in Christ's Sufferings." Period. I'm not trying to prove fully elaborated Catholic doctrines (in this case, our theology of penance) with every biblical passage I am treating. Only a fool would do that. But White gets a lot of mileage by making illogical accusations about straw men of his own making. After all, it "sounds good." And that is the name of the game for the sophist. White obviously couldn't care less about what I was *actually* arguing, *in context*. His game is to make me look foolish and ridiculous, whatever it takes (lying and wholesale, cynical distortion included). Christians "need to" suffer insofar as it is a requirement of the New Testament. *That* was my argument here. See, e.g.,: Philippians 1:29: "For it has been granted to you on behalf of Christ not only to believe on Him, but also to suffer for Him," and 1 Peter 2:21: "To this [suffering] you were called.. ." There are many more such passages. Many Protestants (and Protestant theologies) *minimize* these. It is an undeniable fact, however much White protests.

He writes, "Most Evangelicals do not take it that far, yet still minimize the place of suffering, and hence, of the related notion, penance. This represents a scandalous lack of understanding of the deeper, more difficult aspects of Christianity." I think this represents a scandalous lack of understanding of the deeper, more meaningful works of Calvin, Edwards, the entire body of the Puritans, Bunyan, Spurgeon, Warfield and any number of modern writers.

First, let's get the *context* of what I wrote, lest readers get a warped, out-of-balance idea of it. White deliberately omitted the following passage of mine, which occurs immediately above his last citation above:

> It is only certain strains of evangelical Protestantism (particularly one brand of pentecostal, "name it, claim it" Protestantism, which asserts that believers can have whatever they like merely by "claiming" it and having enough "faith") that try to pretend that suffering is foreign to the Christian life (in extreme cases, not God's will *at all* that we even have sickness, etc.), who ignore this crucial aspect of the passage. They pass right over it as if it weren't even there. (p. 128)

Now, as to White's additional comments: he keeps trying to make out that I am an ignoramus, unacquainted with serious Protestant treatments of suffering. Nothing could be further from the truth. It was *precisely* because of my familiarity with those sorts of writings, that I was very careful to *qualify* my assertions ("only certain strains," "Most . . . do not take it that far," etc.).

Secondly, I am obviously generalizing in a broad manner. To do so does not require a denial that there are many exceptions to the tendency under consideration. An example of a generalization about Catholics would be: "Catholics don't read their Bibles as much as evangelical Protestants do." This is a true and undeniable statement. I recently had an article published in *This Rock* about this very subject. But it also has literally thousands of exceptions. I read the Bible more than many individual Protestants. Etc. White's utter misunderstanding of this aspect of the chapter on penance overlooks this.

Thirdly, as another generalization, only Catholics who fully understand the Church's teaching on suffering and penance would (unfortunately) be more biblically informed and at an advantage to Protestants on this topic (i.e., the average evangelical as an individual probably has a superior understanding of suffering compared to the average Catholic). But that doesn't mean that there is a widespread deficiency in Protestant circles also, regarding this topic.

Fourth, as I showed above, I was critiquing mostly certain pentecostals, who wildly distort this biblical teaching. When I was a Protestant, I read people like Corrie Ten Boom and Elisabeth Elliot: godly women who had suffered much themselves, and who presented a much more biblical view of suffering in the Christian life.

Fifth, here are reflections from three wise Protestants who have a developed theology of suffering, about the widespread deficiency of same in Protestant circles (i.e., it's not just "Dave the ignorant Catholic who [supposedly] isn't acquainted with the best Protestant theology" who is saying this):

> I need no longer try to follow Christ, for cheap grace, the bitterest foe of discipleship, which true discipleship must loathe and detest, has freed me from that. Grace as the data for our calculations means grace at the cheapest price, but grace as the answer to the sum means costly grace. It is terrifying to realize what use can be made of a genuine evangelical doctrine. In both cases we have the identical formula -- "justification by faith alone." Yet the misuse of the formula leads to the complete destruction of its very essence.

> (Dietrich Bonhoeffer, *The Cost of Discipleship*, New York: Macmillan, revised edition, 1959, 54-55)

> . . . several dozen of their children had died because of an error (I believe) in theology. (Actually, the teaching of the Indiana church is not so different from what I hear in

196

many evangelical churches and on religious television and radio; they simply apply the extravagant promises of faith more consistently.)

(Philip Yancey, *Disappointment With God*, Grand Rapids, Michigan: Zondervan, 1988, 26; referring to a church which held that any medical treatment was a denial of faith; hence fifty-two children of sect members had died)

Today all is made to depend upon the initial act of believing. At a given moment a "decision" is made for Christ, and after that everything is automatic . . . We of the evangelical churches are almost all guilty of this lopsided view of the Christian life . . . In our eagerness to make converts we allow our hearers to absorb the idea that they can deal with their entire responsibility once and for all by an act of believing. This is in some vague way supposed to honor grace and glorify God, whereas actually it is to make Christ the author of a grotesque, unworkable system that has no counterpart in the Scriptures of truth . . . To make converts . . . we are forced to play down the difficulties and play up the peace of mind and worldly success enjoyed by those who accept Christ . . . Thus assured, hell-deserving sinners are coming in droves to "accept" Christ for what they can get out of Him . . .

(A. W. Tozer, *A Treasury of A.W. Tozer*, Grand Rapids, Michigan: Baker Book House, 1980, 85-87)

By trying to pack all of salvation into one experience, or two, the advocates of instant Christianity flaunt the law of development which runs through all nature. They ignore the sanctifying effects of suffering, cross carrying and practical obedience. They pass by the need for spiritual training, the necessity of forming right religious habits and the need to wrestle against the world, the devil and the flesh . . . Instant Christianity is twentieth century orthodoxy. I wonder whether the man who wrote

Philippians 3:7-16 would recognize it as the faith for which he finally died. I am afraid he would not.

(A. W. Tozer, *That Incredible Christian*, Harrisburg, Pennsylvania: Christian Publications, 1964, 24-25)

The fact is that the Reformed understanding of the sovereignty of God is so far beyond the crass "suffering by grace = penance for temporal punishments, say your Our Fathers and Hail Marys and fast on Fridays and consider obtaining some indulgences just in case" kind of Catholicism that afflicts millions on our planet that it is truly beyond words to express.

Nice display of White's caricatured, jaded view of Catholicism. It plays well to the anti-Catholic crowd . . .

Yes, suffering is very clearly present in the text. No one doubts this. But what Mr. Armstrong does not seem to understand is that the mere presence of the word does not, to any serious minded reader, include within it the massive mountain of theological baggage connected to suffering/penance/merit as seen in Indulgentiarum Doctrina *and other Roman Catholic magisterial documents and teachings.*

Of course I understand that, and I never claimed *otherwise*. But White sure seems to *think* I did. He is wrong.

Presumption is not exegesis, nor does it amount to confounding the Protestant position.

And creation of straw men and *non sequiturs* are not "rational replies."

Armstrong assumes that the suffering to which Paul refers is identifiable with the sufferings Rome refers to.

I do? That's news to me. Where did I supposedly argue what I don't believe?

Why? He does not say.

For obvious reasons . . . (see previous reply).

He does not even try to tell us how v. 17 is functioning in the entire citadel of Christian truth known as Romans chapter 8. It is just thrown out there, and we are to believe. Sorry, but I've spent far too much time seeking to honor the text and communicate its meaning to others to buy such an obvious ipse dixit.

Just me trying to hoodwink my ignorant heathen Catholic readers again, huh James?

And Phil. 3:10 is not even touched. It is merely cited as one of the "95" verses, no exegesis offered. Just presumption.

It's rather clear, for the purpose I had in this section. If I had exegeted all 95 passages like White wants me to, the book would have been about 900 pages long.

The Bible teaches that Christ's sufferings (and this will come out most clearly in the next section regarding Christ's afflictions) alone avail for our salvation.

Yep. Amen.

Christians suffer as part of their sanctification, or to use the language of Paul later in Romans 8, that process whereby God the Father conforms them to the image of His Son. We do so by the power of the Holy Spirit, so that in our sufferings we die to self, and live to Christ. When a Christian suffers according to God's will, he or she has the promise that nothing can touch them in their suffering that was not ordained by the Father and the Son (Col. 3:3). While our suffering in no way, shape, or form adds to the work of Christ, it is very much a part of God's will. It is never "meaningless," for God does not cause His children to suffer needlessly.

I agree with all of this.

But the fact that my suffering can be used of God to His glory and to the benefit of others (as in the life of Paul) truly has nothing whatsoever to do with Rome's doctrine of penance.

That isn't true, but gets into biblical proofs for penance, from my first book.

These passages may not have been discussed in Dave Armstrong's campus ministry meetings, but a quick review of the sermons and studies at the Phoenix Reformed Baptist Church would disabuse Armstrong of his misunderstandings of what serious Protestants believe about suffering.

I.e., White's twisted caricatures about what he falsely *thinks* I know and don't know about Protestant views . . .

. . . in the course of that debate, took note of the comments of Bishop Lightfoot, the great Anglican scholar, regarding Colossians 1:24 and the term "afflictions" from his commentary on Colossians . . .

Anglicans aren't even *Christians*, according to White's criteria, consistently applied. But that is another matter, when White needs an "ally" against the Great Beast. I have omitted his citation as irrelevant, since (according to the oft-stated purpose of my book), this section examined what *John Calvin* and *Albert Barnes* (not J. B. Lightfoot) wrote about Colossians 1:24.

Hence, to seriously suggest that he is "confounding" Protestants on the basis of Bible passages, Dave Armstrong would have to wrestle with a presentation such as Lightfoot's, . . .

White can go on all day citing commentators I didn't deal with. But my purpose was to show the bias and irrationality so often present in John Calvin and other influential Protestant commentators (not to engage in full-fledged exegesis, for which I'm not qualified).

. . . and would have to establish that in context, both of these passages are indicating that there is some kind of "satisfactory" element to the sufferings of believers that would fit the Roman Catholic concept.

I think these passages are consistent with a Catholic understanding, yes. I'm not claiming that they contain, individually, the full Catholic (developed) doctrine. But Scripture doesn't contain the developed Chalcedonian trinitarian theology, either, so such realities do not concern me. We would expect this.

For obviously, a Protestant can read 2 Corinthians 4:10 and say, "Yes, I die to sin daily, not sacramentally or partially so that I remain imperfect (as in Roman theology), but as the result of the perfect standing that is mine in the righteousness of Christ the Holy Spirit works within me to conform me to the image of Christ and by so doing brings the reality of my union with Christ in His death so that His life will be ever more seen in me." How have I been "confounded" in this passage?

A true critique of what I was doing here would have to deal with Calvin's and Barnes' commentary. A presentation of one Protestant perspective on it and an examination of Protestant dealings with Catholic proof texts are two different things. I'm doing the latter; White the former. Never the twain shall meet.

Armstrong, again, does not offer any exegesis of the cited texts. Instead, he devotes a little over two pages to arguing that in Roman Catholic theology the concept of suffering does not detract from the finished work of Christ, and that Protestants, like Albert Barnes, just don't get it.

Yes; if only anti-Catholics like White could grasp this simple fact.

You can see now why I strongly suggested reading Indulgentiarum Doctrina *when I began this section of the review. When we pray for someone, how are they "helped"? It is not by a transfer of merit. The debt of temporal punishment I owe is not lessened by my prayers, either. I am not adding to the* thesaurus meritorum *by praying or doing good works or suffering (there is no such thing to begin with). And if Armstrong wished to communicate with a serious minded non-Catholic based upon these passages (he is the one claiming the passage confounds Protestants) he would explain why we should understand* qli/yij *to refer to satisfactory sufferings (as opposed to Lightfoot). Of course, no such attempt is made, for I seriously doubt Mr. Armstrong is even aware of the issue, let alone able to interact meaningfully with Lightfoot. But I do note, he has no basis for complaint, since he himself refers to "Catholic exegesis" of the texts on p. 130 (he just doesn't bother to provide it).*

More extraneous *non sequiturs*, with the by-now obligatory insult of my intelligence and thinking ability . . .

Finally, a note on Armstrong's constant attempt to paint Calvin in the worst possible light.

Oh? Does White mean my *citing* the man? Funny that White is most reluctant to defend the nonsense that Calvin so often writes, which I have merely documented. Yet Calvin is doing "exegesis" and I don't have a clue about anything I write about?

In this section he cites Calvin from The Institutes, *but not from Calvin's actual commentary on Colossians 1:24.*

This is untrue. On p. 131 I also cite Calvin from his *Commentaries*. Since White brought this up (a rare instance of actually dealing with an argument of *mine* -- well, "kinda sorta"), I will cite both of Calvin's tirades, to give the reader an idea of the sort of thing I deal with throughout the book. If this casts a bad "light" on Calvin, I ask: whose fault is *that*?:

Indeed, as their whole doctrine is a patchwork of sacrilege and blasphemy, this is the most blasphemous of the whole . . . What is this but merely to leave the name of Christ, and at the same time make him a vulgar saintling, who can scarcely be distinguished in the crowd?

(*Institutes*, III, 5, 3-4)

I then commented (words utterly ignored by White, as usual):

Calvin here is again guilty of presenting a caricature of the Catholic position, whereby it is construed as somehow opposing saints to God or regarding the saints as somehow contributing to the redemption apart from God (the characteristic Protestant dichotomous or "either/or" mindset). Calvin mistakenly *thinks* this is what Catholics hold. In his commentary on this verse, Calvin repeats the falsehoods about the Catholic position, and even urges readers to hate those who are supposedly deliberately corrupting Holy Writ:

Then I cited Calvin's *Commentaries*:

Nor are they ashamed to wrest this passage, with the view of supporting so execrable a blasphemy, as if Paul here affirmed that his sufferings are of avail for expiating the sins of men . . . I should also be afraid of being suspected of calumny in repeating things so monstrous . . . Let, therefore, pious readers learn to hate and detest those profane sophists, who thus deliberately corrupt and adulterate the Scriptures, . . .

This sounds like a familiar charge, doesn't it? As soon as White saw that he couldn't play the "Dave is utterly ignorant about Protestantism" card (after I showed what I had read), he immediately went to the charge of "knowing deception." We see that he follows his master Calvin in this tendency to personal attack at the expense of rational argument. Now, I want to know: how is the above to be regarded as "biblical exegesis"? And if Calvin can lie about Catholics and urge readers to *hate* them, why is it that I can't even critique *tendencies* in Protestant exegetical circles? If White claims I am not doing exegesis (even when I reiterate endlessly that this was not my primary purpose), why doesn't he criticize *Calvin* for failing to do so when *he* is *supposed* to be doing so?!

I thought it would be worthwhile to see what Calvin actually wrote there. Here is the online version [linked]. *Scroll down to the section on Col. 1:24 and note that Calvin, unlike Armstrong, actually addresses the verse in its context prior to responding to Rome's misuse of it. I wonder why Armstrong does not refute Calvin's actual exegesis and commentary? I leave that to the reader to decide.*

I assumed that Calvin would try to exegete the passage, in his *Commentaries*! I dealt with that in Calvin which was the subject matter of my book: the extreme bias present in Protestant commentators when dealing with Catholic claims. When will White *comprehend* this? In this way he wraps up his fallacy-ridden and wrongheaded "critique" concerning penance.

Chapter Six

Refutation of James White Regarding *Moses' Seat*, the Bible, and Tradition
[May 2005]

This will be my final installment in response to Dave Armstrong's The Catholic Verses. *It is not that there are not many more passages that could be addressed, it is just that there is so very little actual exegesis in the book that the real essence of its self-enunciated claim to provide a defense of the Roman Catholic* exegesis *of the text of Scripture has already been refuted, repeatedly, and there is no reason to proverbially beat the dead horse.*

As I pointed out many times in the earlier debates over my book (obviously to no avail, which is a rather annoying and frustrating characteristic of debates with White: he habitually ignores one's clarifications and corrections, even of plain factual matters: this is virtually universally reported by Catholics who have debated him), the book is not, technically, about, or consisting of, exegesis *per se*. He has never grasped this. The fundamental purpose of the book is actually quite *different*. I explained in my Introduction:

> I shall now proceed to offer a critique of common Protestant attempts to ignore, explain away, rationalize, wish away, over-polemicize, minimize, de-emphasize, evade clear consequences of, or special plead with regard to "the Catholic Verses": ninety-five biblical passages

that provide the foundation for Catholicism's most distinctive doctrines. This is not a scholarly work, as I am no scholar in the first place, merely a lay Catholic apologist; but it is not "anti-scholarly," and I will incorporate scholarship wherever necessary to substantiate the argument.

We see, then, what the purpose is. It is more of a *logical* critique of Protestant exegesis and particular tendencies and manifest biases in dealing with certain "Catholic-sounding" verses. It's a somewhat subtle distinction, but a *very* important one, for our purposes. If White doesn't even *comprehend* the *fundamental nature and methodology* of my book, then he can hardly offer a compelling refutation of any part of it with which he deals. One must first *understand* what one purports to refute.

That's rule number one in any debate, and I think White (as a frequent debater, who clearly prides himself on being very good at it) would readily agree with that general principle. I know what my own book is about (as the world's greatest expert on my own book), and if White did also, then he would cease *misrepresenting* (inadvertently or not; I assume the former) what it was about.

He keeps harping on what he seems to think is the plain fact that I wouldn't know how to do proper exegesis if my life depended on it. Well, that may or may not be true. Since I don't claim to be a scholar who specializes in exegesis (or a scholar at all), and my arguments don't depend on that fact, it is a rather moot point. The book is not a commentary. It is a reasoned critique of flaws in historic, mainstream orthodox Protestant commentary; especially those having to do with prior biases brought to the task of exegesis itself.

And one can do that -- point out simple logical flaws and evasions -- without *having* to be an expert on exegesis, or a Bible scholar (that would obviously *help*, but it's not absolutely *necessary* for my particular purpose). One simple example will suffice in illustrating this point. I may not know the slightest thing about trigonometry or calculus. But if I, as an observer of a math professor, notice that there is a simple mathematical error in a complex equation or proof written out by the expert (say, 3 x 4 = 14), it is quite proper and not at all presumptuous for me to point that out, and "correct" the expert.

I don't have to know everything there is to know about trigonometry or calculus, or know as much as the expert knows, or even (in this instance) anything *at all* about it. All I have to know is that 3 x 4 = 12, not 14. Complex, systematic errors can be built upon the simplest of logical errors. And non-experts can point these out.

Likewise, when it comes to historic exegesis and commentary on Holy Scripture, I don't have to be an expert on how to interpret such-and-such a Bible passage (with knowledge of Greek and Hebrew, and eight years of theology, New Testament, Old Testament, etc., etc.) in order to note that someone is ignoring a key aspect of it, or introducing extraneous concerns that have little to do with the verse, or using it to lodge yet another gratuitous and textually irrelevant "dig" at Rome, etc. I don't need to be as brilliant as Calvin and Luther obviously were, in the neutral, non-polemical sense of loving and interpreting Scripture, and providing many true insights which we as Catholics would agree with. It simply doesn't follow.

My book had to do with logical critiques and examinations of underlying assumptions that Protestants bring to the "table of exegesis," and various techniques that are used to dismiss implications that are thought to be too "Catholic." The book is filled with examples of this. It's useless to present twenty of them. One would have to buy the book. But that is the methodology of it. It's a type of apologetic that no one else has yet tried, to my knowledge.

But it's not exegesis per se. It is *about* exegesis (*meta-exegesis*, if you will), not exegesis *itself*. It is much more about human bias, and the effect of prior theologies and predispositions upon exegesis, than about exegesis of texts (considered in isolation). In that way it is even somewhat of a *psychological* analysis, as it deals with our axioms and presuppositions, and how they affect our interpretations (sometimes leading to outright *eisegesis*).

In any event, as long as White keeps falsely claiming that it is simply an exegetical work, he is grossly misrepresenting the book and making a massive straw man, and that strikes me as quite odd, for one who is an author himself, of many books.

One would think that he could at least get the *central purpose* of the book right, before proceeding to critique it. But this ties into my point, too: White despises Catholicism as the purveyor of a "false gospel," so in this instance he has distorted even the *purpose* and *nature* of a work which defends what he despises.

His overwhelming bias disables him from providing a cogent critique. He feels he has to discredit the argument at all costs, even if he falsely portrays it (and myself) in so doing. This need not be *deliberate* (bias works quite well subconsciously), but it is a strong influence nonetheless, whether deliberate or not. Anti-Catholicism will do it's dirty work, every time. And it becomes as easy as breathing, after years of practice.

White has issued endless remarks about how "ignorant" and clueless I am when it comes to the Bible, so I thought it was important to deal with this misguided notion that he has, at some length, right at the beginning of my replies, so readers (especially those who haven't read my book) will be under no delusions as to what my book is *about*; what it is actually *dealing* with, subject-wise.

For example, in the sections relevant to soteriology I would be more than happy for someone to compare the "exegesis" offered by Armstrong with the relevant sections of The God Who Justifies.

As the purposes were fundamentally different in both works (as explained above), the comparison would be completely irrelevant (and invalid).

But I promised to address the one section Armstrong had sent to me prior to the publication of the book. . . . I refer to his section on pp. 43-53 on Matthew 23 and "Moses' Seat." Like the section on Luke 1:28, clearly Armstrong is drawing from his many

Internet articles, cobbling together the most serious attempt mounted in the work. If he does not succeed here, he truly succeeds nowhere in The Catholic Verses.

It's true that I worked very hard on this section, because White's argument provided me with plenty of opportunity to point out serious error. But if I were a reader, I wouldn't put too much stock in White's generalizations about my book, seeing that he doesn't even understand its fundamental purpose.

> **Matthew 23:1-4** 1 Then Jesus spoke to the crowds and to His disciples, 2 saying: "The scribes and the Pharisees have seated themselves in the chair of Moses; 3 therefore all that they tell you, do and observe, but do not do according to their deeds; for they say things and do not do them. 4 "They tie up heavy burdens and lay them on men's shoulders, but they themselves are unwilling to move them with so much as a finger. [White's citation from an undisclosed translation]

In my book, I cited verses 1-3, in the RSV Bible:

> **Matthew 23:1-3**: "Then said Jesus to the crowds and to his disciples, 'The scribes and the Pharisees sit on Moses' seat; so practice and observe whatever they tell you, but not what they do; for they preach, but do not practice.'"

Here begins the longest sustained condemnation of the spirit and practice of Pharisaism in all of Scripture. Indeed, so strong, so compelling is the condemnation here that this passage was embarrassing to many Continental New Testament scholars in post World War II Europe. For most in less conservative circles this passage is considered a later polemic of the Christian church, reflecting a reality many decades removed from the ministry of Jesus. But in reality Matthew 23 "fits" perfectly right where it is. Its broad outlines have been seen throughout the Gospel in the conflict with the Jewish leadership, and it then forms the foundation of the judgment coming upon Jerusalem that appears in chapter 24. The section to which Mr. Armstrong refers begins a long litany of woes pronounced upon the hypocritical attitudes of the scribes and Pharisees. It is, in essence, the introduction to the blistering section that is Matthew 23.

I have no particular beef with this, other than to note that Jesus' condemnations of the Pharisees were of a general nature (there were many corrupt Pharisees), not necessarily of the entire system of Pharisaism itself, considered apart from the behavioral and attitudinal corruptions of the time. Indeed, many aspects of early Christianity were adopted more-or-less wholesale from Pharisaical tradition (rather than from the Sadducees). But Christians of White's general school and outlook, usually take a very dim view of the Pharisees altogether, and don't acknowledge these historical and theological nuances. This is where the influx of Jewish scholarship into New Testament studies and exegesis in recent decades has been very helpful.

In our next section we will review Armstrong's case on Matthew 23 and "Moses' Seat."

In the previous installment of this series I provided an introduction and the comments I made in The Roman Catholic Controversy *regarding the use of Matthew 23:1-3 by Roman Catholic apologists. Let's make sure we understand what is required of the Roman Catholic apologist in order to substantiate their claims. First, there needs to be an identifiable oral tradition regarding "Moses' Seat" that is passed down outside of Scripture. This tradition must grant to the scribes and Pharisees some kind of authority that is not given in Scripture itself,*

It's not necessary that it is *not* in Scripture; only that it is in *harmony* with Scripture, and something alongside it, which is not *opposed* to it, and is, to the contrary, *sanctioned* by it.

and Jesus must be making reference to this tradition, and the resultant authority, and binding His followers thereto. Is that what is going on in Matthew 23?

Something very un-Protestant is "going on" here! I believe that at the very least it is a *difficulty*, or difficult to *explain*, within a Protestant position.

Let's see if Dave Armstrong can provide a positive defense or, will he do what most of the rest of his compatriots do: hope that an attack upon the text will be sufficient to confuse their followers into thinking they have actually provided a meaningful defense of their claims.

Interesting cynical touch . . . Yes, I and "most of the rest of" my "compatriots" sit around at night dreaming up fanciful ways that we can "attack" the biblical text, so as to confuse and mislead our "followers." Is that really what White thinks motivates me and other Catholic apologists and commentators? Apparently so, or he wouldn't have written such a ludicrous thing. I don't (for what it's worth) reciprocate the cynicism. I think White (like most devoted Bible students) sincerely believes that he is interpreting the passage to the best of his abilities, and is trying his best to respect it and let it speak for itself. I think he's dead wrong in his opinion, but I don't have to attack his very *motivations* and *modus operandi* with uncharitable speculations, putting the worst spin on everything he does. That's a major difference between Mr. White and I, and this hostile predisposition will no doubt color his comments throughout (just as I noted in my book with regard to historic Protestant exegesis).

Armstrong begins:

> Jesus teaches that the scribes and Pharisees have a legitimate, binding authority, based on *Moses' seat*, which phrase (or idea) cannot be found anywhere in the Old Testament. It is found in the (originally oral) Mishna, where a sort of teaching succession from Moses on down

is taught. Thus, apostolic succession, whereby the Catholic Church, in its priests and bishops and popes, claims to be merely the custodian of an inherited apostolic Tradition, is also prefigured by Jewish oral tradition, as approved (at least partially) by Jesus himself.

So we see that Armstrong takes "the whole enchilada," so to speak, and sets the highest bar possible, even "prefiguring" Roman apostolic Tradition in the Jewish form, though, he seems to allow a small out for himself with the parenthetic statement, "at least partially." It is hard to know what this refers to at this point.

Mr. White, being the Bible scholar and exegete that he is, is certainly not unfamiliar with the notion of *typology* in Holy Scripture (though you'd never *know* that, reading the above). The *International Standard Bible Encyclopedia* ([*ISBE*] a Protestant work, as will be all sources that I cite, unless indicated otherwise: edited by James Orr, Grand Rapids, Michigan: Eerdmans, 1956), discusses biblical "types":

> The Bible furnishes abundant evidence of the presence of types and of typical instruction in the Sacred Word. The NT attests this fact. It takes up a large number of persons and things and events of former dispensations, and it treats them as adumbrations and prophecies of the future. A generation ago a widespread interest in the study of typology prevailed . . . A type . . . must be a true picture of the person or the thing it represents or prefigures . . . A type always prefigures something future. A Scriptural type and predictive prophecy are in substance the same, differing only in form. This fact distinguishes between a symbol and a type. A symbol may represent a thing of the present or of the past as well as of the future, e.g., the symbols in the Lord's supper. A type always looks to the future; an element of prediction must necessarily be in it.

(Vol. 5, p. 3029)

Presbyterian pastor and writer Peter J. Leithart, writing in *First Things* (November 1997, 12-13), noted that modern evangelicals tend to reject typology (note that the *ISBE* above stated that things were different a mere "generation ago"):

> Modern scholarship has approached the Old Testament in a very different manner. Rejecting typology as fanciful and unscientific, many theologians have treated the Old Testament as a historical document with little or no religious significance for the Church. . . . For all their real differences in approach to the Bible, evangelicals are at one with Protestant modernism in their rejection of typology and, frequently enough, in their belief that Christianity is more or less purely internal, a religion of unmediated individual contact with God.

But the Church fathers interpreted the Bible quite differently, Leithart informs us, noting:

> . . . the typological exegesis of the Bible practiced by patristic and medieval theologians. Typological interpretation assumes that events and institutions of the Old Testament present (to use Augustine's terminology) "latent" pictures of Christ, and the Christ to whom the Old Testament testifies is the *totus Christus*: Head and Body, Jesus and his Church. In this, the fathers and medieval theologians fully agreed with Paul, who wrote that the history of Israel's wanderings in the wilderness were "things written for our instruction." Following the apostolic example, the fathers taught that Israel and "daughter Jerusalem"—and all brides and harlots of Old Testament history—manifest the Church under various guises. . . . the fathers plundered the Old Testament to divine the patterns of history. Because the interpretive path runs from old Israel through Christ to the new Israel, moreover, typology assumes that the New Covenant, like the Old, is concerned with a concrete, historical

213

community. . . . The typological method—by emphasizing that the Church as a real historical institution and communion was prophesied and typified in the Old Testament—provides theological grounding for the Church's efforts to discipline the state.

This has to do with historic exegesis (precisely what my book was about). James White is out of touch with the exegesis of the earliest Christians, even with St. Augustine (whom he views very highly indeed, as I could easily prove from his own remarks), and pre-modernist Protestants. Thus, my delving into typology in the course of the extended argument of my book seems something foreign to him. Typology is no novel notion, either for the fathers or many evangelical commentators through the centuries, but it seems to be for Mr. White.

I can't help that, but in any event, he is free to argue that some *particular* interpretation of mine is unreasonable and implausible, according to the usual cross-referencing, systematics, linguistic considerations, etc. That is an unobjectionable method, but dismissing all types and shadows altogether is quite a bit more difficult to do, in light of historic exegesis: both Catholic and Protestant.

Following these claims Armstrong lists five "anomalous facts" for Protestants, other passages he believes likewise refer to "extrabiblical and oral tradition acknowledged by the New Testament writers." These include 1 Cor. 10:4 and the rock that followed Israel in the wilderness; 1 Pet. 3:19, where Armstrong assumes the passage is drawing from 1 Enoch, together with Jude 14_15 and the citation of 1 Enoch 1:9; Jude 9 and the dispute between Michael and Satan over Moses' body; 2 Tim. 3:8 and the naming of Jannes and Jambres; James 5:17 and the information that the drought had lasted for three years.

White outlines my argument. I will actually *cite* it, so readers know exactly what I stated:

Other examples of extrabiblical and oral tradition acknowledged by the New Testament writers include:

* 1 Corinthians 10:4, where St. Paul refers to a rock which "followed" the Jews through the Sinai wilderness. The Old Testament says nothing about such miraculous movement, in the related passages about Moses striking the rock to produce water (Exod. 17:1-7; Num. 20:2-13). Rabbinic tradition, however, does.

* 1 Peter 3:19, where St. Peter describes Christ's journey to Sheol/Hades ("he went and preached to the spirits in prison"), [and] draws directly from the Jewish apocalyptic book 1 Enoch (12-16). Jude 14-15 directly quotes from 1 Enoch 1:9, and even states that Enoch prophesied.

* Jude 9, which concerns a dispute between Michael the archangel and Satan over Moses' body, cannot be paralleled in the Old Testament, and appears to be a recounting of an oral Jewish tradition.

* In 2 Timothy 3:8, the reference to Jannes and Jambres cannot be found in the related Old Testament passage (Exod. 7:8 ff.).

* James 5:17 mentions a lack of rain for three years, which is likewise absent from the relevant Old Testament passage in 1 Kings 17.

(p. 44)

He concludes his list with these words:

Since Jesus and the Apostles acknowledge authoritative Jewish oral tradition (in so doing, raising some of it literally to the level of written revelation), we are hardly at liberty to assert that it is altogether illegitimate. Jesus attacked corrupt traditions only, not tradition per se, and not all oral tradition. According to a *strict sola Scriptura* viewpoint, this would be inadmissible, it seems to me.

(p. 44)

Immediately the careful reader will note that there seems to be no difference at all in Armstrong's thinking between "authoritative Jewish oral tradition," non-authoritative Jewish oral tradition, and any historical story, whether oral or written.

This is highly curious and inexplicable, since in my very act of mentioning "authoritative Jewish tradition," it follows by simple logic that there must be something to the *contrary* which I (and anyone) could and would label "*non*-authoritative Jewish oral tradition," and indeed, my mention of "corrupt traditions" *presupposes* this. Yet White accuses me of *not* making the very distinctions that I clearly *made*. Go figure . . . this is what happens when the unfortunate tendency to caricature opponents runs head on into simple logic and carefully reading what one's opponent *actually wrote*, before immediately dashing off to tear it apart. For in such a rush, what is "refuted" is often not what the opponent actually wrote or believes. And that creates all sorts of problems and weakness in arguments, and holes large enough to drive a truck through. What "any historical story" is supposed to refer to, is anyone's guess, since context makes abundantly clear that I was referring exclusively to Jewish tradition.

Likewise, he leaves untouched the issues relating to the citation of Enoch, for surely he knows Enoch as a whole is not canonical, hence, is he actually insisting that only a portion of Enoch contains some kind of authoritative, inspired material?

My argument doesn't necessitate regarding all such material as "inspired"; only authoritative and true. Remember how I phrased that to which I was referring: "extrabiblical and oral tradition acknowledged by the New Testament writers." An inspired biblical book might cite any number of non-inspired books as true, insofar as the *portion cited* is concerned. That's exactly what happened in Jude 14-15, where 1 Enoch 1:9 is directly quoted (as the footnote for this verse in my Oxford Annotated RSV Bible states), and is described by the apostle as that which Enoch "prophesied." Whether that counts as "inspired" or not, on that basis, I don't know, and I'll leave that technical question for the appropriate scholars to decide.

But it is perfectly reasonable to conclude that what is cited is *true*, and an instance of true prophecy not different in kind from a prophecy of Jeremiah or Isaiah: whose prophecies are recorded in inspired Old Testament Scripture. And that's just the *point*, isn't it? If Jeremiah's prophecy is regarded as inspired because it is in the Bible (OT), then Enoch's must *likewise* be, because it is in the Bible (NT). Therefore an "extrabiblical tradition" was "acknowledged by the New Testament writers," and my contention is unassailable. White can only try to minimize the implications of this, and attempt to show that it all fits in perfectly with his Baptist, *sola Scriptura* conception of authority, but he can't discount the *fact* of it, because *there it is* . . .

All of these passages have sparked a great deal of discussion in both Protestant and Catholic biblical scholarship, but none of that discussion is referenced here. An allegedly "straightforward" reading is all that is noted.

That's correct. One can't write about everything all the time, and one chooses what to emphasize, where, and how deeply to delve into the subject matter at hand. What does that have to do with anything? White's task is to refute what I have presented. Perhaps he does that later, but he hasn't yet done so, and making *non sequitur* points like this, doesn't bring him any closer to the conclusion of his task. If he wants to deal with these passages, then he can make his argument, and I'll surely respond. One thing at a time . . .

Armstrong moves from here to the specifics of his response to the material in The Roman Catholic Controversy *by stating, "I shall quote the heart of his subtle but thoroughly fallacious argument." He cites the very beginning of the comments, to the point where I note that there is no way to trace this alleged tradition back to Moses, since this refers to an element of synagogue worship that did not come into existence until only a few hundred years prior to the time of Christ. He then writes,*

> White agrees that the notion is not found in the Old Testament, but maintains that it cannot be traced back to Moses. Yet the Catholic argument here does not rest on whether it can be traced historically to Moses, but on the act that it is not found in the Old Testament. Thus, White concedes a fundamental point of the Catholic argument concerning authority and *sola Scriptura.*

White skipped over roughly a page of material (mostly my page 45), where I cited the commentator Albert Barnes at length, and also the Jamieson, Fausset, and Brown commentary, and also noted how Jesus distinguished between good and bad traditions. Since we are centering primarily on my critique of his argument, this is not a major concern.

Yet, on the other hand, it can often be observed in White's replies to Catholics, that he will pick and choose what he wants to respond to, rather than reply to everything (his ignoring of those portions of his opponents' arguments might reasonably be construed as indicating a possibility that they are *difficult* for him to answer, since he skipped over them more or less arbitrarily). The passages of New Testament citing of extrabiblical traditions were not technically related to White's own presentation, either, but he saw fit to mention *them.*

While I wish to wait to respond to the full argumentation until after outlining Armstrong's response, I must point out in passing that "admitting" that Jesus is making reference to a concept that developed during the intertestamental period is hardly relevant to sola scriptura *nor is it a concession to a "fundamental point of the Catholic argument." There is nothing in* sola scriptura *that requires the NT to be silent about developments during the intertestamental period. There is nothing in the doctrine that requires the Bible to remain silent on the form of synagogue worship. This is simply wishful thinking on Armstrong's part, once again.*

I wasn't arguing those things; rather, the topic at hand is whether there is an authoritative extrabiblical tradition, acknowledged by Jesus and the apostles. If *some* parts of those traditions can be cited as true in the New Testament, then it stands to reason that *other* parts can be true (and hence, authoritative) *without* being cited in the New Testament. White simply *assumes* without argument that anything that is fully authoritative *must* be in the Bible. But since that is the issue in dispute, assuming it does no good. It has to be *rationally demonstrated*, with *biblical support*. I've been providing biblical support for my contentions. But these complex points of consideration will obviously have to wait till White presents his "full" response. I presume it will eventually be forthcoming, since White's response consisted of eight parts.

Further, unless I misread Armstrong, he saw a "prefigurement" of the Roman position in the Jewish one regarding tradition; yet, the Jews claimed their traditions did, in fact, go back to Moses, and yet here it seems Armstrong is admitting that the Jews could be wrong about the very origin of their traditions, and yet Jesus would still find the tradition binding.

I argued no such (intrinsically nonsensical) thing. White read that into my statements because he didn't *understand* them (a sadly common occurrence, as we've seen in past installments of this discussion, and will often see again, surely, largely because he vastly underestimates his opponents and considers them much more "ignorant" than they are in fact.

    I was making a *logical point*, reiterating that the Catholic reply to White's *sola Scriptura* arguments does not require proof that Jewish oral traditions go back to Moses; only that some of them were considered authoritative by Jesus and the apostles. For my part, I assume that they *do* go back to Moses, because that is part of the biblical (and historical) record, too, and the early Christians continued this tradition, over against the quasi-*sola Scriptura* position of the Sadducees, the "liberals" of their time). But that aspect was not *logically required* for this particular argument to be effective in its purpose of refutation.

Does it follow that Rome could admit her traditions do not go back to the Apostles but they are still binding? We are not told.

No (now you've been told). It was a silly query to begin with.

Next we encounter the following paragraph:

> White then cites Protestant Bible scholar Robert Gundry in agreement, to the effect that Jesus was binding Christians to the Pharisaical law, but not "their interpretive traditions." This passage concerned only "the law itself," with the "antinomians" in mind. How Gundry arrives at such a conclusion remains to be seen. White's query about the Catholic interpretation, "Is this sound exegesis?" can just as easily be applied to Gundry's fine-tuned distinctions that help him avoid any implication of a binding extrabiblical tradition.

> (pp. 46-47)

One will note that this is at best a partial accounting of the views I noted; but beyond this, there is no meaningful interaction with Gundry's exegesis. And given that I have worked through a number of attempted arguments made by Armstrong in this book, I believe I can say with some foundation that I do not believe Dave Armstrong understands what he would have to do to provide an exegetical response to Gundry or myself or anyone else. He simply does not understand the field. Writing "Is this sound exegesis?" and then in essence saying, "Well, you too!" is a poor substitute for meaningful exegetical interaction, that's for certain.

Here we go with more of White's sadly typical condescension and patronizing of his opponent, leading to lack of argument or no rational argumentation at all. It is "(wishful) meta-analysis" rather than reasoned refutation and a demonstration of exactly how an opponent is in error.

We continue reviewing Dave Armstrong's comments on Matthew 23. He continues with a citation from my book, The Roman Catholic Controversy, *p. 101, on p. 47 of* The Catholic Verses. *However, he does not provide some key elements of the material he is citing, so I will provide the paragraph, but will bold what was skipped, or not included, in the citation:*

This appears to be the tired old charge of citing out of context. Not every instance of partial citation is incorrect or out-of-context citation. But it is one of the oldest rhetorical tricks in the book. Let's see if White can make a positive case that I have misrepresented him at all or neglected "key elements" in his presentation. It is all the more comic and ironic, that a man who *habitually ignores* his opponents' arguments and skips over huge amounts of the others' words to rush to what he wishes to express (the present exchange is no exception to that rule), would nitpick about someone not citing absolutely every one of his words. Here is his citation, as he wishes it to be:

> **Indeed, the Lord's unwillingness to become an "ecclesiastical rebel" is in perfect harmony with the Scriptural teaching on the subject of authority in the church.** There was nothing in the tradition of having someone read from the Scriptures while sitting on Moses' seat that was in conflict with the Scriptures, **and hence, unlike the corban rule which we saw earlier in Matthew 15, Jesus does not reject this traditional aspect of Jewish synagogue worship. He does not insist upon anarchy in worship in the synagogue anymore than His apostle Paul would allow for it in the worship of the church at Corinth.** It is quite proper to listen to and obey the words of the one who reads from the Law or the Prophets, for one is not hearing a man speaking in such a situation, but is listening to the very words of God.

Now, it is a measure of Armstrong's understanding of the issues involved in exegesis that he responds in these words:

This is true as far as it goes, but it is essentially a *non sequitur* and amounts to a "reading into," or eisegesis of the passage (which is ironic, because now *White* plays the role of "a man speaking" and distorting "the very words of God").

And he is merely assuming what he is trying to prove, which is no logical argument; it's a fallacy.

He then repeats the text, as if this somehow proves his point.

The point was that the text was more general than White's arbitrary restriction of it, in order to conform to the arbitrary and unbiblical notion of *sola Scriptura*, and the rejection of tradition as understood by the Church throughout the centuries.

Now I am going to try to read Armstrong's work in the most positive light and assume that the next few pages, as they have paragraphs starting with "first" and "second" and so on, are his attempt to substantiate the assertion that my words are reading into the text something that is not there.

How thoughtful of him . . . imagine the novelty of granting one's opponent the courtesy of acknowledging that he means what he obviously means!

Of course, to do this, he will have to do something more than just assume his own reading is exegetically sound. He will have to provide solid, positive argumentation.

That's right, and this works *both ways*, doesn't it?

Let's see how well he fares. His first paragraph reads:

First, it should be noted that nowhere in the actual text is the notion that the Pharisees are *only* reading the Old Testament Scripture when sitting on Moses' seat. It is an

222

assumption gratuitously smuggled in from a presupposed position of *sola Scriptura.*

Quite true, but does it not likewise follow that it is a gratuitous assumption that Jesus is actually telling His disciples to embrace extra-biblical traditions that parallel Rome's---an assumption smuggled in from a presupposed position of sola ecclesia*?*

First of all, "*sola ecclesia*" is a false description of the Catholic system of authority. This is not a Catholic term (whereas *sola Scriptura* is the Protestant's own terminology for *his* principle). We don't believe in "Church alone." We believe in the "three-legged stool" of Bible, Church, and Tradition, which is quite a different concept indeed. But White seems to think that he succeeds in rational argument by caricaturing opposing positions. The implicit reasoning seems to be: "if you don't accept Bible Alone, you must believe in Church alone," as if there are not *other* possible positions besides this stark contrast: one extreme to another.

Secondly, I agree that everyone has presuppositions that they bring to the table. But the presuppositions have to be *tested* to see if they can stand up, and if they are *harmonious with biblical teaching*. Whether "extra-biblical traditions" are involved remains to be proven; that's what our discussion is largely about. White's task, however, in line with his own beliefs, is to prove that they are definitely *not* involved, and he can't do that by simply assuming without argument his system of *sola Scriptura*, which *rules out* such an eventuality *beforehand*. Thus far, he has given no one any reason to believe that such traditions are *absolutely absent* in the New Testament accounts under consideration.

Thirdly, it should be noted that in my book, I am critiquing White's attempt to deny that extra-biblical Tradition could possibly be in play in these passages. All I have to do is cast doubt on his "proofs" along these lines, and show that they are not adequate to their task. Technically (i.e., logically), I don't even have to prove that such traditions *are* there, in order to refute *his* argument, because his reasoning is somewhat similar to the following scenario:

1. James says he can prove that there are no children in the schoolyard from 2 to 3 PM.

2. His proof is that the school allows children there only from 12 to 1 PM.

3. Therefore, no children are there from 2 to 3.

Does this prove that no children are there from 2 to 3? Of course not. All it proves (assuming the documented truthfulness of #2) is that if children are there from 2 to 3, that it is against school rules. It doesn't prove that no children are there, because it has simply assumed what it is trying to prove, by appeal to a rule which may or may not be broken in fact or actuality. It doesn't rest upon actual observation of the schoolyard. Likewise, a critic of the argument does not have to prove that a child was actually *there* from 2 to 3, to disprove the above argument, because it is fallacious of its own accord. The analogy to the present case are as follows:

children = extra-biblical traditions

schoolyard = Christianity

school rules concerning what is permitted = *sola Scriptura*

conclusion (#3) = presupposed, unproven, axiomatic, dogmatic assertions of Protestantism with regard to what is permitted and not permitted in Christianity

All this being the case, both sides have to strive to make a plausible biblical case for their own position. Since the Bible is the authority both sides agree upon, it is the "field" where the argument can succeed, using the agreed-upon standard of Divine

Revelation.

Remember, the Corban rule of Matthew 15, which Jesus specifically rejected on the basis of Scripture, was one of the Pharisees' favorite "Mosaic traditions," claiming divine authority. Was Jesus contradicting Himself? Surely not. And so the point clearly is, what understanding of the text is consistent with Jesus' own practices when faced with such things as the Corban rule elsewhere?

This doesn't prove White's contentions of "no extra-biblical traditions" *at all*, because to prove that Jesus opposed *one* tradition doesn't say anything at all about whether He opposed *all* such traditions. He Himself made this distinction clear in Mark 7:3-9. St. Paul also makes it abundantly clear that there is a legitimate tradition and a false tradition of men. So White can't simply assume that the "approved" category of tradition is nonexistent. This is exceedingly weak reasoning; in fact, it proves nothing whatsoever.

Secondly, the specific example of the Corban rule (Matthew 15:5) is actually simply another proof that Jesus did *not* reject *all* tradition (which is the issue at hand), and this is quite simple to demonstrate. He was rebuking this *particular* Pharisaical tradition as a *corruption* of the *larger tradition* of proper sacrifice, which He did not abrogate at all; quite the contrary: He continued to participate in the old sacrificial system. Thus, *The New Bible Dictionary* (edited by J. D. Douglass, Grand Rapids, Michigan: Eerdmans, 1962) states:

> The Old Testament sacrifices . . . were still being offered during practically the whole period of the composition of the New . . . Important maxims are to be found in Mt. 5:23-24, 12:3-5 and parallels 17:24-27, 23:16-20; 1 Cor. 9:13-14. It is noteworthy that our Lord has sacrifice offered for Him or offers it Himself at His presentation in the Temple, at His last Passover, and presumably on those other occasions when He went up to Jerusalem for the feasts. The practice of the apostles in Acts removes all

225

ground from the opinion that after the sacrifice of Christ the worship of the Jewish Temple is to be regarded as an abomination to God. We find them frequenting the Temple, and Paul himself goes up to Jerusalem for Pentecost, and on that occasion offers the sacrifices (which included sin-offerings) for the interruption of vows (Acts 21; cf. Nu. 6:10-12).

(p. 1122 in the article, "Sacrifice and Offering")

I thought the reader might appreciate a little balance being gained as to whether Jesus opposed all tradition. White wants to mention only the times where Jesus rejected one particular tradition. It's important to get the *whole New Testament picture* and not just one small part of it, ignoring the rest.

Is it Armstrong's, or that which sees this as the beginning of the condemnation of the Pharisees that takes up the rest of Matthew 23, and hence is actually restricting *the authority of the Pharisees?*

Matthew 23 is not necessarily about "restricting the authority of the Pharisees" at all. It is about Pharisaical *hypocrisy*, as anyone who knows the passage at all, is well aware, and also about their legalistic corruptions of the legitimate Mosaic Law (which is what Jesus found hypocritical). But condemning hypocrisy and corruption is not the same as condemning the thing that they are being hypocritical about and distorting. The fact remains (and it is obvious in the New Testament) that much of the Pharisaical tradition was retained by Christianity (as sanctioned by our Lord Jesus and St. Paul).

The answer is clear. If Armstrong is going to claim an exegetical *basis for Rome's position, he cannot simply* assume *it. So far, that is all he is doing.*

I provided more than enough of that, in my (admittedly biased) opinion, to cast significant doubt on White's argument, in the book. Even if I didn't provide sufficient exegetical argument in the book, I *certainly* have added much biblical cross-referencing and relevant data in this paper (far more than White's brief, passing references, such as to the Corban rule), which White would have to deal with, if he thinks his argument can withstand the scrutiny of proper examination.

But it is almost a certainty that this dialogue will never get to the stage of a second round, judging by virtually all past experience with White for ten years. As soon as the discussion gets really interesting and biblical and logical, he is no longer interested, and either flees altogether or becomes insulting. I don't blame him, since he has such a weak and insubstantial case, in the present instance.

In any event, I submit that I have provided *far* more biblical support for *my* position than White has for *his*, at least as far as we have gotten. Perhaps he'll produce a "golden bullet" in subsequent installments. I keep waiting for at least an *attempt*, but it never comes . . .

I would like to expand, momentarily, on a thought with which I closed the last installment in this series. Mr. Armstrong is right to say that the text does not provide us with a direct listing of what the Pharisees did or did not teach when speaking in the synagogue. That can only be determined on the basis of other texts, if at all . . .

Good. But it's not like we are historically ignorant; as if no source outside of the Bible can help us learn what they taught (or the subsequent history of Judaism).

(and I believe such texts as Matthew 15 do tell us a good bit about that).

We learn some things, but not nearly enough for White's sweepingly negative, unqualified rejection of both the Pharisees and also of tradition outside the bounds of what *sola Scriptura* permits.

227

But is it truly a "gratuitous" assumption on my part, based upon sola scriptura *to believe that there is no warrant here for believing that the text is relevant to an establishment of some second source of divine authority in the views of the Lord Jesus?*

Yes. It's presuppositional-type apologetics, which is not particularly compelling for anyone who does not already accept it on faith.

I firmly believe so, and once again the grounds for this is not a gratuitous assumption, but that wonderful thing called context. *As I pointed out originally, these words are the introduction to a lengthy pronouncement of woe and judgment upon the scribes and Pharisees.*

I dealt with the context of Matthew 23 and the Pharisees in general and their theological relationship to early Christianity in the last installment. White's fallacy is that He sees Jesus rebuking them for hypocrisy and corruption, and incorrectly, illogically concludes that He therefore must deny that they have any authority *at all*.

    This has been the usual historic Protestant response (especially among those, who -- like Baptists and even Lutherans -- want to drive a big, unbiblical wedge between Law and Grace, as if they are literally antithetical). The *Moses' seat* issue (as well as continued Christian observance of sacrifices and matters of the Law in one form or another) precisely shows that they still *do* have authority. This can be fully harmonized with Matthew 23 and the scathing denunciations, rightly-understood. No problem there . . .

    But White has a *huge* problem squaring this other data with the notion that Jesus was *absolutely rejecting* both the Pharisees and tradition outside the Bible (however one defines "Bible" at that early stage of canonization). I give more biblical evidences for my position in my book, which I will cite as necessary, in due course. White may or may not respond to those, with either a real rational reply, or just more boilerplate and standard, ultimately ineffective *sola Scriptura* rhetoric, which doesn't truly take into account the nature or strength of objections.

As we will see, Armstrong is forced, in his attempt to force Matthew 23 into his theological mold, to speak of how indebted the early Christians were to the Pharisees, and to in essence speak positively about them.

I don't have to force it into *any* "mold"; I simply have to highlight, document, and follow the *facts*: from the Bible and history. I don't need to force those facts into anything that they aren't. *White* is the one who must do that, because the facts in this instance go *against* his "pet theory." Therefore, *he* is the one forced (by necessity of his unproven presuppositions) to *minimize* any positive historical fact concerning the Pharisees, or any of their contributions to early Christian theology. He can certainly try to do this, but he won't succeed, because the historical evidences are too compelling.

And while one may well say positive things about Pharisees in various contexts (I would argue the issue of their traditions would not be one of those contexts),

Again, he can try to argue and believe this way, but it won't succeed, because there were *plenty* of these traditions that the early Christians adopted wholesale. It's impossible to make a blanket condemnation of all their traditions. *Jesus* didn't do that, so neither should Mr. White.

. . . this passage in Matthew 23 is singularly contradictory to such a discussion.

Not in the *slightest*, as already shown in my last reply. This is very simple logic, but White commits a rather elementary (but momentous in its results) fallacy, which is common when one is trying to defend a position in the teeth of contrary facts; the facts and logic are the first thing to go.

The fact of the matter is that Armstrong's comments do not flow from the text at all. His position does not start with a recognition of the context of the text being examined. Instead, he clearly proceeds from the position demanded of him by Rome.

Sheer nonsense. Anyone can see that I have incorporated the context into my analysis, and it has not been a happy result for White's position. White is far more forced by his *sola Scriptura* position to interpret the passage in a particular (eisegetical) way, than I am forced by "Rome." It so happens that nothing here contradicts Catholic teaching about tradition. *Plenty*, however, contradicts Protestant false, unbiblical tradition of *sola Scriptura*.

The fact that these words must be heard in a condemnatory, not congratulatory, context, must be kept in mind. And when we do this, we see that the fact that these men sat in positions of leadership within the people of God only increases their guilt. This theme will build to a crescendo in the following verses.

This doesn't undermine the fact that Jesus told His followers to "practice and observe whatever they tell you" (thus, they have authority), "but not what they do; for they preach, but do not practice" (authority does not preclude hypocrisy and bad example; and the latter do not forbid continuing authority) -- Matthew 23:1-3.

Armstrong continues:

> Secondly, White's assumption that Jesus is referring literally to Pharisees sitting on a seat in the synagogue and reading (the Old Testament only) -- and that alone -- is more forced and woodenly literalistic than the far more plausible interpretation that this was simply a term denoting received authority.
>
> (p. 47)

Of course, my whole point (and this is clear when the sections DA did not include are read with the citation) is that Jesus is addressing synagogue worship and the position the Pharisees have taken in that worship. The disciples (and the crowds, v. 2) would know to what He referred by the mere reference to Moses' seat, and to the primary functions in synagogue worship of that seat. It was a position of honor to read from the Word of God, and Jesus' admonition is to do what they tell you in that *context, but not to do what they* practice.

If by this, White means more than a literal sitting in the seat, then good. His phrase, "sitting on Moses' seat" suggested to me a literal chair, and folks sitting in it. I stand corrected if I misread him. Hypocrisy is still being referred to, and that is a different issue from authority.

If Armstrong wishes to expand Moses' seat beyond the role it had in the synagogue and include within it some kind of "received authority" including the ability to bind men to extra-scriptural traditional teachings (which is, after all, what Armstrong is driving at), . . .

The Pharisees did indeed believe in "extra-scriptural traditional teachings." This is the whole *point.* There was plenty of "tradition in that tradition," both written and oral. Thus, if these Pharisees still possessed authority, according to our Lord Jesus, then that would obviously include oral tradition as well, because that's what they believed in their system. They weren't bound to arbitrary, man-made rules of faith such as *sola Scriptura.* But we mustn't have *that*! We must pretend that this authority extended only to a *sola Scriptura*-like, Bible-Only mentality, completely overlooking the role of tradition (particularly oral) in mainstream Pharisaical thought.

They *had* authority, and we know the *nature* of this authority. It's a simple historical question, easily answered. But if one doesn't like the *implications* of the answer, then one starts minimizing, ignoring, dismissing things that go against one's pet hypothesis (as White is -- quite openly -- doing presently).

This type of dynamic and "canned response" was *exactly* what my book dealt with: the processes of rationalization and evasion that occur when faced with "anomalous" biblical and historical facts. White is a classic, almost quintessential case of this process-in-progress. That's why I cited him regarding Moses' Seat. I heartily thank him for being such a picture-perfect textbook example of the very thing my book was devoted to examining.

. . . some explanation must be offered for why Jesus specifically limits their authority as He does.

I see no specific limits. Where are they? White thinks he sees some. Let's see what he can come up with:

He tells His disciples and the crowds not to do what they do. Well, what do they do? The rest of Matthew 23 tells us. In essence, they were hypocrites (v. 28).

Exactly, just like many Christians *today* are. For example, there are some Christians who are such hypocrites and rigid legalists that they can't even recognize certain entire classes of *other* Christians, or acknowledge any good thing that other Christians (whom they define as non-Christians and in "darkness" on no legitimate grounds whatsoever) *do* -- even when they would totally *agree* with that particular thing! So the worst aspects of the corruptions of the Pharisees definitely live on today, in the equally-unworthy traditions of certain backward, muddleheaded, irrationally and uncharitably judgmental, theologically obtuse sectors of Christianity.

And what was one of the main ways they demonstrated their hypocrisy? Matthew 15:1-8 tells us: the binding of extra-biblical traditions upon men's backs in contradiction to the Word of God.

This was one particular corruption of a tradition, that was unbiblical, or contrary to the Bible. That doesn't prove that *no* legitimate tradition *whatever* exists: one that is not technically included in the letter of the Bible, yet in harmony with it. White would love the text to prove all *that*, but it clearly does *not*, so all he can do is engage in wishful thinking, and greatly exaggerate the implications of the text: basically *read into it* what he wants to see (which is both eisegesis and fallacious circular reasoning). The *text itself* cannot at all hold all the weight which White is attaching to it. And other clear biblical texts (many of which I've already noted) contradict White's interpretation of *this* one.

So, if Jesus told His disciples and the crowds that they should not "do according to their deeds," is He not telling them that they must examine those deeds by some standard and judge them to be wanting?

Yes. If one particular tradition of theirs contradicts the Bible, then it is a *false* tradition, and people ought not to be bound to it. That is, if they commit the hypocrisy of not making sure their actions are in harmony with the Law, rightly understood in the light of the Bible, then they should not be imitated in that respect. We have no disagreement insofar as *that* goes.

And what is that standard? The answer is clear.

It sure is: the Bible and received, correct tradition, which is consistent with that Bible.

That is why I said Jesus was not telling the crowds to quit the synagogue or begin a revolution by throwing the Pharisees out, but He was freeing them from the ungodly control the Pharisees had over the "am ha'aretz," the "people of the land," who were told by the Pharisees that unless they acted and lived like them, they would never have the grace of God.

We mustn't imitate sinners. I couldn't agree more.

No, Jesus says, for they are hypocrites, and He is about to pronounce an entire series of woes upon them.

Indeed; yet he doesn't take away their *authority*. As that is the subject at hand (is there an authority not technically, strictly confined to the words of the Bible?), most of the above argumentation of Mr. White is a *non sequitur*, and much ado about nothing, *accomplishing* nothing. As we (hopefully) get into more specifics and substantiation for each of our views, that will become all the *more* clear.

But one must give White credit for trying so hard to support a position which is so impossible to uphold, based on the biblical record. You know: give him an E for effort . . . it's very tough to "prove" something that is untrue. It takes a *lot* more work, and is incomparably more frustrating.

At this point Armstrong opines,

> It reminds me of the old silly Protestant tale that the popes speak infallibly and *ex cathedra* (*cathedra* is the Greek word for seat in Matthew 23:2) only when sitting in a certain chair in the Vatican - because the phrase means literally "from the bishop's chair" - whereas it was a figurative and idiomatic usage).
>
> (pp. 47-48)

Of course, I have never made such a statement, . . .

I never stated that he *did*; but only that his sort of reasoning here *reminded* me of that particular instance of mistaken Protestant reasoning. They misunderstood *ex cathedra* to be referring always to a literal chair (rather than to authority). White is doing roughly the same thing, by limiting the usage in Matthew 23 to the synagogues. Thus, my analogy was quite apt.

. . . but the fact remains that in the context of the condemnation of the Pharisees in Matthew 23, the identity of "Moses' seat" and its function in synagogue worship is central.

White (as we have seen so often) simply assumes his interpretation, and proceeds onward, without seeming to realize that he needs to establish the validity of his premises first. He can't just *assume* that Moses' seat refers strictly to the literal seat in the synagogues, from which the Pharisees taught. In my book, shortly after this, I cited both *The Eerdmans Bible Dictionary* and *The International Standard Bible Encyclopedia*, in favor of my position as to what the term *meant*. Without proper definitions, discussions go nowhere. So White is off on his tangent of restricting the term to synagogue teaching, and is off-base, because his definition is faulty to begin with.

If one allows the function of Moses' seat to be removed from the discussion (as Armstrong does), you lose the connection with the condemnation of the Pharisees: the reason they are hypocrites is because they should *know better: they read from the Scriptures on a regular basis, and then turn around and do away with that teaching by their traditions, and those traditions result in actions that are contrary to the Word.*

A particular function in a synagogue is not required for the condemnations of Jesus to make sense. They need not read the Scripture in a synagogue to know what it teaches. We agree that their traditions in some (or many) cases ran contrary to Scripture. But they don't have to read in the synagogue for that to be the case. Nor do they have to not accept extra-biblical tradition for it to be the case. And White still is neglecting to see that Jesus told people to *obey their teachings*. These teachings included extra-biblical tradition, because the Pharisees *believed in oral tradition*, received by Moses at the same time he received the Ten Commandments. He can't overcome this, no matter how hard he tries.

This is why you do as they say in the context of the synagogue worship, but you do not do what they do.

This is eisegesis (reading into the text), in my opinion, relying upon the already highly questionable definition of *Moses' seat* that White has been utilizing. No such qualification is in the text itself, restricting it to synagogue worship. So White has a bad definition, and desperate exegesis, to shore up an already abysmally weak position.

Since we know Christ held men accountable to have known the Corban rule was contrary to God's Word, and the Pharisees taught this, even claiming it came from Moses, then clearly we must allow the limitation of the function of Moses' seat to stand. And this Armstrong will not allow.

It's not up to me to "allow" or disallow. I'm only going by the definition of the term that the scholars who have properly studied such things have given me. We can't redefine terms whatever way we like them, like a wax nose.

He misconstrues the proper recognition of the synagogue context of Moses' seat, and hence the limitation of its purview, with a woodenly literalistic idea about whether one is standing or sitting. He writes,

> Jesus says that they sat "on Moses' seat; so practice and observe whatever they tell you." In other words, because they had the authority, based on the position of occupying Moses' seat, they were to be obeyed. It is like referring to a chairman of a company or committee. He occupies the "chair"; therefore he has authority. No one thinks he has the authority only when he sits in a certain chair reading the corporation charter or the Constitution or some other official document.

> (p. 48)

Notice the importance of this to Armstrong's argument: he must create an authority that resides in the Pharisees separate from their place in the worship of God's people in the synagogue. So, instead of the biblical limitation of their authority to the role they have taken in the synagogue, Armstrong speaks of the Pharisees

236

(who are about to be condemned roundly) as having an inherent authority, and hence they are to be obeyed. Yet in Matthew 23, what is to be obeyed is not an inherent authority in the scribes and Pharisees, but, as the "therefore" of v. 3 shows us, the reason for obedience is the seat of Moses, not an authority separate from it. But having missed this distinction, Armstrong continues, "Yet this is how White would exclusively interpret Jesus' words." No, White would not force Jesus into internal contradiction, ignore the fact that He holds His disciples and the crowd accountable for exercising judgment on the deeds of the Pharisees (even those deeds they based upon "tradition"), and rip this section out of its role as the introduction not to the lauding *of the scribes and Pharisees, but their condemnation.*

This is just more building of a house of cards on top of the fallacies already listed. Catholic apologist "Matt1618" -- responding in an Internet paper to Protestant apologist Ron Rhodes ("Reasoning From the Scriptures with Ron Rhodes"), illustrates the weakness of such a position (italics substituted for bolding):

> His words are practice and observe *whatever* they tell you. How can Rhodes say that this is not authoritative? . . . Here Jesus legitimizes this tradition. Yes, he later castigates the Pharisees because they don't practice what they preach. But he binded them to *whatever* they told them. Thus, it is an authoritative statement that binds people to obey them, even if they can be hypocrites. 'Whatever', makes it another authoritative source that followers must obey.

Rhodes even tried to use the Corban rule of Matthew 15, just as White did, but (also like White) inconsistently, as "Matt1618" notes:

> I see the double standard of Rhodes. In the earlier chapter when he mentioned Matthew 15 to say that tradition had no binding authority, he did not balance that by

mentioning Matthew 23 at all, when Jesus said that whatever they tell you to do from Moses' seat, you obey them. Now, when Jesus legitimizes that authority, he mentions Matthew 15. If he was going to use Matthew 15 to help give insight to Matthew 23, he should have given us Matthew 23 to give insight to Matthew 15. But Rhodes does not do that. Of course, what Jesus condemned is non-legitimate traditions, that caused people to disobey commandments in Matthew 15. That was an illegitimate tradition. However, in Matthew 23 he recognized the binding authority of another tradition. Apparently, Jesus as God accepted a tradition that was binding on believers as noted in this passage.   . . . the Pharisees cannot trace themselves back to Moses. However, there is authority recognized by the Jewish tradition that had passed on this authority to the Pharisees and scribes. We also see that this Moses' seat referred to the right to interpret the Mosaic law. Jesus validated that right, independent of Scripture. The acceptance of succession is also noted. The Pharisees are seen as legal successors. This gives precedence for succession of the apostles. By the way, Jews had no concept of Sola Scriptura.

"Matt 1618" then cites two Protestant statements on *Moses' seat*, from fellow Catholic apologist Steve Ray's copious research:

Sitting on 'Moses seat' referred to a place of dignity and the right to interpret the Mosaic law. The scribes were the successors and the heirs of Moses' authority and were rightfully looked to for pronouncements upon his teaching . . . Jesus does not appear to challenge this right". *Encyclopedia of the Bible*, ed. Walter A. Elwell [Grand Rapids, Mich: Baker Book House, 1988], 2:1498, as quoted in Stephen Ray, *Upon This Rock*, [San Francisco, Ca, Ignatius Press, 1999], p. 47, fn. 62.

DA Carson writes "Moreover, 'to sit on X's seat' often means to succeed X" (Exod 11:5;12:29; 1 Kings 1:35, 46; 2:12; 16:11;2 Kings 15:12; Ps. 132:12; crf. Jos Antiq. VII, 353 [xiv.5] XVIII, 2 [i.1]. This would imply that the 'teachers of the law' are Moses' legal successors, possessing all his authority - a view the scribes themselves held...*Panta hosa* ('everything') is a strong expression and cannot be limited to 'that teaching of the law that is in Jesus' view a faithful interpretation of it'; they cover *everything* the leaders teach, including the oral tradition as well' Gaeberlein, *Expositor's Bible Commentary*, 8:472), as quoted in Stephen Ray, *ibid.*, p. 47 fn. 62.

Steve Ray added, right after this:

Carson later dismisses the whole passage by relegating it to irony, which even James White rejects.

(p. 47, footnote 62)

New Testament exegete Floyd V. Filson concurs with the same general understanding of Moses' seat:

The scribes, mostly Pharisees, copied, taught, and applied the Mosaic Law. They were pledged to obey and teach both the written law and the oral tradition, which they claimed was an integral part of the Law, *received through a direct succession of teachers going back to Moses . . .* Moses' seat [was a] synagogue chair which symbolized the origin and authority of their teaching. Jesus does not challenge their claim; he seems here to approve it.

(*A Commentary on the Gospel According to St. Matthew*, New York: Harper & Row, 1960, 243; emphasis my own)

But continuing with his misunderstanding he cites from the Eerdman's Bible Dictionary, *likewise seemingly not understanding that the definition offered is not at all contrary to what I have written.*

That's not true. It referred to a general judicial authority. Here is the citation (which White curiously omitted, seeing that he made a big deal out of my not citing all of his words). Readers can decide for themselves what it entails:

> References to seating in the Bible are almost all to such as a representation of honor and authority . . . According to Jesus, the scribes and Pharisees occupy "Moses' seat" (Matt. 23:2), having the authority and ability to interpret the law of Moses correctly; here "seat" is both a metaphor for judicial authority and also a reference to a literal stone seat in the front of many synagogues that would be occupied by an authoritative teacher of the law.
>
> (p. 48 of my book; *Eerdmans Bible Dictionary*, edited by Allen C. Myers, Grand Rapids, Michigan: Eerdmans, 1987; English revision of *Bijbelse Encyclopedie*, edited by W. H. Gispen, Kampen, Netherlands: J. H. Kok, revised edition, 1975; translated by Raymond C. Togtman and Ralph W. Vunderink, 919-920)

The ISBE is likewise noted, and its definition, "It is used also of the exalted position occupied by men of marked rank or influence, either in good or evil." Of course, in this case, it is in reference to evil men, as the rest of Matthew 23 demonstrates. Armstrong continues,

> White makes no mention of these considerations, but it is difficult to believe that he is not aware of them (since he is a Bible scholar well acquainted with the nuances of biblical meanings). They do not fit in very well with the case he is trying to make, so he omits them. But the reader is thereby left with an incomplete picture.
>
> (p. 49)

Actually, it is Armstrong who has the incomplete understanding of my own position, as has been demonstrated. On that basis he, seemingly, accuses me of purposefully omitting these "considerations" so as to strengthen my case, or worse, deceive my readers.

I'm only pointing out that one's bias can lead one to many strange tactics, in order to avoid a conclusion that one doesn't want to accept. I've never made an accusation of deliberate deception with regard to White (or almost any *other* theological opponent, for that matter), but White had no scruples about accusing *me* of that very thing in the earlier dialogue we engaged in concerning my book. I guess this is a bit of projection, which is misplaced, to put it mildly.

In the next section Armstrong comes out fully with his insistence that Jesus was here binding Christians to the oral traditions of the Pharisees, and this will certainly provide the fullest basis for the complete rejection and refutation of his reading of Matthew 23.

Not *all* oral traditions; only those which are consistent with the Bible. In other words, I was trying to demonstrate that such traditions exist, that they are positively mentioned in the Bible, and practiced by Jesus and the apostles, and that, therefore, *sola Scriptura* is contradicted.

But I wish to pursue White's argument that the Pharisees' authority was strictly confined to the synagogues. For example, we have the incident of St. Paul and the high priest. High priests (or any priests) had little directly to do with the synagogue, by definition, because they offered *sacrifice*, and that was done at the Temple. Yet they had authority. In this case, Ananias, the high priest, was a Sadducee, and, according to ISBE, a scoundrel: "lawless and violent . . . haughty, unscrupulous, filling his sacred office for purely selfish and political ends" (vol. 1, p. 129). But Paul thought he had authority. Here is what I wrote in my book, on page 50:

Paul shows the high priest, Ananias, respect, even when the latter had him struck on the mouth, and was not dealing with matters strictly of the Old Testament and the Law, but with the question of whether Paul was teaching wrongly and should be stopped (Acts 23:1-5). A few verses later Paul states, "I am a Pharisee, a son of Pharisees" (23:6) and it is noted that the Pharisees and Sadducees in the assembly were divided and that the Sadducees "say that there is no resurrection, nor angel, nor spirit; but the Pharisees acknowledge them all" (23:7-8). Some Pharisees defended Paul (23:9).

So here is a case of the high priest, who sacrifices at the Temple, being granted authority by the Apostle Paul. So much for White's argument that Jesus granted authority only to Pharisees in synagogues who read the Bible in services, in *Moses' seat*. Secondly, he was a scoundrel, which disposes of White's continual reiteration that Jesus strictly limited Pharisaical authority, because some of them were bad men, and because He sternly rebuked them for hypocrisy. Thirdly, the Sadducees were on a lower theological plane than the Pharisees, and adopted "liberal" or dissenting views on may doctrines which Pharisees and Christians alike accepted, as noted above. But Paul *still* thinks they have authority! Fourth, Paul had rebuked this man (for having him struck) in much the same terms that Jesus had rebuked the authorities:

> God shall strike you, you whitewashed wall! Are you sitting to judge me according to the law, and yet contrary to the law you order me to be struck?" (Acts 23:3)

After he was informed that it was the high priest (23:4), Paul (for some odd reason) quickly changed his tune:

> I did not know, brethren, that he was the high priest; for it is written, "You shall not speak evil of a ruler of your people." (Acts 23:5)

A *what*???!!! I thought these people *had* no authority other than to sit and read the Bible publicly??? Obviously, being a "ruler" of a people entails more than that. So the analogy to Jesus' rebuke of the Pharisees is very close. And this time it has nothing whatsoever to do with synagogues, and the person is in an even higher position of authority than the Pharisees (in fact, he was the president of the Sanhedrin when Paul appeared before it).

Shortly afterwards, "some of the scribes of the Pharisees' party" defended Paul:

> We find nothing wrong in this man. What if a spirit or an angel spoke to him? (Acts 23:9)

Now how can all this be squared with White's scenario? I dare say that it cannot be. Likewise, his commentary on Jesus' statements about Moses' seat is based on a woefully inadequate understanding of the power that the Pharisees yielded, and on related passages such as this one.

Dave Armstrong "shows his cards" so to speak, and in so doing reveals the true motivation behind his use of Matthew 23, in these words:

> Thirdly, because they had the authority and no indication is given that Jesus thought they had it only when simply reading Scripture, it would follow that Christians were, therefore, bound to elements of Pharisaical teaching that were not only nonscriptural, but based on oral tradition, for this is what the Pharisees believed.

(p. 49)

What "cards" or "true motivation"? Interest in historical truth and in presenting the beliefs of others accurately? I happily plead guilty to those accusations. Whatever "motivation" I had was already plainly presented in the subtitle in this chapter: *Oral and Extrabiblical Tradition in the New Testament*. So why would White or anyone else think I am "revealing" anything at this "late stage" of the chapter? I was simply stating a rather obvious fact (based on what we know about the Pharisees' belief system). Because that fact disagrees with White's preconceived notions of what is "supposed" to be New Testament teaching, he has to either deny it or melodramatically pretend that my straightforward acknowledgment of it is itself an inaccurate presentation. It's fascinating to observe.

Here we see the full impact of Armstrong's reading, and, I believe, misreading of the entire opening to Matthew 23. The full power of sola ecclesia is here seen, . . .

As stated before, the Catholic position is not *sola ecclesia* . . .

. . . for when you can turn the opening phrases of condemnation of the Pharisees for their hypocrisy into a binding of believers to Pharisaical traditions that are explicitly condemned therein, you are obviously operating with a very, very strong external authority.

This is, of course, an absurd characterization of my position, as if I am contending that Jesus condemned some traditions out of one side of His mouth, and bound believers to the *same* traditions out of the other side. This is a very clever tactic, but it doesn't hold up well when exposed. My true position is that *some* Pharisaical traditions were *corrupt* (therefore, Jesus condemned them), but when they taught traditions which were perfectly consistent with the Bible, then folks were bound to those. It could be that White is unaware of the Hebrew idiom, whereby "everything" does not mean "*absolutely* everything *without a single exception, ever*." Christians were not bound to teachings or commands which were against God or the Bible. But most of Pharisaical teaching was good, since Jesus and Paul followed it themselves, for the most part (as I showed previously). As a fundamentalist might say: "if it's good enough for *Paul*, it's good enough for me!" "Gimme that old time tradition, gimme that old time tradition . . . "

But before we go further, let's document the two lengthy citations from Protestant sources, that White chose to omit from his reply (remember, how in the beginning, he complained about my less-than-total citation of his argument), because doing so would work against his plan to portray my argumentation as strictly "Catholic" and based on that "external authority," rather than biblically based and historically grounded, as confirmed by Protestant sources (which he can't accuse of being biased in favor of the Catholic position and therefore, readily dismissible, because Catholicism is the "Beast," "Whore of Babylon," etc.). Here they are, from pages 49-50:

> . . . the Torah was not merely 'law' but also 'instruction', i.e., it consisted not merely of fixed commandments but was adaptable to changing conditions . . . This adaptation or inference was the task of those who had made a special study of the Torah, and a majority decision was binding on all . . .

> The commandments were further applied by analogy to situations not directly covered by the Torah. All these developments together with thirty-one customs of 'immemorial usage' formed the 'oral law' . . . the full development of which is later than the New Testament. Being convinced that they had the right interpretation of the Torah, they claimed that these 'traditions of the elders' (Mk 7:3) came from Moses on Sinai.

> (J. D. Douglas, editor, *The New Bible Dictionary*, Grand Rapids, Michigan: Eerdmans Pub. Co., 1962, 981-982)

> Likewise, *The Oxford Dictionary of the Christian Church* notes in its article on the Pharisees:

> Unlike the Sadducees, who tried to apply Mosaic Law precisely as it was given, the Pharisees allowed some interpretation of it to make it more applicable to different situations, and they regarded these oral interpretations as of the same level of importance as the Law itself.

(Cross, F. L. and E. A. Livingstone, editors, Oxford: Oxford University Press, 2nd edition, 1983, 1077)

This is the central assertion, in my opinion, and hence will be the primary focus of my response (which, to the shock of some, I will, eventually, get to).

I am shocked that White responded *at all.* I'll be even *more* shocked if he actually tries to interact with my present reasoning, and either retract his opinions where necessary or fully defend them against the present scrutiny.

Next, Armstrong makes the interesting observation that the Pharisees did indeed have their "traditions" that were extra-biblical,

Correct. Now this is either historically verifiable or it is not. I have provided the documentation, especially in my last reply. This discussion needs to proceed on the grounds of *verifiable historical fact,* not presuppositionalism or wishful thinking. Also, I should reiterate that "extra-biblical" is not the same thing as "non-biblical" or "unbiblical" or "contrary to the Bible" or "a contradiction against the Bible." It simply means "traditions that are not included in the letter of the Bible, but which are in perfect *harmony* with the Bible." But a certain kind of Protestant (of which White is one) hears "extra-biblical" and they immediately equate that with "fallible [rather than infallible] traditions of *men* [rather than of God] which are obviously *contrary* to Scripture and not *allowed* by Scripture." Ironically, *this* is contrary to Scripture, not the notion of tradition per se. But White labors under these false premises, and that weighs down the discussion and prevents it from ever becoming constructive, for those who think as he does.

. . . and since he is seeking to present as positive a picture of the Pharisees as possible, . . .

So was St. Paul, obviously, since, after all, he called *himself* a Pharisee (Acts 23:6). That's pretty "positive," I would submit. That said, I am "seeking" historical *truth*, not trying to pull off a silly ploy of selectively presenting facts that back me up and oppose what I oppose. We see that *White* is the one who wants (from all appearances) to avoid certain uncomfortable biblical and historical facts. Thus, he passed over the two extremely relevant citations from Protestant sources, which I happily provided for readers, a little bit above.

Those who have a weak case in the first place almost invariably pick and choose things from their opponents' arguments, leaving out particularly damaging bits of evidence and argumentation. It's one of the oldest tricks in the book. But I'm not interested in "debater's tricks." I'm interested in the truth. Period. I don't deny that Mr. White has the same motivation.

. . . he identifies the Sadducees as the "Jewish sola Scripturists and liberals of the time," an odd combination when one thinks about it.

This is no more odd than "Protestants and *sola Scripturists*." Neither position is a biblically based one. Nor is it "odd" in light of the fact that it was Protestantism and its Bible Only rule of faith that produced (in terms of cultural milieu) what we know and love as modern liberal theology (and many of the larger modern cults and heresies, such as Mormonism, Jehovah's Witnesses, and Christian Science). The ancient Arians, for example (who thought Jesus was created, and were similar to Jehovah's Witnesses) believed in Scripture Alone, whereas the orthodox trinitarian Church believed in apostolic succession, tradition, and Church authority. It has always been those who accept a *larger tradition*, beyond, but in harmony with Holy Scripture, who preserve *orthodoxy*. Thus, Pharisees, preserved the ancient Jewish theological tradition that developed into Christianity. Sadducees and their Bible-Only position, were rapidly rejecting several tenets which Christianity accepted, as noted previously.

In support of what he realizes is, in fact, his central assertion (the third point just noted), . . .

I didn't "realize" anything. I consistently and openly developed my arguments from the beginning of the larger chapter on "Bible and Tradition."

Armstrong seeks to establish more positive connections to Pharisaism (in reference to a passage that begins the longest denunciation of them in all of Scripture--don't let that irony pass) by asserting that:

> . . . it was precisely the extrabiblical (especially apocalyptic) elements of Pharisaical Judaism that New Testament Christianity adopted and developed for its own---doctrines such as resurrection, the soul, the afterlife, eternal reward or damnation, and angelology and demonology (all of which the Sadducees rejected).

Exactly. Now, the *interesting* thing would be to see what White thinks of *that*, since he believes that Jesus' view of the Pharisees was either totally or overwhelmingly condemnatory. But (not surprisingly at all), White doesn't tell us. In the meantime, he opted to pass over the second half of this paragraph. Here it is:

> The Old Testament had relatively little to say about these things, and what it did assert was in a primitive, kernel form. But the postbiblical literature of the Jews (led by the mainstream Pharisaical tradition) had plenty to say about them. Therefore, this was another instance of Christianity utilizing nonbiblical literature and traditions in its own doctrinal development.
>
> (p. 50)

Immediately the reader is probably surprised to discover that Christian beliefs in these areas are actually found in the traditions of the Pharisees (it is hard to refrain from refuting this directly from the previous chapter, but I shall do so for the moment) rather than from the Scriptures themselves, . . .

This is a classic, blatant, example of one of White's many false, irrational dichotomies. Let me rephrase what he is arguing here, to make it more clear from a logical standpoint:

General undeniable premise or axiom: Christian beliefs didn't come from *nowhere*, and had historical pedigree (going back to Noah, Abraham, Moses, and David, among others).

> 1. *White's major unproven premise / conclusion* (as his "argument" is *logically circular*, the two are identical): Christian beliefs came solely from the Scriptures themselves.

> 2. *Dave's query*: from what theological / cultural background did the Scriptures *come*? (answer: the Jews). And which Jewish group preserved that heritage most fully, without giving up indispensable doctrines? (answer: the Pharisees).

> 3. *White's hidden minor premise (#2)*: What comes from Scripture cannot also come from a particular people, or school of the same people.

> 4. *Dave's assertion*: many Christian beliefs can be derived historically from the Pharisees.

> 5. *White's ultimate premise / conclusion*: Christian beliefs could not in any way be derived from the Pharisees because they were derived from Scripture.

The fallacy here is obvious. No argument was made; instead, a false dichotomy is accepted. But it is patently obvious that it is false, by the example of biblical inspiration:

1. God wrote inspired Scripture. It is, in fact, "God-breathed" (*theopneustos*).

2. Men [inspired and enabled by God] wrote inspired Scripture.

3. *Conclusion (by White's "logic")*: this can't *be*! One or the *other* had to write it, because it is a contradiction!

4. *Historical Christian conclusion (Protestant, Catholic, and Orthodox alike)*: both statements (#1 and #2) are true. God wrote through men, and preserved inspiration and infallibility despite human error.

White's conclusion might hold for Islam, where it is believed that the Koran came down from heaven, written and delivered by Allah, with no human participation whatever, but not in Christianity. Therefore, his previous reasoning collapses by analogy:

> Christian doctrine came from God through the Bible, but the Bible came through the Jews (culturally, historically) and Jewish writers (in terms of individual documents).

Both notions are true. But James White can't see that, because the sort of Reformed presuppositional apologetics that he espouses is proudly, self-consciously circular in its "logic."

. . . let alone from the very traditions Jesus condemned so thoroughly (remember, we have only a few examples of explicit Pharisaical traditions on the lips of Jesus, but the Corban rule is one of them, and remember the Lord's view of such things).

White apparently believes that if you repeat a half-truth or a fallacy enough times, people will start believing it. How many times now has he repeated this *non sequitur* (in light of all the relevant considerations)? Seven, eight times now?

Armstrong's next point is to continue seeking to prop up the Pharisees as a group, pointing out that Paul respected Ananias in Acts 23:1-5, and that Paul said he was a Pharisee, "a son of Pharisees" (Acts 23:6). I believe the reader can judge for himself the relevance to the point at hand.

Yes, so do I. So I'm delighted that White breezily dismisses a highly important consideration and thinks it to be of no relevance or force whatsoever. I happen to think that it is, and I offered an actual argument in the previous installment for why I think so (citing my *entire paragraph*, rather than merely summarizing it). One continues to hope that White will raise himself to the level of rational argument in many of these crucial issues that he either mocks or cavalierly dismisses. I think people would be more impressed, were he to try that.

Next he misunderstands the reason why I cited the incident in Nehemiah 8, assumes I am trying to draw a parallel to the Pharisees and Moses' seat (I was simply pointing out the centrality of the Word of God in worship, revival, and its reading in the gatherings of God's people)

Fair enough, but then, that doesn't resolve anything in this dispute, as no Christian of any stripe would *deny* this. I hear far more Scripture at every Catholic Mass than I ever did in Protestant services in my 13 years as an evangelical Protestant.

and can't help but include yet another unfounded "swipe" by writing,

> He (White) conveniently neglects to mention, however, that Ezra's Levite assistants, as recorded in the next two verses after the Evangelical-sounding *Amens*, "helped the people to *understand* the law" (8:7) and "gave the sense, so that the people *understood* the reading" (8:8).
>
> (p. 51)

Of course, I could respond that it is Mr. Armstrong who "conveniently neglects to mention" that such an observation is utterly irrelevant to either my use of the text, nor my understanding of Scriptural sufficiency. The fact that instruction was offered is perfectly in line with what I do as an elder in the church every Lord's Day;

That's right, but that is not the sense in which the text is relevant to this discussion, which has to do with *historical Judaism*, and what *they* believed, not present-day (historically "Johnny-come-lately") Baptist ecclesiology, and what *it* holds, with regard to the issue of Bible and Tradition. White is consistent with his own false premises, in his own religious practice, but he can't apply those to the ancient Jews. That is where his inconsistency lies.

further, to be relevant to Armstrong's position, this instruction would have to include the binding of extra-biblical traditions upon the people, which, of course, is not *what the text says.*

It's relevant precisely because the Jews then, and the Pharisees later, held to oral tradition, which was incorporated into its understanding and interpretation of Scripture. We know that from the historical record. It's true that the text does not specifically *mention* this, but once we understand what the Jews have historically believed about oral tradition (cultural background being a very important consideration in good exegesis), it is far more plausible to conclude that it was part of this "instruction"; far more than engaging in historical revisionism, superimposing the 16th century Protestant innovation of *sola Scriptura* onto the text and Jewish worldview, and concluding that *only* Scripture was discussed, and that no "extra-biblical" tradition *whatsoever* was involved. History, as so often, tilts the discussion decisively in the "pro-traditional" (or "proto-Catholic") direction. But let's also include my next paragraph (since White did not), which greatly clarified my meaning and intent:

So this supposedly analogous example (that is, if presented in its *entirety*; not selectively for polemical purposes) does not support the position of White and Gundry that the authority of the Pharisees applied only insofar as they sat and *read* the Old Testament to the people (functioning as a sort of ancient collective Alexander Scourby, reading the Bible onto a cassette tape for mass consumption), not when they also *interpreted* (which was part and parcel of the Pharisaical outlook and approach).

(p. 51)

Gratuitous swipes at a person's character and honesty based upon ignorance of that person's beliefs are one element of reading "apologetic" literature that I find very distasteful.

I made no such swipe (and *vehemently deny* that I did). I think White is honestly, sincerely engaging the text, according to his worldview and theology. But I think he is severely (sincerely) *biased*, and often operates on false and inadequately examined premises, which often leads to atrocious and false conclusions. But if White finds this so "distasteful," then why did he make *precisely* this accusation against *me* in our earlier runaround over my book? (italics added):

> *Armstrong simply doesn't understand the process of scholarly examination of a text, and as a result, runs headlong into walls* trying to act like *he does.*

(1-1-05)

> *This kind of* utterly amazing mishandling of Scripture *is sad to observe, let alone to realize it has appeared in publication.*

(1-2-05)

White is quick to accuse me falsely, without sufficient grounds, of what *he* clearly did to *me*. In Christian circles, we call that *hypocrisy*, and I *do* openly accuse White of *that*, but not dishonesty. And this is doubly ironic, since we are discussing the Pharisees, and White endlessly repeats his mantra that Jesus accused them of hypocrisy, which we all knew already, so it adds nothing to the discussion. My explanation fully incorporates that fact into the analysis.

Next we have an odd, brief explosion of a complete straw-man argument:

> One does not find in the Old Testament individual Hebrews questioning teaching authority. *Sola Scriptura* simply is not there. No matter how hard White and other Protestants try to read it into the Old Testament, it cannot be done.
>
> (p. 51)

For some, this is a form of argument, but for most, it is little more than another "confession of faith." What teaching authority did individual Hebrews not *question?*

I'm delighted that Mr. White is inquisitive enough to *ask*. That indicates a willingness to learn. Good for him! To give just two examples of many:

> 1) Deuteronomy 17:8-13: *the Levitical priests* had binding authority in legal matters (derived from the Torah itself). They interpreted the biblical injunctions (17:11). The penalty for disobedience was death (17:12), since the offender didn't obey "the priest who stands to minister there before the LORD your God." Cf. Deuteronomy 19:16-17, 2 Chronicles 19:8-10.
>
> 2) Ezra 7:6,10: *Ezra, a priest and scribe*, studied the Jewish law and taught it to Israel, and his authority was

254

binding, under pain of imprisonment, banishment, loss of goods, and even death (7:25-26).

I think that with a possible death penalty lurking in the background, most folks would be inclined to obey. But we know that they were often disobedient, as all of us are at one time or another. In any event, there was clearly a strong authoritarianism in place, even regarding matters of interpretation of Scripture.

The OT Papacy? The Vatican in Jerusalem? We aren't told.

I would love to hear a counter-response, not only to this, but to *all* my argumentation.

It is ironic indeed, in a passage where Jesus instructs His disciples and the crowds to examine the teachings and actions of the Pharisees, discern right from wrong, and not follow them into false behavior, that Armstrong can find in this passage a basis for such rhetoric.

It's not only "ironic," it is absolutely untrue that I did this. In this statement I wasn't commenting on Matthew 23 at all; I was making a *general observation*, in opposition to White's tendency to absurdly superimpose *sola Scriptura* onto the Old Testament and the Jews. The immediate context was an indirect comment on the passage I cited two paragraphs before: Nehemiah 8 (also in the Old Testament; last time I checked). Quite odd. But this isn't the first time that White has completely misconstrued and/or misrepresented some argument of mine, and it sure won't be the last.

Armstrong ends his presentation with two more main points.

White skipped yet another two paragraphs from my book, but for the sake of space, I won't cite those. I am replying at all under the assumption that this was a "point-by-point" rebuttal attempt from White (which I assumed, as it had eight parts). But alas, it is not. Why am I not surprised?

255

First, he draws from his own anecdotal experience as a Protestant to assert that "individual Christians" have the right and duty to rebuke their pastors for "unbiblical" teaching. I find it odd that Roman Catholics will lionize those who stood up to the corrupt Papacy in the past, and then turn around and demonize a non-Catholic who would seek biblical fidelity from his or her leaders. Be that as it may, yes, every member of Christ's body has the duty to believe the truth, and, if there is trouble in the camp, so to speak, to bring his or her concerns to the elders (note Armstrong doesn't seem to understand the plurality of elders polity position). He relates a bad experience he had in what sounds like a single-pastor situation, not realizing that in the biblical model the local church is not under the control of a despot, but under the direction of a group of men who fit the qualifications laid out in 1 Timothy 3 and Titus 1. This changes the dynamic greatly, for instead of a one-on-one "power struggle" you have one of the sheep bringing a concern which may be valid, or may be based upon ignorance or misunderstanding, to a group of men, not just a single person.

This is not the time to get into a broad ecclesiological discussion (nor of the fine points of private judgment and *sola Scriptura*). White's "plural elder" ecclesiology is not at all the predominant position, even among the hundreds of Protestant denominations. White then cynically summarizes my next four-paragraph argument and dismisses it with no real argument of his own. As I am sick to death of that tactic by now, I won't even bother quoting his remarks, since he grants me no such courtesy.

So, with all of that said (probably took me more room to review/summarize his position than he spent in the book itself!), I move to my response, and I promise to keep it as brief as possible. I could not resist the temptation to respond a bit as we were going along, but I wish to outline a response to the entire argument that should be useful to anyone encountering the use of Matthew 23 by Roman Catholic apologists. I shall do so in our next, and possibly final, installment.

It's clear that White is now setting the stage for a general argument that will utterly ignore all or most of the particulars of my argument. As such, it will be worthless as a "response" because it won't be specific enough.

Regular readers of this blog are already well aware of the fact that in almost every instance of apologetic conflict with the various religions of men the issue comes down to either the validity and accuracy of the Bible as the Word of God, or, to the proper exegesis of the text of the Bible itself. And surely that is the case here as well.

It certainly is. White and I only disagree as to where the improper exegesis lies. After repeating a citation, White opines:

We have already pointed to the many problems with the far-reaching attempt of Armstrong to find in the introduction to the announcement of judgment upon the Pharisees its polar opposite. Rather than seeing the main point in Jesus' words (the hypocrisy of the scribes and Pharisees, and the judgments coming upon them), Armstrong's commitment to Rome helps him to find the opposite: Jesus hasn't gotten around to condemning the Pharisees yet; instead, he starts off lauding them as possessors of divine tradition passed down from Moses himself! The screeching transition into the condemnation of them is hard to imagine, but keeping this text consistent with the surrounding inspired material has never been a high priority of those who interpret via Roman decree.

I thoroughly answered this charge. White, throughout has simply assumed what he is trying to prove, with the following shallow "reasoning":

1. Jesus rebuked the Pharisees.

2. Therefore, they are utterly evil, and nothing good can come from them.

3. Therefore, He couldn't possibly have been granting them any authority at all; He must have meant something else.

Very briefly I wish to note that the listing of passages Armstrong provided regarding alleged "oral tradition" include some which simply refer to the passing down of historical incidents or facts, which does nothing more than prove that ancient men kept historical records just as modern men do. History does not have to be inspired to be recorded or referenced.

I agree. I wasn't trying to prove that it always was.

Further, it seems odd to believe that supernatural knowledge could be granted to the writers of Scripture in various portions and yet, when it comes to the NT writers, they must be enslaved to merely human sources.

Yes it *is* odd, but who *believes* this?

In any case, it is a huge leap to move from "NT writers did not limit themselves to solely the Scriptures as their source of knowledge" (i.e., they knew other books had been written, they knew of history, and they knew of current events, and used these things in their teaching and exhortation) to "the biblical writers embraced the idea of extra-biblical tradition as inspired and equal to the Tanakh."

I have given my reasons for believing that such a tradition was authoritative (not "inspired." which is another White red herring).

As we documented many times in the initial responses to Mr. Armstrong's book, he is unaware of what he must provide on an exegetical basis to substantiate a particular reading of any text, let alone a disputed one.

The usual charge of profound ignorance . . .

Armstrong is here presenting the simplified version of what has been presented by others, like David Palm, in a more scholarly format . . .

White then goes off on a tangent of the question of oral tradition itself, with long quotes intended originally for David Palm. As this is not the topic at hand, it is irrelevant to our current discussion. I won't be diverted by this tactic.

These questions are just as applicable to Armstrong as they were years ago in this context.

As I said, that's another discussion. Here the topic was supposedly Moses' seat. We've seen how bankrupt White's arguments have been. He claimed in Part VI that he was ready to issue his actual "response." I have yet to see it, and now it's already on to Part VIII, after marveling at White's weakest, most irrelevant presentation yet.

But let us hurry to the real issue:

What a novel concept! Here we are at Part VIII and White is now prepared to arrive at the "real issue." I suppose some people are slow learners. Maybe White will give us something of significant substance *this* time, at long last.

Armstrong wrote,

> ...Christians were, therefore, bound to elements of Pharisaical teaching that were not only nonscriptural, but based on oral tradition, for this is what the Pharisees believed.

Armstrong assumes no distinction between practice, interpretation, or doctrine, regarding the teaching of the Pharisees, ignoring the function of the seat of Moses in the synagogue, and assuming an entire mountain of later Roman Catholic concepts in the process.

Huh? Is this an argument? No; once again, it is a declarative statement, and largely a *non sequitur*. I have made my case at great length, and have now defended it at almost equally great length. At no time have I assumed "an entire mountain of later Roman Catholic concepts." I don't have to do that for my argument to succeed, and it would be dumb and historically anachronistic anyway. I didn't do it, but White (with more of his patented cynical wishful thinking) thinks I did. As usual, he provides no proof of his curious charges. What else is new? If most of his "arguments" are logically circular, it shouldn't surprise us that his "accusations" are also circular and incoherent.

But there is a simple, easy way of determining if Armstrong's central assertion is true (indeed, without it, the rest of his argument is vacuous and irrelevant): are we to seriously believe that the opening words of the condemnation of the Pharisees and scribes for their hypocrisy and opposition to God's truth are in fact commendations of the theology of the Pharisees, so that their extra-biblical traditions are to be taken as normative for Christians? Let's test this theory.

No argument again; just a repetition of his earlier remarks. I guess this must be what White does in his oral debates: he plays to the crowds with boilerplate and *non sequiturs* and straw men. I could see how that would work with your average anti-Catholic, but it won't fly with mainstream Protestants or Catholics or open-minded individuals trying to decide between the two presented positions.

And yet, in the immediately preceding chapter, *the Lord Jesus had defended the truth about the resurrection (did He get this truth* from the Pharisees *or did the Pharisees simply believe the truth about the subject?) against the Sadducees, had He not? And how did He do so? If we are to believe Armstrong, he would do so by reference to Pharisaical tradition, since, as he said, the Old Testament is not clear enough, and besides, it is much clearer in the oral traditions, correct? Of course not!*

I dealt with this false dichotomy last time. White, almost more than anyone I have ever seen, is such a prisoner of his false premises and presuppositions, that he makes some amazingly weak arguments, yet thinks they are so compelling. This is a striking example of one such "argument."

How did Jesus respond?

> Matthew 22:29-33 29 But Jesus answered and said to them, "You are mistaken, not understanding the Scriptures nor the power of God. 30 "For in the resurrection they neither marry nor are given in marriage, but are like angels in heaven. 31 "But regarding the resurrection of the dead, have you not read what was spoken to you by God: 32 'I AM THE GOD OF ABRAHAM, AND THE GOD OF ISAAC, AND THE GOD OF JACOB '? He is not the God of the dead but of the living." 33 When the crowds heard this, they were astonished at His teaching.

Did Jesus appeal to Pharisaic traditions? Surely not. He took His opponents directly back to the text of Scripture itself, held them accountable for the words as if God had spoken them directly to them that very day, and proved that God is the God of the living, not of the dead. And please note the reaction of the crowds: they were astonished at His teaching. This was not the first time.

Jesus appealed to Scripture in making arguments. Wow, what an astounding realization! I'm delighted that White informed me of this little-known fact. I'll have to remember this (and so I take out my handy-dandy notebook to record the momentous tidbit of truth from White).

This has nothing whatsoever to do with whether Jesus respected Pharisaical traditions or not. He *did* because He *observed* several of them. White's reasoning is as silly as saying that, because I emphasize almost exclusively biblical argumentation for Catholic doctrines in my first two books, that therefore I must not accept Catholic tradition. It proves exactly nothing. The assumption would be dead wrong in my case, and it is exceedingly likely (if not certainly) just as wrong with regard to our Lord Jesus.

White continues on with this sort of utterly irrelevant argumentation, which resolves nothing in our discussion, concluding that "He did not argue from tradition, but from the Scriptures" (as if there is an *absolute separation* of the two in the first place: this is yet another of White's false, unbiblical dichotomies).

This is just the opposite of the conclusions we would draw from Armstrong's position.

Since White adopts *one* side of a false dichotomy; he assumes that we Catholics must adopt the *other* extreme side. But of course, a false dichotomy is just that: *false.* We don't accept "tradition-only" as a viable option for anything. Our position is Bible-Tradition-Church: all in harmony with each other. *Sola Traditio* is just as silly as *sola Ecclesia*, and neither is the Catholic position. But note how White vainly tries to *make* it so. That's what we call a "straw man," folks.

But most compellingly the interpretation offered by Armstrong (and others) falters with finality when we ask a simple question: even if we were to grant all the inserted ideas about the centrality of "tradition" here, the fact is that Armstrong's interpretation goes directly against Jesus' own teaching in Matthew 15. You just cannot make these two passages fit together.

This is the passage concerning the Corban rule, which we have already dealt with, and disposed of, as any sort of successful objection at all.

Note the text: 1) These are Pharisees, the very ones Armstrong refers us to as carrying divine traditions as those who have seated themselves in Moses' seat. 2) The Pharisees begin with reference to one tradition (note it is behavioral in orientation, interpretive of other laws, not doctrinal or revelational) and the Lord respond by reference to a completely different tradition-- but both are encompassed by the one phrase, "the tradition of the elders," which, no matter how hard Armstrong may try, is definitional of the entire body of tradition to which he wishes to bind us via his reading of Matthew 23. 3) If Armstrong is right, the Corban rule to which Jesus refers here would be properly defined by the Pharisees and properly taught from "Moses' seat." Does it not follow, inexorably, that for Jesus' followers to do as He commands in both *Matthew 15 and Matthew 23 that they would have to exercise the very discernment and examination of the Pharisees' teaching that Armstrong decries? The Corban rule was just as much a part of "oral tradition" as anything else. It was an "interpretation" of the law concerning a man's duties to his parents as well as the laws dealing with giving to the temple and its worship. But it was a false teaching, as Jesus here makes clear. It was an allegedly divine tradition that men* should have *examined* and rejected *on the basis of their own reading of the Scriptures.*

That's right: people should reject corrupt traditions. No argument there . . . this gets back to a statement I made earlier, concerning the modern misunderstanding of Hebrew idiom of "everything" and "all." It was not understood in the sense of having no exceptions whatsoever. That was a later, more logical, "Greek" mode of thinking. So it is entirely possible in the Hebrew mind that the Pharisees could have authority, while they might teach some things that are corrupt, and to be rejected (just as civil governments have authority, but in extreme cases, must be disobeyed, in matters of conscience). But by and large, they were authoritative. This is no contradiction; a *paradox*, maybe, but not another of White's false dichotomies.

In fact, it seems plain beyond contradiction that Jesus is here teaching the Scriptures are so clear and compelling on this point in relationship to honoring one's father and mother that there is surely no need for a magisterium to tell you this, for the "magisterium" of the day was telling you just the opposite!

Here White smuggles in his prior disposition of *sola Scriptura*, which doesn't follow simply from Scripture being clear enough to clinch a particular argument. That can be, and often is, true, but it has no inherent implication that, therefore, authority does not exist, or exists only in a provisional sense. White's general fallacy here is arguing from the particular to the general, and "throwing out the baby with the bathwater." Just because one corrupt tradition was rebuked does not mean that Pharisaical authority was null and void. He can't prove his case from the single case of the Corban rule. All the relevant data must be taken into consideration. But White refuses to do that because it doesn't help his superficial "case" for the matter to be examined too closely. We mustn't do that!

But how could Jesus say these things about the Pharisees, who had seated themselves in Moses' seat, in Armstrong's scenario? He couldn't!

No??!! He can say them just like Paul rebuked Peter. If someone is being a hypocrite, or has corrupted one aspect of their teaching, they should be rebuked. White seems to have forgotten that God made an eternal covenant with David, which wasn't broken even by murder and adultery.

But if we simply allow the context to speak, and realize Matthew 23:1-3 is not a positive statement about the Pharisee's authority, but the beginning of their condemnation, and their having seated themselves in Moses' seat in the synagogue only adds to their condemnation (but has absolutely nothing whatsoever to do with later Roman Catholic theories of authority or tradition), then we find a consistent reading of Jesus' words.

This is not a plausible interpretation at all, as shown in previous installments, at great length.

In Conclusion

While there is much more that could be said, we have certainly said enough. Mr. Armstrong was unwise to sub-title his book, "95 Bible Passages That Confound Protestants" when he is manifestly ill equipped to provide the "goods" to back up his claims. His work is convincing only to the already convinced, but surely not to anyone who is actually familiar with what is necessary to show respect to God's Word by handling it aright. It is truly my prayer that the time I have invested in demonstrating the lack of substance in this work will help those who are seeking to minister the gospel of grace to those who have been ensnared by Rome's false and deceptive "gospel."

I thank Mr. White for a clear summary of his position (and derision). I will pass on my own summary, preferring to let what I have already written speak for itself. I continue to await a substantive, rational, biblically sound reply to my argument from James White.

Chapter Seven

Critique of James White's Arguments on 1 Corinthians 3:10-15 and Purgatory
[3 March 2007]

[1 Corinthians 3] 10 According to the grace of God which was given to me, like a wise master builder I laid a foundation, and another is building on it. But each man must be careful how he builds on it.
11 For no man can lay a foundation other than the one which is laid, which is Jesus Christ.
12 Now if any man builds on the foundation with gold, silver, precious stones, wood, hay, straw,
13 each man's work will become evident; for the day will show it because it is to be revealed with fire, and the fire itself will test the quality of each man's work.
14 If any man's work which he has built on it remains, he will receive a reward.
15 If any man's work is burned up, he will suffer loss; but he himself will be saved, yet so as through fire.

[Bible version not listed]

This passage of Paul's first epistle to the church at Corinth has prompted much discussion down through church history. The context of the preceding ten verses is really quite simple: Paul is discussing the problems that exist in the Corinthian congregation. He has used harsh words with them, referring to them as "men of flesh" and "infants in Christ." He refers to the strife and jealousy that exists among them. He zeroes in on their partisanship: the fact that they are saying "I am of this Christian leader or that one." He reminds them that leaders are but servants of the Lord, and that it was the Lord that even gave those servants the opportunity to preach the gospel to them. He writes in verse 6, "I planted, Apollos watered, but God was causing the growth." God used Paul and Apollos as means, but the growth was caused by God, not by the Christian leaders themselves. At this point then Paul begins to speak of the role Christian leaders have in the work of the Church. Note his words:

> 8 Now he who plants and he who waters are one; but each will receive his own reward according to his own labor. 9 For we are God's fellow workers; you are God's field, God's building.

Verse 8 provides the first reference to "reward," and it is clearly in the context of the Christian leaders who labor in the work of ministry. It will be significant to note that the phrase "receive a reward" in verse 8 is identical *in terminology to the same phrase in verse 14. Since in this context we know that the planting and watering mentioned goes back to Paul and Apollos, the topic remains consistent throughout this passage. Paul then speaks of himself and Apollos as "God's fellow workers," and they labor in this high calling in God's field. He uses two terms, field and building, but picks up only on the second, "God's building." A fellow worker of God works in building God's building, and that building is the church.*

White attempts to make the passage apply only to *Christian workers*; those in ministry; the ordained, etc. I think this fails because, while there are indeed references to Christian workers: those who evangelize and teach, etc., there are just as many indications that Paul *also* generalizes his teaching. Even beyond that, one must remember that Paul is writing to the entire church at Corinth. The all-inclusiveness of what he is writing about is indicated more than once:

268

3:11: For no other foundation can *any one* lay . . .

3:12: Now if *any one* builds on . . .

3:14: If the work which *any man* has built . . .

3:15: If *any man's* work is burned up, . . .

The next two verses after the passage under consideration (also the context) are clearly general: intended for all in the Corinthian church to whom he is writing:

> [16] Do you not know that you are God's temple and that *God's Spirit dwells in you*? [17] If *any one* destroys God's temple, God will destroy him. For God's temple is holy, and *that temple you are*.

Anyone who has God's Holy Spirit inside of him is a Christian, because all who are truly God's are indwelt with the Holy Spirit. This can't possibly refer to simply Christian workers. Paul continues the general language in the next verse (3:18):

> . . . If *any one* among you thinks that he is wise in this age, let him become a fool that he may become wise.

Moreover, in verse 4:5 Paul refers again about rewards after death:

> Therefore do not pronounce judgment before the time, before the Lord comes, who will bring to light the things now hidden in darkness and will disclose the purposes of the heart. Then *every man* will receive his *commendation* from God.

Most of the entire context of the passage (both before and after) is in generalized language. Paul even explains exactly why he mentioned himself and his co-worker Apollos:

[6] I have *applied all this to myself and Apol'los for your benefit*, brethren, that you may *learn by us* not to go beyond what is written, that none of you may be puffed up in favor of one against another. [7] For who sees anything different in you? What have you that you did not receive? If then you received it, why do you boast as if it were not a gift?

As usual, Paul uses his own example (by the grace of God) as one to *imitate* (4:14-16). Thus, we see the parallelism of the example of himself as a Christian worker and apostle applied generally to *all* Christians. Note how he writes in 3:7:

So neither he who plants nor he who waters is anything, but only God who gives the growth.

That was in the immediate context of his work with Apollos. But he clearly generalizes that to all Christians in similar language in 4:7:

For who sees anything different in *you*? What have you that you did not receive? If then *you* received it, why do you boast as if it were not a gift?

In other words, all men are under God; He gives the grace; we cooperate with Him in that grace or can reject it (see. e.g., 9:24-27). And man's works will ultimately be judged and rewarded or burned up. Therefore, considering all of this relevant context (especially 4:5-6), it is clear that the "purgatorial" judgments in 3:13-15 apply to all men, not just Christian workers.

This then brings us to the main passage. Verses 10-15 give us an illustration of how weighty it is to minister in the church, and how God will someday manifest the motivations of the hearts of all those who have engaged in that work.

He sure will (see also James 3:1), but this passage applies to *all* men, as just shown.

Then in verses 16-17 Paul adds a further warning, speaking of God's certain judgment upon those who do not build, but instead tear down, or destroy. There is an obvious movement between 10-15 and 16-17, for in 10-15 the metaphor remains the construction of a building upon a foundation; in 16-17 this switches to the metaphor of the temple of God, already constructed.

3:16 and 3:17b plainly refer to (indwelt) Christians, so it stands to reason that the preceding section of 3:11-15 does also. Paul only provided himself as an example of the general principle that all we have is from God, by His grace (3:7 <---> 4:7), and we can choose to build upon that grace and empowerment or destroy it. But the hypothetical person referred to in 3:17a is not saved in the end, since God "destroy[s]" him. This is a different notion entirely from that of 3:15, where a person's work is "burned up" but he is "saved, but only as through fire."

Further, in 10-15 the "certain ones" are those who are indeed building upon the foundation, even if they have less than perfect motivations or understanding; the certain one in verses 16-17 is not building anything at all, but is instead tearing down and ruining what has already been built. This distinction is important as well, as we shall see.

If distinctions are so important to the biblical exegete Mr. White, it seems to me that he would notice that 3:16 is talking about Christians (the Corinthians, in terms of direct address) but 3:17 (and even then only the first half) about someone who is ultimately damned.

> 10 According to the grace of God which was given to me, like a wise master builder I laid a foundation, and another is building on it. But each man must be careful how he builds on it. 11 For no man can lay a foundation other than the one which is laid, which is Jesus Christ.

Paul continues the context, insisting that by God's grace he has laid a foundation, knowing that others would build upon that same foundation. This foundation, of course, refers to the work of ministry in building up the church that he has engaged in. But there is an element of personal responsibility that is part of ministry in Christ's church: a man must be "careful" how he builds upon the foundation, which Paul reminds us is holy. The only foundation of the church is Jesus Christ Himself. So just as we are to have an attitude of fear and trembling when considering that it is the holy God who is at work within us, working out our salvation (Philippians 2:12-13), so the minister is to recognize that ministry in the church is a holy task, and he must "look well" (a literal understanding of the Greek) upon how he goes about this work. This leads to further expansion upon this thought in the following section.

That's all fine and good, except to note that the entire passage applies to all, not just Christian workers, and the key verses of 3:13-15 clearly refer to all men.

> 12 Now if any man builds on the foundation with gold, silver, precious stones, wood, hay, straw, 13 each man's work will become evident; for the day will show it because it is to be revealed with fire, and the fire itself will test the quality of each man's work.

The first thing to see in v. 12 is that we are still talking about the same group: Christian workers. Those under discussion build upon the foundation. We will see that in vv. 16-17 Paul refers to a different group, those who do not build, but instead tear down.

That's not at all certain, or even likely, in my opinion.

So we have one group who build upon the one foundation, but with different quality "materials." Now obviously, the terms gold, silver, precious stones, wood, hay and straw, are all figures of speech, metaphors. Christian leaders are not known for having an abundance of gold, silver, or precious stones, let alone is the "building" being done here a literal activity either. These are terms referring, as Paul himself puts it, to "the quality of each man's work." Some labor selflessly and in obscurity with motivations pure and honorable, while others have mixed motivations, tinged to a lesser or greater degree by selfishness and vainglory (cf. Phil 2:3-4). During this lifetime we cannot necessarily know which Christian leaders, even within the bounds of orthodox teaching and practice, are doing what they do with motivations that are pleasing to God. But Paul is reminding us that such will not always be the case: God will reward those who have labored diligently for His glory in that day when all the secrets of men's hearts will be revealed.

More of the same category error . . .

Paul says that each man's work "will become evident, for the day will show it." The nature of the Christian minister's work will be plain and clear: the lack of clarity that exists during this lifetime will no longer cloud our vision at the judgment. What a tremendously sobering thought for those who labor in building upon the foundation of Jesus Christ! God, who searches the hearts, will reveal our true motivations on that day!

The revelation of whether one's ministerial works are precious and lasting, or surface-level and temporary, will be accomplished "by fire." Obviously, fire differentiates, at the most basic level, between gold and wood, silver and straw, precious stones and stubble. The precious elements withstand the fire's presence, whereas the others are consumed in their entirety. Given that it has already been established that gold and silver, etc., are figures for the quality of men's works, so it follows inexorably that "fire" refers to a testing that makes its verdict as clear as the destruction of wood, hay, and stubble by the raging flames of a fire. The works that were not done to God's glory are destroyed, while those works having the proper character pass through unharmed.

This is a good description of purgatory indeed. Sin isn't "done to God's glory" so to the extent that are works were sinful, they (and we) will be judged. It's striking that Protestants like White cannot see that this is exactly what the doctrine of purgatory entails.

> 14 If any man's work which he has built on it remains, he will receive a reward. 15 If any man's work is burned up, he will suffer loss; but he himself will be saved, yet so as through fire.

The context continues, unbroken. Note the repetition of the preceding concept of "building" on the "foundation." If a man's work, built upon the foundation of Christ in the church, remains in the presence of the judgment of God, he receives a reward. But in direct parallel, if another worker's labors are burned up, he will suffer loss. The opposite of the reception of a reward is to suffer loss. The Greek term Paul uses is translated by the vast majority of recognized translations as "suffer loss," and there is a reason for this. Despite the fact that you can render the term as "punish," its normative meaning, especially in the NT, refers to experiencing the opposite of gain (i.e., loss), and often what is not gained is found in the immediate context of the words use. For example:

> More than that, I count all things to be loss in view of the surpassing value of knowing Christ Jesus my Lord, for whom I have suffered the loss of all things, and count them but rubbish so that I may gain Christ, (Philippians 3:8)

Obviously, this does not mean Paul has been "punished," but has "suffered the loss" of all things. The same is true in Jesus' use of the term:

> "For what will it profit a man if he gains the whole world and forfeits his soul? Or what will a man give in exchange for his soul? (Matthew 16:26, see also Mark 8:36, Luke 9:25)

In 1 Corinthians 3:15, the term is used in a context that provides a direct correlation to the term: the one whose work remains receives a reward, so the one whose work is burned up does not, hence, they suffer loss (for further information on this word, see TDNT 2:888). We are reminded, however, that despite the seriousness of the loss of reward for the Christian worker, we are still talking about those who have found salvation in the perfect righteousness of Jesus Christ. Paul tells us that despite suffering loss, these are saved, "yet so as through fire." This in no way makes the judgment of the motivations of Christian workers a trivial matter: it is obvious that for Paul, who himself faced this test, it was not. But it also safeguards against the misuse of his teaching. No one can argue that one's salvation is based upon the works one does: this is not his teaching here, nor anywhere else.

I agree with the last sentence in particular. Paul doesn't teach salvation by works, which is the Pelagian heresy. Nor does the Catholic Church. But both teach that good works inevitably follow true saving faith and justification.

A man is justified before God by the imputation of Christ's righteousness to him, and the imputation of the man's sin to Christ, the perfect substitute, who bears in His body the sins of His people upon Calvary (Romans 3:20-4:8). But this is not his subject here.

Indeed, and so I won't critique the typical Protestant soteriological errors implied.

The context has remained constant: the revelation of the motivations of the hearts of Christian workers.

I believe I have shown that to be untrue, with much contextual contrary evidence.

In a perfect world it would not be necessary to go beyond the mere exegesis of the text to understand Paul's meaning and intention. But we do not live in such a world. In God's providential wisdom, we live in a time when the church must struggle against false teaching and false teachers (Acts 20:24ff).

Has there ever been a time when this was *not* true?

Specifically, the truth of God's sovereign grace is attacked by Roman Catholicism, and its man-centered sacramentalism.

Sacramentalism isn't "man-centered"; it is "man-directed" by God, since sacraments are physical means to obtain God's grace.

One of the most egregious attacks upon the finished nature of Christ's work on Calvary is the dogma of purgatory.

It doesn't attack it at all. It is no essentially different than what White himself admits occurs in whatever he calls the process described in 1 Corinthians 3:10-15.

We have often engaged in debate on this topic (see, for example, the debate against Fr. Peter Stravinskas on this topic, May, 2001). Rome attempts to enlist this passage in support of its doctrine, but in the process engages in gross eisegesis of the text, missing its plain meaning, and inserting concepts utterly foreign to Paul's theology.

We'll see about that.

Just a few items should be noted that, in light of the preceding comments, should be sufficient for any person not committed to the ultimacy of Roman authority.

I want *many*! If there are many, then surely White can produce them, rather than refer to something he has not demonstrated. Furthermore, it is obvious that White has his own "authority" of a sort: Baptist traditions that are virtually as impenetrable as any Catholic dogmas.

First, the passage is about Christian workers, not all the Christian faithful.

I beg to differ, per my arguments above.

Next, the passage says nothing about the purification of individuals. Works are tested in this passage.

Technically, our works or sins are separate from us as people, yet we make them part of us. They can become ingrained in our character and (seemingly) our very being. Protestants take it even further than Catholics, and believe that we have a sin nature, so that entails the sins being very close to ourselves indeed. So I think this is a distinction without a difference. If my sins are purged from me, I feel that as a judgment of myself because I have made those sins my own and attached myself to them.

Rome teaches souls are purified from the temporal punishment of sins by suffering satispassio *in purgatory: but there is nothing about temporal punishments,* satispassio, *or suffering of individuals for their sins, in this passage. All these are extraneous to the text itself.*

Not at all, as just shown. In fact, Protestants are fond of citing 2 Corinthians 5:21 to demonstrate that Jesus took on our sins. He suffered so greatly that Paul uses graphic language of equation of even our holy Lord Jesus with sin:

> For our sake he made him to be sin who knew no sin, so that in him we might become the righteousness of God.

If even Jesus can be described in such a way, when He did not and could not ever sin, surely fallen human beings are closely identified with *their* sins. This is shown repeatedly in Scripture, when character judgments are made about people: that they are "evil" -- as contrasted to the "good" persons (e.g., Mt 12:35; Lk 6:43-45; Phil 3:2; 2 Tim 3:13; Heb 3:12, 10:22; Rev 22:11; throughout Proverbs and Psalms, etc.) or to be characterized in terms of some serious sin, as if it sums up their entire character (see, e.g., Paul's list of such people in 1 Corinthians 6:9-10, and the similar Rev 22:15).

Further, the insertion of the Roman concepts into the passage turns it on its head. Remember, those with works of gold, silver, and precious stones (i.e., Christian workers who had godly motivations) appear in this passage: their works are subject to the same testing as the others. If this "fire" is relevant to purgatory, then are we to assume that even those with godly motives "suffer"? Are there no saints involved in building upon the foundation?

Sin runs far deeper than good or bad motives. It runs the whole gamut of human behavior.

But most telling is this: the fire of which Paul speaks reveals. It does not purge. If this were the fire of Rome's purgatory, it would not simply demonstrate that gold is, in fact, gold, or hay is truly hay. The sufferings of purgatory are supposed to sanctify and change a persons soul, enabling them to enter into the very presence of God! If this passage supported Rome's position, it would speak of purifying the gold, making it more pure, spotless, precious, and ready for God's presence. It would speak of the fire removing wood or other "impurities" from a person's soul, not simply telling us that the works a Christian minister did were or were not done with God's sole glory in mind. But the text speaks of a revelation of the quality of a man's work, which is wholly incompatible with Rome's use of the passage.

This is silly quibbling about words, ending with an extravagant claim that doesn't follow: more distinctions without a difference. The fact remains that Holy Scripture often speaks in these terms. To purify a person is to remove their sins and imperfections. Purgation of this type is precisely a negative work of getting rid of contamination, just as in metal-working. If the impurities are gotten rid of the final product is more pure.

Likewise with the stains and impurities of sin on human souls. To get rid of them *is* to purify the person. See, for example, 2 Corinthians 7:1: ". . . let us cleanse ourselves from every defilement of body and spirit, and make holiness perfect in the fear of God." (cf. Ps 51:7; Ecc 12:14; Is 1:25; 4:3-4; 6:5-7; 48:10; Jer 9:7; Dan 11:35; Zech 13:9; Mal 3:2-3; 2 Cor 5;10).

In 2 Corinthians 5:10 the person is judged based on what he has done. So the person is purified based on his works, which is exactly what we see in 1 Corinthians 3; just with a little bit different terminology.

One might follow the "metal analogy" further and observe that even gold and silver (the better works in Paul's word-picture) have to be *refined* (see 1 Chr 28:18; 29:4; Ps 12:6; Rev 3:18). The relatively more righteous Christians with more works and faith (those whom White says have "godly motives") therefore also have to undergo this process of purification and purging.

Modern Roman Catholics have started to move away from the term "fire" (though this was, inarguably, what attracted the attention of Rome to the passage in the first place), and seek to focus more upon the suffering of a loss, so that only the second group is seen as being relevant to purgatory. Of course, this is made possible by the constant repetition of the assertion, "Rome has never officially declared the meaning of this passage, nor that there is fire in purgatory, nor that purgatory is a place, nor that we experience time in purgatory..." etc and etc. The fact that one can go into history and determine with great clarity what was taught and believed only a few centuries ago does not seem to matter.

If Mr. White wishes to assert a contradiction, let him produce one and we'll examine it. I won't do his work for him.

Finally, it should be noted that in Roman Catholic theology, a person sent to purgatory has already been judged to be in need of further purging (sanctification) before entering into the presence of God. Yet, there is no mention of such a judgment here; in fact, most RC interpretations see this as the judgment itself.

The language is quite similar in thrust and intent to the passages above. It is a common biblical theme: a purging or refining of God's people: the ones who will be saved. What could be plainer than "saved, but only as through fire"? That practically sums up the doctrine of purgatory in six words.

An Example From Roman Catholic Scholarship: The Jerome Biblical Commentary

A fascinating example of the divide between what the text says and what a Roman Catholic needs it to say is provided by the Jerome Biblical Commentary. *Note the interpretation provided by this Roman Catholic source:*

> 10. Developing the metaphor, Paul describes his ministry and the responsibility of all who follow him, as they build upon the foundation he has laid. 11. Christ, as the unique foundation, may be an allusion to Is 28:16 or Ps 118:22 (cf. Eph 2:20 and 1 Pt 2:6-8). This Christ, Preached by Paul, dwells in the hearts of the faithful (Eph 3:17) and communicates his Spirit to them. Succeeding preachers must take care how they build on this foundation. 13. the Day: The Lord's Day when Christ returns as victorious judge (1 Thes 5:4). fire: It is to test the quality of various building materials. Fire is the customary biblical metaphor describing the might and majesty of the divine judgment. it: Probably the neut. pron. auto refers to ergon, "work." The fire tests the work, destroying what is of poor quality and perishable. 14. A wage will be paid only for good, durable work. 15. The man whose work will not endure the searching test of judgment will suffer a loss. Like one escaping from a burning house, he will be saved, but his work and his reward will be lost. This metaphor clearly teaches the responsibility of ministers of the gospel, who will be rewarded or punished for the manner in which they have fulfilled their ministry. That the

preacher will be saved implies that his sins were not serious and have not ruined the Christian community, because God destroys such a one.

To this point all is well: the Roman Catholic exegete follows the text, sees the context, recognizes the meaning of the words. But since Rome has defined more than this in her teachings, something must be said about purgatory:

Although the doctrine of purgatory is not taught in this passage, it does find support in it. The metaphor suggests an expiatory punishment--which is not damnation--for faults that, although not excluding salvation, merit punishment. When Paul wrote this epistle he was still hoping for the coming of the Lord's Day in his lifetime. Consequently, he locates this expiatory punishment at the final judgment.

Where does one find the basis, in the exegesis offered by the commentary itself, for the assertion that there is an "expiatory punishment" in the passage, especially when this involves, in the Roman context, the punishment of the person and not an examination of the works he performed?

As I have argued above, the two amount to the same thing: to purge one's sins is to purge the person himself, because he has made the sins his own: part of himself.

All of the elements of Rome's concept of purgation, including temporal punishments, satispassio, *etc., are absent from both the text and the interpretation offered by the commentary itself, and yet we have the unfounded assertion that while the text does not teach purgatory, purgatory finds support within the text.*

Of course it does. It refers to a "fire" that is refining and "revealing", that will be a "test" for every man's "work" (that's temporal punishment of suffering indeed), a situation where a man will "suffer loss" and yet still be saved. How much clearer does it have to be? Now, of course we won't find a fully-developed medieval conception of purgatory, but it is foolish to expect that anyway, just as it would be to expect to find full Chalcedonian Christology and trinitarianism in all its glorious nuanced complexity. That is true of all doctrines, so why should purgatory be an exception?

. . . The passage is not difficult at all, and without the insertion of anachronistic Roman Catholic concepts that developed centuries later, there really would not be any meaningful question about its teaching.

Further below I shall briefly survey prominent Church Fathers' views on the passage (particularly, St. Augustine's). We shall see whether the doctrine of purgatory was only a later medieval development, or whether it was present in its essentials during the patristic period.

. . . There is, of course, nothing contradictory between asserting that the motivations of Christian workers will be made known at the end of time and that those who had pure motives will receive a reward and those who did not will suffer loss (not "will suffer" as in a judicial sense of "satispassio"). There is nothing in justification by grace through faith alone that is in any way out of harmony with such a revelation of motivations, an opening of hearts.

If only Mr. White had eyes to see it, he would realize that Protestant teaching of differential rewards, and the "judgment seat of Christ" etc., is not all that different from the biblical, Catholic, apostolic, patristic doctrine of purgatory. It might even be argued that the main distinction is one of length of time. Protestants tend to see these judgments of Christians as more or less instantaneous (just as they view salvation); Catholics think it is more of a process. But the basic concept is present in both systems. That's what White has to content himself mostly with nibbling around the edges; griping about *satispassio* and so forth.

. . . Of course, Paul makes no such emphasis here, or anywhere else [i.e., that one might be saved as a direct result of his works]. *The judgment is of works relative to reward, not to salvation. All judged here were Christian workers: their salvation was already a matter of fact.*

It's true that the persons referred to in the passage we are considering are all saved. But White's first sentence is demonstrably untrue. It is rather easy to prove this, too. Whenever the Bible reveals what takes place at judgment, it is, I believe, always the case that human works are discussed and judged and made relevant to salvation or damnation. We don't see "Protestant language" of "you had great faith alone in Me, and firmly believed in TULIP; enter into glory!" All that we find is examination of works. Surely, this is a startling biblical reality that a Protestant has to grapple with. St. Paul himself (in evangelical Protestants' favorite book of his by far: Romans) makes this crystal-clear in Romans 2:5-13 (cf. Mt 7:19-21, 24; 16:27; 25:31-35; Lk 18:18-25; 1 Pet 1:17; Rev 22:12). All this, and yet White feels able to make a blanket statement: "The judgment [not just in *this* passage, but "anywhere" in Paul] is of works relative to reward, not to salvation."

This is little more than rhetoric. When one considers the highly anachronistic interpretations offered by Rome of all the passages relevant to purgatory, as well as such passages as John 19:26, or Luke 1:28, speaking of "desperate attempts" becomes almost humorous.

White would certainly be able to relate to "desperate attempts" at special pleading exegesis.

Roman Catholic apologists live in a world where double-standards abound. When speaking to their own followers, terms like "always" abound, as if there is a unified, consistent, easily discerned "tradition" to which to refer. But, as soon as anyone points out counter-citations from those same sources, all of a sudden we begin to hear either about how that was an early

Father speaking "as a private theologian" and "not for the universal church," or, the spirit of Newman arises to make all historical issues "go away" since we can just rely upon "development" anyway.

Let us see what patristic support Mr. White can drum up for his position. Perhaps the Church fathers, too, will be found to be neck-deep in double standards and manage to somehow believe in a doctrine that White sees nowhere in the Bible at all?

Consider, for example, the breadth of the beliefs represented by Tertullian or Gregory the Great---no serious scholar suggests that what Tertullian believed regarding prayers for the dead, for example, is the same as what Gregory the Great believed about purgation after death.

Of course they wouldn't, since Gregory lived some 400 years later and much development had taken place. The same holds for the Trinity. This is how it *always* is. So White provides no great illumination for anyone with even a working knowledge of the history of Christian doctrine and its development.

Not only had there been a number of developments during the intervening centuries, but the sources Gregory accepted as relevant were much wider (and less orthodox) than those used by Tertullian. . . . Tertullian speaks of prayers for refrigerium for those who have died. This is nothing like Gregory; Augustine's view is different than either one. Origen's entire theology was wildly off-base, so throwing him into the mix is hardly a positive thing for anyone interested in truly biblical theology.

I find it fascinating, then, given White's present disdain for Origen and his "wildly off-base" errors in relation to "truly biblical theology," that he cited him no less than three times in defense of the *theology of God* (pretty important biblical theology there), prefaced by the description of "early Christian sources" and "Fathers" – in his website paper, "Did the Early Church Believe in the LDS Doctrine of God?"

He is also quick to utilize Origen when it comes to citing the smattering of fathers who thought Mary sinned (several references in his papers). So I guess Origen is a good, solid "Christian source" when he agrees with White; otherwise, he is relegated to "wildly off-base," and if a Catholic cites him in support of a Catholic doctrine, he can thus be dismissed with a sweeping insult.

Likewise, when White thought he could enlist Origen in another paper of his against papal primacy, we find no negative comment about the Church father. He is, apparently, only as good or as orthodox as the extent of his agreement with White.

. . . *men who would not recognize the modern Roman dogma at all.*

I love the gratuitous "at all" tacked onto the end. That is quite debatable, to put it mildly.

. . . *I would assert that true textually-based exegesis is not something* [a Catholic] *can faithfully engage in anyway (i.e., this would involve a fundamental contradiction of his beginning commitment to Rome's authority).*

Is that so? This is quite the novel interpretation of the position of a Catholic exegete, in light of the fact that the Catholic Church has only expressly defined very few texts. Mr. White again shows his rank ignorance of Catholic thinking and conception of authority. Protestants arguably have far more restrictions on how they can interpret biblical passages, because they are so fond of isolated proof texts, where just one meaning is allowed.

If anyone wants to deny this, I would suggest attempting to argue with White that Romans 9 can be interpreted in any way other than the strictly Calvinist one. Or let anyone try to present to White some of the many passages that plainly teach baptismal regeneration, and observe how he *must* maintain that they do *not*, because his Baptist dogmas won't allow it. The same thing holds for passages about true Christian believers falling away from God.

Thus, the "commitment to prior authority" canard absolutely works both ways. It is not only Catholics who are bound to doctrinal constrictions: *all* Christians who believe *anything* are, and all appeal to Scripture to back up their claims.

. . . the Greek term translated "suffer loss" . . . the context does not support the rendering "punishment," as the phrase is directly parallel to verse 14.

The Greek word is *zemioo* ("suffer loss" -- 1 Cor 3:15). Mr. White claims that "punishment" would not be the correct meaning in our passage, but Greek linguists differ with him:

> 1.a. Disadvantage may take the form of monetary or material "loss" or "damage." b. It may also be moral or spiritual in the sense of "hurt" or "ruin," with a subjective nuance of "unpleasantness."

> . . . The same sense [1.b.] is probable (rather than "penalty") in 1 Cor. 3:15 in contrast to the reward of v. 14. What is at issue is "hurt" or "loss" in a general sense, not in a financial sense or as loss of salvation . . .

> (Gerhard Kittel, *Theological Dictionary of the New Testament*, translated and abridged by Geoffrey W. Bromiley, Grand Rapids, Michigan: Eerdmans, 1985, 299)

Likewise, Thayer's *Greek-English Lexicon* (Grand Rapids, Michigan: Baker Book House, 1977, word #2210, p. 272) defines *zemioo* in this instance as "to sustain damage, to receive injury, suffer loss." All of this is perfectly consistent with the apostolic, patristic, biblical, Catholic doctrine of purgatory, where one experiences "loss" and "hurt" and "damage" and "injury" (to our egos and pride and sense of self-sufficiency, no doubt) and it is quite "unpleasant," just as our trials and tribulations in this life are, but all to good purpose.

Chapter Eight

Reply to James White on the Council of Nicaea and Its Relationship to Pope Sylvester, St. Athanasius' Views, and the Unique Preeminence of Catholic Authority
[2 April 2007]

      This was a reply to Mr. White's article, "What Really Happened at Nicea?" (*Christian Research Journal*, Spring 1997). I shall cite everything in White's article that I disagree with and reply point-by-point, as is my custom. I don't pick and choose and ignore everything that might be a bit more difficult to interact with. This will be completely my own response: that of an apologist and non-scholar who appeals to the Church historians who *are* scholars, regarding such questions. Mr. White's footnotes will be noted in bracketed numbers, and appear in their totality at the end of the chapter (not italicized)

* * * * *

Summary

The Council of Nicea is often misrepresented by cults and other religious movements. The actual concern of the council was clearly and unambiguously the relationship between the Father and the Son. Is Christ a creature, or true God? The council said He was true God. Yet, the opponents of the deity of Christ did not simply give up after the council's decision. In fact, they almost succeeded in overturning the Nicene affirmation of Christ's deity. But faithful Christians like Athanasius continued to defend the truth, and in the end, truth triumphed over error. The conversation intensified quickly. "You can't really trust the Bible," my Latter-day Saints acquaintance said, "because you really don't know what books belong in it. You see, a bunch of men got together and decided the canon of Scripture at the Council of Nicea, picking some books, rejecting others." A few others were listening in on the conversation at the South Gate of the Mormon Temple in Salt Lake City. It was the LDS General Conference, and I again heard the Council of Nicea presented as that point in history where something "went wrong," where some group of unnamed, faceless men "decided" for me what I was supposed to believe. I quickly corrected him about Nicea — nothing was decided, or even said, about the canon of Scripture at that council. [1] I was reminded how often the phrase "the Council of Nicea" is used as an accusation by those who reject the Christian faith. New Agers often allege that the council removed the teaching of reincarnation from the Bible. [2] And of course, Jehovah's Witnesses and critics of the deity of Christ likewise point to that council as the "beginning of the Trinity" or the "first time the deity of Christ was asserted as orthodox teaching." Others see it as the beginning of the union of church and state in light of the participation of the Roman Emperor, Constantine. Some even say it was the beginning of the Roman Catholic church.

THE BACKGROUND

Excepting the apostolic council in Jerusalem recorded in Acts 15, the Council of Nicea stands above other early councils of the church as far as its scope and its focus. Luther called it "the most sacred of all councils." [3] When it began on June 19, 325, the fires of persecution had barely cooled. The Roman Empire had been unsuccessful in its attempt to wipe out the Christian faith. Fourteen years had elapsed since the final persecutions under the Emperor Galerius had ended. Many of the men who made up the Council of Nicea bore in their bodies the scars of persecution. They had been willing to suffer for the name of Christ. The council was called by the Emperor Constantine.

Leading bishops in the church agreed to participate, so serious was the matter at hand.

Bishops? "Church"? Why is it that, invariably, when a "low church" Baptist like White, who believes in congregational Church government (the furthest thing from episcopacy and hierarchy, let alone apostolic succession and authoritative tradition), and only in "bishops" insofar as a *local elder* is the equivalent of one – starts talking about the early Church, all of a sudden he casually tosses out words like "bishop" and "church" (in the sense of one unified body)?

Moreover (here is the main point), he does so matter-of-factly, with none of the disdain and derision and palpable animus that characterizes treatments of the same entity among current-day Christians.

Apparently, there was such a thing as "*the* Church" in this period, but somewhere along the line (Protestants differ as to *when*) it disappeared. But one Christian communion continues to hold ecumenical councils and to have bishops and an institutional sense of what the Church is, precisely like the Councils of Jerusalem and Nicaea: strangely enough, the same one that James White reads out of Christianity altogether. How incredibly odd and ironic that is.

To understand why the first universal council was called, we must go back to around A.D. 318. In the populous Alexandria suburb of Baucalis, a well-liked presbyter by the name of Arius began teaching in opposition to the bishop of Alexandria, Alexander. Specifically, he disagreed with Alexander's teaching that Jesus, the Son of God, had existed eternally, being "generated" eternally by the Father. Instead, Arius insisted that "there was a time when the Son was not." Christ must be numbered among the created beings — highly exalted, to be sure, but a creation, nonetheless.

Very similarly to the present-day heresy of Jehovah's Witnesses, The Way International, and the Christadelphians . . .

Alexander defended his position, and it was not long before Arius was declared a heretic in a local council in 321. This did not end the matter. Arius simply moved to Palestine and began promoting his ideas there. Alexander wrote letters to the churches in the area, warning them against those he called the "Exukontians," from a Greek phrase meaning "out of nothing." Arius taught that the Son of God was created "out of nothing." Arius found an audience for his teachings, and over the course of the next few years the debate became so heated that it came to the attention of Constantine, the Emperor. Having consolidated his hold on the Empire, Constantine promoted unity in every way possible. He recognized that a schism in the Christian church would be just one more destabilizing factor in his empire, and he moved to solve the problem. [4] While he had encouragement from men like Hosius, bishop of Cordova, and Eusebius of Caesarea, Constantine was the one who officially called for the council. [5]

White is clearly trying to avoid anti-Catholic polemics and rhetoric here (because he was writing for a periodical that is *not* anti-Catholic, begun by Walter Martin: the Protestant cult-fighter -- whom I had the pleasure to meet -- who did not consider Catholicism one of the heretical cults). To understand his own thought that lies behind these casual statements, one would have to note, for example, what he wrote on his private *sola Scriptura* discussion list (where I was an invited member), less than a year before he wrote this article (on 7-15-96):

> I simply encourage everyone on the list to read any decent modern *historical* source, Roman Catholic or Protestant, on the subject of Nicea and the role of the bishop of Rome. The idea that the council was called by, presided over by (through representatives), or was merely conditional until ratified by, the bishop of Rome as the head of the church, is a-historical, untenable, and to my knowledge, not promoted by any serious historian in our age. Oh yes, there are many Roman Catholics who, *for solely theological reasons*, might promote this idea, but it

is anachronism in its finest form, and shows to what length people will go to maintain a tradition.

All agree that Constantine called the council. But that's not the same as a denial that the pope and his legates were central figures in the authority structure. Note that White claims that no "decent" historian "Roman Catholic or Protestant" would argue otherwise. White himself concedes later in his article that Constantine did not preside over the council, in terms of setting the agenda for the theology and proclamations:

What really was Constantine's role? Often it is alleged (especially by Jehovah's Witnesses, for example) that, for whatever reasons, Constantine forced the "same substance" view upon the council, [10] or, at the very least, insured that it would be adopted. This is not the case. There is no question that Constantine wanted a unified church after the Council of Nicea. But he was no theologian, nor did he really care to any degree what basis would be used to forge the unity he desired. Later events show that he didn't have any particular stake in the term homoousios *and was willing to abandon it, if he saw that doing so would be of benefit to him. As Schaff rightly points out with reference to the term itself, "The word...was not an invention of the council of Nicea, still less of Constantine, but had previously arisen in theological language, and occurs even in Origen [185-254] and among the Gnostics...." [11] Constantine is not the source or origin of the term, and the council did not adopt the term at his command.*

With regard to the dynamics of the ecclesiastical authority exercised at Nicaea, the key to understanding lies in White's own subtle phrase, "encouragement from men like Hosius." Hosius (also known as Ossius: c. 257-357) had, in fact, close ties to Pope Sylvester (r. 314-355). If Hosius played a central role in convincing the emperor to convene the council, then indeed, the pope was a key player, and persuaded Constantine to make possible what he wanted to bring about. We don't know much about Pope Sylvester (or, "Silvester"), but what we do know is perfectly consistent with a Catholic conception of papal authority. Warren Carroll observed:

> The recommendation for a general or *ecumenical* council . . . had probably already been made to Constantine by Ossius, and most probably to Pope Silvester as well (9). . . Ossius presided over its deliberations; he probably, and two priests of Rome certainly, came as representatives of the Pope. (10)
>
> (*The Building of Christendom*, Christendom College Press, 1987, 11)

Dr. Carroll, in his footnotes 9 and 10 on pages 33-34, provides very fascinating additional historical insight:

> 9. Victor C. De Clercq, *Ossius of Cordoba* (Washington, 1954), pp. 218-226; Charles J. Hefele, *A History of the Councils of the Church*, ed. William R. Clark (Edinburgh, 1894), I, pp. 269-270.
>
> De Clercq thinks that Ossius had already recommended the council to Constantine before the synod of Antioch [March or April 325], which merely joined in the prior recommendation; in view of the close relationship between Ossius and Constantine . . ., this would seem probable . . .
>
> That Pope Silvester I was informed from the first about plans for the Council of Nicaea there is no good reason to doubt, . . .
>
> We know that later, at the 6th Ecumenical Council in Constantinople (680), it was stated as accepted fact - though very much against the interest of the partisans of the episcopate of Constantinople, where the Council was held, who sought to build up their see as a rival to Rome - that "Arius arose as an adversary to the doctrine of the

Trinity, and Constantine and Silvester immediately assembled the great Synod of Nicaea" (Hefele, loc. Cit.) . . .

Constantine's personal role in the calling of the Council of Nicaea does not, from the available evidence, seem to be any greater than the personal role of Emperor Charles V in convening the earlier sessions of the Council of Trent . . .

10. De Clercq, *Ossius*, pp. 228-250; Hefele, *Councils*, I, 36-41; Timothy D. Barnes, *Constantine and Eusebius* (Cambridge, MA, 1981), pp. 214-215. De Clercq's arguments on this often controverted point are powerfully convincing; his conclusion, that Ossius' representing Pope Silvester at Nicaea is only a 'possibility,' is too modest or too cautious or both. The whole history of the calling of the Council of Nicaea, and the whole history of the Church in the empire for the preceding decade, suggest that Pope Silvester would have designated Ossius for this role. At the Ecumenical Council of Ephesus a century later, Bishop Cyril of Alexandria presided and signed the acts of the Council first, without reference to his role as chief representative of the Pope, and his signature was immediately followed by those of two bishops and a priest specifically designated as representing the Pope - just as in the acts of the Council of Nicaea, Ossius signed first as presiding officer without reference to his representing the Pope, followed by two priests identified as the Pope's legates. The two situations are exactly parallel; yet in the case of the Council of Ephesus we know for a fact that Cyril of Alexandria had been designated the Pope's representative. The whole creates a strong presumption that the same was true of Ossius at Nicaea.

The *Encyclopedia Britannica* (1985 edition), informs us ("Hosius," vol. 6, p. 77):

Prompted by Hosius, Constantine then summoned the first ecumenical Council of Nicaea (325) . . .

Likewise, *The Oxford Dictionary of the Christian Church* (edited by F. L. Cross, 2nd edition, Oxford University Press, 1983, 668), a very reputable non-Catholic reference, largely concurs:

. . . from 313 to the Council of Nicaea [Hosius] seems to have acted as ecclesiastical adviser to the Emperor Constantine . . . it was apparently in consequence of his report that the Emperor summoned the Nicene Council. There are some grounds for believing that here he presided, and also introduced the *Homoousion*.

Catholic apologist David Palm added in a letter of 7-16-97:

Here is a quotation from Gelasius [of Cyzicus] the Eastern priest-historian writing about A.D. 475, stating explicitly that Hosius the bishop of Cordova was in effect a papal legate at the council of Nicea. So much for the notion that the popes did not preside at the earliest councils. The translation is mine; it's fairly literal but functional, I hope:

Hosius himself, the famous Beacon of the Spaniards, held the place of Sylvester, bishop of great Rome, along with the Roman presbyters Vito and Vincent, as they held council with the many [bishops].

(*Patrologia Graece* 85:1229)

Furthermore, *This Rock* magazine (p. 27, June 1997), offers the following information:

The Graeco-Russian liturgy, in the office for Pope Silvester, speaks of him as actual head of the Council of Nicaea:

> Thou hast shown thyself the supreme one of the Sacred Council, O initiator into the sacred mysteries, and hast illustrated the Throne of the Supreme One of the Disciples.

(From Luke Rivington, *The Primitive Church and the See of Peter*, London: Longmans, Green, 1894, p. 164)

The late Dr. Warren Carroll replied to a critical post by an Orthodox participant on my discussion list, on 8-19-97:

> It is true, and I state, that there is no specific evidence that Ossius was specifically designated as a papal representative at Nicaea. But I maintain that it is highly probable, for the reasons given. Ossius may very well have been--in fact, I would say that he probably was-- suggested or even "nominated" as president of the Council by Emperor Constantine, who obviously had complete confidence in him. But since the Pope sent two men to represent him at the Council, it seems unreasonable to me that he would not have confirmed the presiding officer if he were not to designate one of his representatives for that position.
> 　The records of the Council make it clear that Ossius, not Constantine, presided (Eusebius' vague reference to "several presidents" cannot stand against the records of the Council itself). Constantine was present and did intervene; he promised the Council of Nicaea his support and protection, which he gave it; it might well not have been held but for him. But the presence of papal representatives, specifically designated as such, means it must have had at least the Pope's approval, otherwise he would not have sent them. All the successful ecumenical councils of the first six centuries of the Church required

the cooperation of both Pope and Emperor, and we know that all the others had that. Only for Nicaea, because of our dearth of information about Pope Silvester, is there room for doubt about the Pope's role.

More evidence can be brought to bear along these lines. Protestant historian Philip Schaff writes:

> . . . from Rome the two presbyters Victor or Vitus and Vincentius as delegates of the aged pope Sylvester I . . . Of the Eastern bishops, Eusebius of Caesarea, and of the Western, Hosius, or Osius, of Cordova,1325 had the greatest influence with the emperor. These two probably sat by his side, and presided in the deliberations alternately with the bishops of Alexandria and Antioch. . . . Then Hosius of Cordova appeared and announced that a confession was prepared which would now be read by the deacon (afterwards bishop) Hermogenes of Caesarea, the secretary of the synod. It is in substance the well-known Nicene creed with some additions and omissions of which we are to speak below. It is somewhat abrupt; the council not caring to do more than meet the immediate exigency. The direct concern was only to establish the doctrine of the true deity of the Son. . . . Almost all the bishops subscribed the creed, Hosius at the head, and next him the two Roman presbyters in the name of their bishop. This is the first instance of such signing of a document in the Christian church.

> (*History of the Christian Church*, Vol. III: *Nicene and Post-Nicene Christianity*, Grand Rapids, MI: Eerdmans, 5th revised edition, 1910, Chapter IX, § 120. The Council of Nicaea, 325, 624, 627-629)

We know the sort of attitude that Ossius of Cordova had towards the meddling of emperors in the Church and theology, from the evidence of his "protest" letter (the only writing of his that is known to exist) to Constantius II: Roman emperor from 337-361:

> You have no right to meddle in religious affairs. God has given you authority over the Empire, But He has given us authority over the Church. In matters of faith it is you who must listen to our instructions.

> (in Henri Daniel-Rops, *The Church of Apostles and Martyrs*, translated by Audrey Butler, London: J. M. Dent & Sons, 1960, 558)

> Cease, I entreat you, and remember that you are a mortal. Fear the day of judgment and keep yourself pure against it. . . . as he who would steal the government from you opposes the ordinance of God, even so do you fear lest by taking upon yourself the conduct of the Church, you make yourself guilty of a grave sin. It is written, "Render unto Caesar the things that are Caesar's and unto God the things that are God's." Therefore it is not permitted to us to bear rule on earth nor have you the right to burn incense. I write this out of anxiety for your salvation.

> (from James Shotwell and Louise Loomis, *The See of Peter*, New York: Columbia University Press, 1927, 578; cited in Roland H. Bainton, *Early Christianity*, New York: D. Van Nostrand Co., 1960, 168-169)

It doesn't require any great stretch of logic or imagination, then, to hold (albeit speculatively) that Ossius was presiding solely or primarily over the Council of Nicea, in the actual theological discussion, with the two Roman legates of the Pope, as opposed to Constantine doing so (unless Ossius had a radical change of mind or suffered from a split personality). Daniel-Rops believes that Constantine's "ecclesiastical counsellors, Ossius in particular and the prelates of Antioch . . . persuaded him to convene a plenary council of Christendom . . ." (*ibid.*, p. 468)

Ossius had presided at the Synod of Antioch the year before (324), when Arius was condemned, and was also a leader at the important Council of Elvira in Spain (306). He also presided over the orthodox Council of Sardica (343, in modern-day Sofia, Bulgaria), which vindicated St. Athanasius, among other things, and gave "the first legal recognition of the bishop of Rome's jurisdiction over the other sees and was, therefore, the basis for further development of his primacy as pope" (*Encyclopaedia Britannica*, 1985, Vol. X, 450, "Sardica, Council of").

Historian Michael Grant of Cambridge and Edinburgh University gives some indication of the prominence of Ossius at the Council of Nicaea:

> It is not certain who was selected as chairman of the Council -- probably several persons in turn, including Ossius, were appointed to preside over its meetings. . . . On somebody's advice -- probably that of Ossius once again -- Constantine decided to pronounce that Jesus was *homoousios* with God, 'of one substance'.
>
> (*Constantine the Great*, New York: Charles Scribner's Sons, 1993, 172-173)

Catholic historian Philip Hughes gives further evidence of Ossius' prominence:

> Who it was that proposed to the council this precise word [*homoousios*], we do not know. An Arian historian says it was the bishop of Alexandria and Hosius of Cordova. St. Athanasius, who was present at the council, says it was Hosius.
>
> (*The Church in Crisis: A History of the General Councils: 325-1870*, Garden City, New York: Doubleday / Hanover House, 1961, 33)

Another Catholic historian, John L. Murphy, adds, regarding the pope:

> The Roman Pontiff, Sylvester I, was apparently not consulted before Constantine acted, but he ratified the move by sending two legates to the gathering, the Roman priests Victor and Vincentius. It was in this way that the "head" of the college of bishops convoked the meeting -- what the authors refer to as the "formal convocation."

> (*The General Councils of the Church*, Milwaukee: The Bruce Publishing Company, 1960, 28)

Nicea did not come up with something "new" in the creed. Belief in the deity of Christ was as old as the apostles themselves, who enunciated this truth over and over again. [14] References to the full deity of Christ are abundant in the period prior to the Council of Nicea. Ignatius (died c. 108), the great martyr bishop of Antioch, could easily speak of Jesus Christ as God at the opening of the second century. More than once Ignatius speaks of Jesus Christ as "our God." [15] When writing to Polycarp he can exhort him to "await Him that is above every season, the Eternal, the Invisible, (who for our sake became visible!), the Impalpable, the Impassible, (who for our sake suffered!), who in all ways endured for our sake." [16] Ignatius shows the highest view of Christ at a very early stage, when he writes to the Ephesians: "There is only one physician, of flesh and of spirit, generate and ingenerate, God in man, true Life in death, Son of Mary and Son of God, first passible and then impassible, Jesus Christ our Lord." [17] Melito of Sardis (c. 170-180), a much less well-known figure, was tremendously gifted in expressing the ancient faith of the church regarding the deity of Christ:

> And so he was lifted up upon a tree and an inscription was provided too, to indicate who was being killed. Who was it? It is a heavy thing to say, and a most fearful thing to refrain from saying. But listen, as you tremble in the face of him on whose account the earth trembled. He who

299

hung the earth in place is hanged. He who fixed the heavens in place is fixed in place. He who made all things fast is made fast on the tree. The Master is insulted. God is murdered. The King of Israel is destroyed by an Israelite hand. [18]

This is all true. White likes and accepts development of doctrine when he agrees with its theological result. But he inconsistently frowns upon it when it doesn't come out his Baptist anti-Catholic way, and expresses a fuller Catholic concept. We shall see how he applies this double standard in dealing with the papacy, in relation to the same council and statements of various Church Fathers prior to 325.

Nicea was not creating some new doctrine, some new belief, but clearly, explicitly, defining *truth against error.*

Yes; that is exactly what Catholics believe about development of doctrine.

The council had no idea that they, by their gathering together, possessed some kind of sacramental power of defining beliefs: they sought to clarify biblical truth, not to put themselves in the forefront and make themselves a second source of authority.

Now this is where White starts to become inaccurate, by anachronistically superimposing his *sola Scriptura* rule of faith onto the ancient Church, when it doesn't fit at all. He mentioned the council of Jerusalem early in his article. This was the biblical model for Church councils. And this council had absolute authority over Christians. It announced a decree, not simply on the basis of a democratic vote, but grounded in supernatural guidance of the Holy Spirit (in effect, infallibility):

> For *it has seemed good to the Holy Spirit and to us* to lay upon you no greater burden than these necessary things: that you abstain from what has been sacrificed to idols and from blood and from what is strangled and from

300

unchastity. If you keep yourselves from these, you will do well. Farewell. (Acts 15:28-29)

The Apostle Paul then went out and delivered this binding teaching:

As they went on their way through the cities, they *delivered to them for observance* the *decisions* which had been reached by the *apostles and elders* who were at Jerusalem. (Acts 16:4)

This is not *sola Scriptura*. It is as far from that as it gets. This is binding Church authority, derived from an authoritative council. There is no reason to believe (though we don't have a lot of documentation) that the Council of Nicaea regarded itself as any less binding. Indeed, White accepts the Nicene Creed that came from it, and grants it a high authority. He does this because he makes a prior (correct) judgment that it is in line with *Holy Scripture*, but he does it nonetheless.

Even here, however, White doesn't fully accept the Nicene Creed, because it contains the line, "I acknowledge one Baptism *for the remission of sins*," and as a Baptist, White rejects sacramental baptism altogether, as well as the baptismal regeneration "remission of sins") that is taught in the Nicene Creed, and indeed held virtually universally in the ancient Church.

The twenty canons of the council, as translated in the Schaff-Wace edition of the Church Fathers, exhibits this authority in many places:

Canon Three: "The Great Synod has stringently forbidden . . ."

Canon Six: ". . . if any one be made bishop without the consent of the Metropolitan, the Great Synod has declared that such a man ought not to be a bishop."

Canon Fourteen: ". . . the Holy and Great Synod has decreed . . ."

Mr. White apparently thinks that ecumenical councils were the equivalent of modern-day gatherings of evangelical theological societies: people shoot the breeze, present papers, influence each other, and the latest fashionable theological ideas and denominational traditions are bandied about, but this is only to "clarify" and is not "authority." Nothing is binding; only the Bible is that (but interpreted by *whom*, of course, is always the dilemma).

Actual Protestant historians, on the other hand, present a vastly different conception of ecumenical councils such as Nicaea. For example, Philip Schaff (note what the great St. Athanasius himself states about Nicaea):

> The synodical system in general had its rise in the apostolic council at Jerusalem, . . . The *jurisdiction* of the ecumenical councils covered the entire legislation of the church, all matters of Christian faith and practice (*fidei et morum*), and all matters of organization arid worship. The doctrinal decrees were called *dogmata* or *symbola*; the disciplinary, *canones*. At the same time, the councils exercised, when occasion required, the highest judicial authority, in excommunicating bishops and patriarchs. The *authority* of these councils in the decision of all points of controversy was supreme and final. Their doctrinal decisions were early invested with infallibility; the promises of the Lord respecting the indestructibleness of his church, his own perpetual presence with the ministry, and the guidance of the Spirit of truth, being applied in the full sense to those councils, as representing the whole church. After the example of the apostolic council, the usual formula for a decree was: *Visum est Sprirtui Sancto et nobis*. Constantine the Great, in a circular letter to the churches, styles the decrees of the Nicene council a *divine* command; a phrase, however, in reference to which the abuse of the word *divine*, in the language of the Byzantine despots, must not be forgotten. Athanasius says, with reference to the doctrine of the divinity of Christ: "What God has spoken by the council

of Nice, abides forever." [Schaff cites Isidore and Basil the Great similarly, in this footnote] The council of Chalcedon pronounced the decrees of the Nicene fathers unalterable statutes, since God himself had spoken through them. The council of Ephesus, in the sentence of deposition against Nestorius, uses the formula: "The Lord Jesus Christ, whom he has blasphemed, determines through this most holy council." Pope Leo speaks of an "*irretractabilis* consensus" of the council of Chalcedon upon the doctrine of the person of Christ. Pope Gregory the Great even placed the first four councils, which refuted and destroyed respectively the heresies and impieties of Arius, Macedonius, Nestorius, and Eutyches, on a level with the four canonical Gospels. In like manner Justinian puts the dogmas of the first four councils on the same footing with the Holy Scriptures, and their canons by the side of laws of the realm.

(*Ibid.*, Chapter V: The Hierarchy and Polity of the Church, *§ 65. The Synodical System. The Ecumenical Councils*, 331, 340-342)

Many more such appraisals of the authority of ecumenical councils could easily be brought forth, no doubt. But I won't belabor the point, because it is so evident. White even contends that the bishops assembled in Nicaea had "no idea" that they were there to authoritatively define and decree theological beliefs and dogmas. This is astonishing, breathtaking historical anachronism and revisionism. It simply flows from White's Anabaptist biases.

This can easily be seen from the fact that Athanasius, in defending the Nicene council, does so on the basis of its harmony with Scripture, not on the basis of the council having some inherent authority in and of itself.

But no one is saying that the council has to be pitted against Scripture! That's merely typically Protestant dichotomous reasoning. Councils are in harmony with Scripture, but they still have authority to make binding decrees. In other words, to defend a council on the basis that it agrees with Scripture, is not to deny its authority.

Note his words: "Vainly then do they run about with the pretext that they have demanded Councils for the faith's sake; for divine Scripture is sufficient above all things; but if a Council be needed on the point, there are the proceedings of the Fathers, for the Nicene Bishops did not neglect this matter, but stated the doctrines so exactly, that persons reading their words honestly, cannot but be reminded by them of the religion towards Christ announced in divine Scripture." [19]

Amen. But how does this *change* anything? *Of course* St. Athanasius thought the council was in accord with Scripture. What does White think he would have done: think it was more harmonious with the sayings of Confucius or the Buddha? White is citing St. Athanasius' work, *De Synodis* (available online), from section 6. But Athanasius was no Baptist believer in *sola Scriptura* (a thing that was invented out of expedience in the 16th century). Why don't we look at some *other* things that the great saint says in the same work, that don't quite fit into White's picture of Church authority. It's easy to pick out where someone extolls Holy Scripture. But if references to tradition, the Church, and apostolic succession are ignored, a false, inaccurate, incomplete picture is formed. St. Athanasius *also* writes in the same treatise (my italics):

> 3. What defect of teaching was there for *religious truth in the Catholic Church*, . . .

> 5. . . . about the faith they wrote not, 'It seemed good,' but, *'Thus believes the Catholic Church;'* and thereupon they confessed how they believed, in order to show that their own sentiments were not novel, but *Apostolical*; and what they wrote down was no discovery of theirs, but is *the same as was taught by the Apostles.* . . .

7. Having therefore no reason on their side [referring now to the Arian heretics] , but being in difficulty whichever way they turn, in spite of their pretences, they have nothing left but to say; 'Forasmuch as **we** *contradict our predecessors, and transgress the traditions of the Fathers*, therefore we have thought good that a Council should meet; but again, whereas we fear lest, should it meet at one place, our pains will be thrown away, therefore we have thought good that it be divided into two; that so when we put forth our documents to these separate portions, we may overreach with more effect, with the threat of Constantius the patron of this irreligion, and may supersede the acts of Nicaea, under pretence of the simplicity of our own documents.' . . .

10. Copy of an Epistle from the Council to Constantius Augustus.

> We believe that what was formerly decreed was *brought about both by God's command* and by order of your piety. For we the bishops, from all the Western cities, assembled together at Ariminum, both that *the Faith of the Catholic Church* might be made known, and that gainsayers might be detected. For, as we have found after long deliberation, it appeared desirable to adhere to and maintain to the end, *that faith which, enduring from antiquity, we have received as preached by the prophets, the Gospels, and the Apostles* through our Lord Jesus Christ, Who is Keeper of your Kingdom and Patron of your power. . . .

54. This is why the Nicene Council was correct in writing, what it was becoming to say, that the Son, begotten from the Father's essence, is coessential with Him. And if we too have been taught the same thing, let us not fight with

shadows, especially as knowing, that they who have so defined, have made this confession of faith, not to misrepresent the truth, but as vindicating the truth and religiousness towards Christ, and also as destroying the blasphemies against Him of the Ario-maniacs. For this must be considered and noted carefully, that, in using unlike-in-essence, and other-in-essence, we signify not the true Son, but some one of the creatures, and an introduced and adopted Son, which pleases the heretics; but when we speak uncontroversially of the Coessential, we signify a genuine Son born of the Father; though at this Christ's enemies often burst with rage. What then I have learned myself, and have heard men of judgment say, I have written in few words; but do you, *remaining on the foundation of the Apostles, and holding fast the traditions of the Fathers*, pray that now at length all strife and rivalry may cease, and the futile questions of the heretics may be condemned, and all logomachy; and the guilty and murderous heresy of the Arians may disappear, and the truth may shine again in the hearts of all, so that all every where may 'say the same thing' (1 Cor. i. 10), and think the same thing, and that, no Arian contumelies remaining, it may be said and confessed in every Church, 'One Lord, one faith, one baptism' (Eph. iv. 5), in Christ Jesus our Lord, through whom to the Father be the glory and the strength, unto ages of ages. Amen.

St. Athanasius makes a number of statements that do not blend very well at all with some supposed, mythical adherence to *sola Scriptura*:

But, beyond these sayings, let us look at *the very tradition, teaching, and faith of the Catholic Church from the beginning, which the Lord gave, the Apostles preached and the Fathers kept.*

(To Serapion of Thmuis 1:28)

However here too they introduce their private fictions, and contend that the Son and the Father are not in such wise "one," or "like," *as the Church preaches*, but, as they themselves would have it.

(*Discourse Against the Arians*, III, 3:10)

. . . inventors of unlawful heresies, *who indeed refer to the Scriptures, but do not hold such opinions as the saints have handed down*, and receiving them as the traditions of men, err, . . .

(*Festal Letter* 2:6)

See, we are proving that this view has been *transmitted from father to father*; but ye, O modern Jews and disciples of Caiaphas, *how many fathers can ye assign to your phrases*?

(*Defense of the Nicene Definition*, 27)

For, *what our Fathers have delivered*, this is truly doctrine;   .   .   .

(*De Decretis* 4)

Hence, Protestant patristics scholar J. N. D. Kelly summarizes Athanasius' exceedingly un-Baptist, un-evangelical outlook on authority:

So Athanasius, disputing with the Arians , claimed [*De decret. Nic. syn.* 27] that his own doctrine had been handed down from father to father, whereas they could not produce a single respectable witness to theirs . . . the ancient idea that the Church alone, in virtue of being the home of the Spirit and having preserved the authentic apostolic testimony in her rule of faith, liturgical action and general witness, possesses the indispensable key to

Scripture, continued to operate as powerfully as in the days of Irenaeus and Tertullian . . . Athanasius himself, after dwelling on the entire adequacy of Scripture, went on to emphasize [*C. gent.* I] the desirability of having sound teachers to expound it. Against the Arians he flung the charge [*C. Ar.* 3, 58] that they would never have made shipwreck of the faith had they held fast as a sheet-anchor to the . . . Church's peculiar and traditionally handed down grasp of the purport of revelation.

(*Early Christian Doctrines*, San Francisco: HarperCollins, fifth revised edition, 1978, 45, 47)

The relationship between the sufficient Scriptures and the "Nicene Bishops" should be noted carefully. The Scriptures are not made insufficient by the council;

No one is saying it is. Catholics believe in material sufficiency of Scripture, just not *sola Scriptura*. They are two vastly different things.

rather, the words of the council "remind" one of the "religion towards Christ announced in divine Scripture." Obviously, then, the authority of the council is derivative from its fidelity to Scripture.

The authority comes from the fact that it is assembled bishops in agreement with the pope, who agree with the Scripture because they are guided by the Holy Spirit. It doesn't follow that their authority is thereby lessened. The authority was binding. White cannot accept that because, for him, the individual always reigns supreme, and judges councils and popes and received traditions based on private judgment and individualistic sectarianism and innovative, corrupt denominational traditions. He merely substitutes one tradition (the true, received, apostolic one) for another (private traditions of men, which may or may not be true), and therefore, sometimes he departs from the consensus of apostolic succession (using the same principle that the Arians used with regard to the doctrine of Christ). In other words, *sola Scriptura* was the heretical, Arian rule of faith, whereas the Catholic rule held by Athanasius and other orthodox fathers, was apostolic succession and the three-legged stool of Church-Scripture-Tradition.

CANON #6

While the creed of the council was its central achievement, it was not the only thing that the bishops accomplished during their meeting. Twenty canons were presented dealing with various disciplinary issues within the church. Of most interest to us today was the sixth, which read as follows:

> Let the ancient customs in Egypt, Libya, and Pentapolis prevail, that the Bishop of Alexandria have jurisdiction in all these, since the like is customary for the Bishop of Rome also. Likewise in Antioch and the other provinces, let the Churches retain their privileges. [20]

This canon is significant because it demonstrates that at this time there was no concept of a single universal head of the church with jurisdiction over everyone else. While later Roman bishops would claim such authority, resulting in the development of the papacy, at this time no Christian looked to one individual, or church, as the final authority. This is important because often we hear it alleged that the Trinity, or the Nicene definition of the deity of Christ, is a "Roman Catholic" concept "forced" on the church by the pope. The simple fact of the matter is, when the bishops gathered at Nicea they did not acknowledge the bishop of Rome as anything more than the leader of the most influential church in the West. [21]

The essential silliness of this claim will become apparent, with just a little reflection. White expects the papacy to be full-blown and developed at this fairly early stage in 325. If it isn't, he'll reject it on that basis (along with supposed lack of biblical evidence). Yet he won't apply the same standard to *other*

309

doctrines that he himself believes in. The most obvious of these is *the Two Natures of Christ*. The full development of that had to wait for another 126 years: until the *Council of Chalcedon in 451*; famously led by Pope St. Leo the Great. So if *Christology* itself was not yet fully formulated, why does White demand that the *papacy* has to be?

A related example is the *divinity or deity or Godhood of the Holy Spirit*. This is trinitarian theology: central to all of Christian doctrine. Yet this was not even *discussed* at Nicaea. The council basically stated only that it "believed in the Holy Spirit." The full divinity of the Holy Spirit was only explicitly stated 56 years later: at the Ecumenical *Council of Constantinople in 381*, over against the Macedonian heresy.

Thirdly, there is the *canon of Holy Scripture* itself, which was not to be formulated in its lasting form until 393 (68 years later). The first list of the New Testament books as we have them today was from Athanasius in the year 367. At the time of the Council of Nicaea, James, 2 Peter, 2 and 3 John, and Jude were still being disputed. James was not even *quoted* in the west until around 350! Hebrews was still being questioned in the west and was slow to gain acceptance as canonical, as was Jude. Sts. Cyril of Jerusalem, John Chrysostom, and Gregory Nazianzen questioned the canonicity of Revelation.

Moreover, the Epistle of Barnabas and Shepherd of Hermas were regarded as biblical books in the famous Codex Sinaiticus of the late fourth century. Lastly, when the *Councils of Hippo (393) and Carthage (397)* decreed the canon of Scripture, this included the deuterocanonical books, or so-called "Apocrypha" that James White does not accept. That was only changed in the 16th century among Protestants.

Fourthly, John Henry Cardinal Newman has pointed out that the doctrine of *purgatory* (which James White rejects) has far more evidence in its favor in patristic writings than *original sin*, in this relatively early period.

Furthermore, a mere 18 years later, at the Council of Sardica in 343 (presided over by Hosius / Ossius), papal primacy was explicitly asserted, in canons 3-5, and 9.

More explicit recognitions of papal primacy and supremacy in both east and west explode in the fourth century. They didn't come out of nowhere. They were consistent developments of what came before, in less developed form.

Modern Christians often have the impression that ancient councils held absolute sway, and when they made "the decision," the controversy ended. This is not true. Though Nicea is seen as one of the greatest of the councils, it had to fight hard for acceptance. The basis of its final victory was not the power of politics, nor the endorsement of established religion. There was one reason the Nicene definition prevailed: its fidelity to the testimony of the Scriptures.

One must differentiate (as Athanasius and the fathers did) between true authority and the ever-present obstinacy of heretics and schismatics to spurn such authority. Folks can always refuse to accept Church teaching. The heretical Arians did with regard to Nicaea. But that didn't prove that the council lacked authority: only that they lacked obedience and a Catholic principle of authority.

The Arians followed a *sola Scriptura* method, divorced from the precedence of received tradition. And so they were led astray. And so it has always been" when the heretics separated biblical interpretation from authoritative teaching of the Church, they strayed into false doctrine. Hence St. Irenaeus constantly appeals to tradition and apostolic succession, over against *merely* citing the Scriptures, as the heretics were wont to do (my italics):

> When, however, they are confuted from the Scriptures, they turn round and accuse these same Scriptures, as if they were not correct, nor of authority, and [assert] that they are ambiguous, and that the truth cannot be extracted from them by those who are ignorant of tradition . . .

> It comes to this, therefore, that *these men do now consent neither to Scripture or tradition.*

. . . But, again, when we refer them to *that tradition which originates from the apostles*, [and] which is *preserved* by means of the successions of presbyters *in the Churches*, they *object to tradition*, saying *they themselves are wiser*.

. . . Suppose there arise a dispute relative to some important question among us, should we not have *recourse to the most ancient Churches with which the apostles held constant intercourse*, and learn from them *what is certain and clear* in regard to the present question? For how should it be if the apostles themselves had not left us writings? Would it not be necessary, [in that case,] to *follow the course of the tradition which they handed down* to those to whom they did commit the Churches?

(*Against Heresies* 3, 2:1 / 3, 2:2 / 3, 4:1)

But as I noted above, White doesn't believe that Nicaea was totally faithful to the "testimony of the Scriptures," because he rejects the *baptismal regeneration* that was plainly taught in the Nicene Creed. he doesn't care that this was held only by heretics in the early Church. In *that* respect, he is very much like the Arians who can't produce the evidence of tradition passed down for their false beliefs, and so pretend that Scripture supports them.

Yet, in the midst of this darkness, a lone voice remained strong. Arguing from Scripture, fearlessly reproaching error, writing from refuge in the desert, along the Nile, or in the crowded suburbs around Alexandria, Athanasius continued the fight. His unwillingness to give place — even when banished by the Emperor,

We have seen that he didn't argue from Scripture Alone. He was a Catholic, who accepted the binding, infallible nature of an authoritative Church, tradition, and apostolic succession, as the true interpreters of the truths of Scripture. He wasn't a "lone voice" at all. As Schaff noted of the post-Nicene period:

> The whole Western church was in general more steadfast on the side of Nicene orthodoxy, and honored in Athanasius a martyr of the true faith.

(*Ibid.*, vol. III, 634)

Protestant historian Roland Bainton concurs:

> The West was orthodox, but Asia Minor leaned towards Arianism.

(*Early Christianity*, New York: D. Van Nostrand Co., 1960, 69)

The east had a host of heretical patriarchs, while no pope was ever an Arian or even a semi-Arian. White tries to make out that Pope Liberius fell into heresy: "Even Liberius, bishop of Rome, having been banished from his see (position as bishop) and longing to return, was persuaded to give in and compromise on the matter." To do this, he cites Philip Schaff, but on the same page cited (p. 636 of his Volume III), Schaff noted: "He died in 366 in the orthodox faith, which he had denied through weakness, but not from conviction."

There is some dispute among historians over whether Liberius caved in at all (one strong piece of evidence against the assertion being the strange silence of Emperor Constantius on the matter). The choices are basically that he caved in under pressure, or didn't at all. Patrick Madrid observed, mentioning Liberius' "two years of imprisonment, exile, and harassment" by the emperor Constantius:

> But we can't forget that he was under extreme duress, mentally and physically, and was being coerced with the threat of torture and execution if he didn't sign. . . . when forced to do something wrong through coercion and

threats of violence or death, a person isn't guilty of the deed as he would be if he had total freedom.

(*Pope Fiction*, Rancho Santa Fe, California: Basilica Press, 1999, 142-143)

disfellowshipped by the established church, and condemned by local councils and bishops alike — gave rise to the phrase, Athanasius contra mundum: *"Athanasius against the world."*

Yes; he was "disfellowshipped" by eastern bishops, but not western ones. As already noted above, he appealed to Pope Julius I (339-342), who reversed the wrong and unjust decisions of the eastern bishops, and was also vindicated by the western council of Sardica in 343. This was rather common among many of the great saints of the east; for example, a bit later in history, St. Basil the Great (371), St. John Chrysostom (404), St. Cyril of Jerusalem (430), and St. Flavian of Constantinople (449), all appealed to, and were supported or sheltered by the popes and the Latin Church. As I wrote in one paper:

> The East all too frequently treated its greatest figures much like the ancient Jews did their prophets, often expelling and exiling them, while Rome welcomed them unambiguously, and restored them to office by the authority of papal or conciliar decree. Many of these venerable saints (particularly St. John Chrysostom), and other Eastern saints such as (most notably) St. Ephraim, St. Maximus the Confessor, and St. Theodore of Studios, also explicitly affirmed papal supremacy.

So yes, Athanasius fought against a lot of heretical people, but it was basically the eastern patriarchs and rulers who opposed him, not the west or the Church of Rome, headed by the popes. He wasn't totally alone in terms of Europe; he had all of that massive support behind him. Therefore, his case can't be spun as an instance of a lone, Luther-like "*sola Scriptura* guy" with Scripture in hand against the corruption of the Catholic

314

Church. Quite the contrary . . . that is simply mythical revisionism.

Convinced that Scripture is "sufficient above all things," [25]

Of course it is; that is different from saying it is the only final authority in Christianity. I have already shown from the same work that this was cited from, how thoroughly Catholic in his views on authority Athanasius was.

Athanasius acted as a true "Protestant" in his day. [26]

Really? It is a strange Protestant who would appeal to a pope to be restored to his see. Most Protestants don't even believe in *bishops*, which is what Athanasius was appealing *about*, let alone the *papacy*, which is what he was appealing *to*. That's acting like a true "Protestant"? Hardly. Nor is his belief in the supreme authority of ecumenical councils. The fallacy is that he was using the Bible alone to fight the Arian heretics. He was not.

Like the other Church fathers, he used Scripture, tradition, Church, and apostolic succession, regarded as a cohesive unit, to oppose them. This is simply not the Protestant methodology. When Luther opposed the Church and argued in favor of doctrinal innovations, he appealed to Scripture Alone and opposed infallible councils and popes. That is exactly the *opposite* of what Athanasius. That is the true Protestant method.

Athanasius protested against the consensus opinion of the established church, . . .

Only in the east, not the west. The east was no more the whole of the "established church" then, than it is now. The Catholic Church is universal, by definition, not sectarian.

. . . and did so because he was compelled by scriptural authority.

Orthodox Christians believe in Scriptural authority, yes. I do it all the time in my apologetics. It doesn't make me anything remotely

315

like a Protestant. It was the same with Athanasius. Protestants don't "own" Holy Scripture.

Athanasius would have understood, on some of those long, lonely days of exile, what Wycliffe meant a thousand years later: "If we had a hundred popes, and if all the friars were cardinals, to the law of the gospel we should bow, more than all this multitude." [27]

Hardly, since he appealed to a pope for safety and restoration of his bishopric. It's quite amusing that White actually tries to pit Athanasius against popes (it's difficult to believe that he is ignorant of all this part of Athanasius' history), when, for example, *The Oxford Dictionary of the Christian Church* observes:

> [I]n 339 he was forced to flee to Rome, where he established close contacts with the Western Church, which continued throughout his life to support him.
>
> (p. 101, "Athanasius")

If Athanasius was on the right side, and Rome and the west supported him, then how can they be demonized, as the anti-clerical Wycliffe tries to do? They were on the side of the angels, too! And not just popes; also the bishops of the Council of Sardica in 343 . . . So all of a sudden episcopacy and hierarchy (i.e., orthodox ones, united with the pope) become very *good* things, in defense of Christian, biblical truths. But White (being a Baptist and anti-Catholic) doesn't *like* that, so he engages in historical revisionism and anachronism of the most brazen, tunnel vision sort.

Nicea's authority rested upon the solid foundation of Scripture.

That is, except when it taught baptismal regeneration, according to Mr. White . . .

The authority of the Nicene creed, including its assertion of the homoousion, is not to be found in some concept of an infallible church, but in the fidelity of the creed to scriptural revelation. It speaks with the voice of the apostles because it speaks the truth as they proclaimed it. Modern Christians can be thankful for the testimony of an Athanasius who stood for these truths even when the vast majority stood against him. We should remember his example in our day.

This is, as is abundantly clear by now, a distortion of what Athanasius believed. White shows himself abominably ignorant of basic historical facts regarding Athanasius. Philip Schaff, example, holds that Athanasius was neither a "proto-Protestant" nor a "proto-Catholic" (which is enough to profoundly differ with White's estimation):

> . . . Voight . . . makes Athanasius even the representative of the formal principle of Protestantism, the supreme authority, sufficiency, and self-interpreting character of the Scriptures; while Mohler endeavors to place him on the Roman side. Both are biassed, and violate history by their preconceptions.

(*Ibid.*, vol. III, 607)

Schaff, being a Protestant, can't bring himself to see that Athanasius was a full-fledged Catholic, but, being an honest, fair-minded, accurate historian, neither can he fudge the facts and exhibit excessive Protestant bias like White does, so as to make out that Athanasius held to "the formal principle of Protestantism." Athanasius was, in fact, thoroughly Catholic in his understanding of authority. Schaff simply is unaware of that because he (like many many Protestants, scholars or not) lacks understanding, too, of the proper nature of Catholic authority, then and now. But at least he knows the facts of what Athanasius actually *believed*, unlike Mr. White. He is simply mistaken as to whether what Athanasius believed is consistent with Catholic teaching on authority and the rule of faith. It is indeed.

317

[White's footnotes]:

1 The Council of Nicea did not take up the issue of the canon of Scripture. In fact, only regional councils touched on this issue (Hippo in 393, Carthage in 397) until much later. The New Testament canon developed in the consciousness of the church over time, just as the Old Testament canon did. See Don Kistler, ed., *Sola Scriptura: The Protestant Position on the Bible* (Morgan, PA: Soli Deo Gloria Publications, 1995).

2 See Joseph P. Gudel, Robert M. Bowman, Jr., and Dan R. Schlesinger, "Reincarnation — Did the Church Suppress It?" *Christian Research Journal,* Summer 1987, 8-12.

3 Gordon Rupp, *Luther's Progress to the Diet of Worms* (New York: Harper and Row Publishers, 1964), 66.

4 Much has been written about Constantine's religious beliefs and his "conversion" to Christianity. Some attribute to him high motives in his involvement at Nicea; others see him as merely pursuing political ends. In either case, we do not need to decide the issue of the validity of his confession of faith, for the decisions of the Nicene Council on the nature of the Son were not dictated by Constantine, and even after the Council he proved himself willing to "compromise" on the issue, all for the sake of political unity. The real battle over the deity of Christ was fought out in his shadow, to be sure, but it took place on a plane he could scarcely understand, let alone dominate.

5 Later centuries would find the idea of an ecumenical council being called by anyone but the bishop of Rome, the pope, unthinkable. Hence, long after Nicea, in A.D. 680, the story began to circulate that in fact the bishop of Rome called the Council, and even to this day some attempt to revive this historical anachronism, claiming the two presbyters (Victor and Vincentius) who represented Sylvester, the aged bishop of Rome, in fact sat as presidents over the Council. See Philip Schaff's comments in his *History of the Christian Church* (Grand Rapids: Eerdmans, 1985), 3:335.

6 Athanasius's role at the council has been hotly debated. As a deacon, he would not, by later standards, even be allowed to vote.

But his brilliance was already seen, and it would eventually fall to him to defend the decisions of the Council, which became his lifelong work.

7 The Latin translation is *consubstantialis*, consubstantial, which is the common rendering of the term in English versions of the final form of the Nicene Creed.

8 Modalism is the belief that there is one Person in the Godhead who at times acts as the Father, and other times as the Son, and still other times as the Spirit. Modalism denies the Trinity, which asserts that the three Persons have existed eternally.

9 Schaff, 3:624.

10 The only basis that can be presented for such an idea is found in a letter, written by Eusebius of Caesarea during the council itself to his home church, explaining why he eventually gave in and signed the creed, and agreed to the term *homoousios*. At one point Eusebius writes that Constantine "encouraged the others to sign it and to agree with its teaching, only with the addition of the word 'consubstantial' [i.e., *homoousios*]." The specific term used by Eusebius, *parakeleueto*, can be rendered as strongly as "command" or as mildly as "advise" or "encourage." There is nothing in Eusebius's letter, however, that would suggest that he felt he had been *ordered* to subscribe to the use of the term, nor that he felt that Constantine was the actual source of the term.

11 Schaff, 3:628.

12 Someone might say that this demonstrates the *insufficiency* of Scripture to function as the sole infallible rule of faith for the church; that is, that it denies *sola scriptura*. But *sola scriptura* does not claim the Bible is sufficient to answer every *perversion* of its own revealed truths. Peter knew that there would be those who twist the Scriptures to their own destruction, and it is good to note that God has not deemed it proper to transport all heretics off the planet at the first moment they utter their heresy. Struggling with false teaching has, in God's sovereign plan, been a part of the maturing of His people.

13 For many generations misunderstandings between East and West, complicated by the language differences (Greek remaining predominate in the East, Latin becoming the normal language of

religion in the West), kept controversy alive even when there was no need for it.

14 Titus 2:13, 2 Pet. 1:1, John 1:1-14, Col. 1:15-17, Phil. 2:5-11, etc.

15 See, for example, his epistle to the Ephesians, 18, and to the Romans, 3, in J. B. Lightfoot and J. R. Harmer, eds., *The Apostolic Fathers* (Grand Rapids: Baker Book House, 1984), 141 and 150.

16 Polycarp 3, *The Apostolic Fathers,* 161.

17 Ephesians 7, *The Apostolic Fathers,* 139.

18 Melito of Sardis, *A Homily on the Passover,* sect. 95-96, as found in Richard Norris, Jr., *The Christological Controversy* (Philadelphia: Fortress Press, 1980), 46. This homily is one of the best examples of early preaching that is solidly biblical in tone and Christ-centered in message.

19 Athanasius, *De Synodis,* 6, as found in Philip Schaff and Henry Wace, eds., *Nicene and Post Nicene Fathers*, Series II (Grand Rapids: Eerdmans, 1983), IV:453.

20 *Nicene and Post Nicene Fathers*, Series II, XIV:15.

21 For those who struggle with the idea that it was not "Roman Catholicism" that existed in those days, consider this: if one went into a church today, and discovered that the people gathered there did not believe in the papacy, did not believe in the Immaculate Conception of Mary, the Bodily Assumption of Mary, purgatory, indulgences, did not believe in the concept of transubstantiation replete with the communion host's total change in accidence and substance, and had no tabernacles on the altars in their churches, would one think he or she was in a "Roman Catholic" church? Of course not. Yet, the church of 325 had none of these beliefs, either. Hence, while they called themselves "Catholics," they would not have had any idea what "Roman Catholic" meant.

22 Ammianus Marcellinus, as cited by Schaff, *History of the Christian Church* (Grand Rapids: Eerdmans, 1985), III:632.

23 For a discussion of the lapse of Liberius, see Schaff, III:635-36. For information on the relationship of Liberius and the concept of papal infallibility, see George Salmon, *The Infallibility of the Church* (Grand Rapids: Baker Book House,

1959), 425-29, and Philip Schaff, *The Creeds of Christendom* (Grand Rapids: Baker Book House, 1985), I:176-78.

24 Jerome, *Adversus Luciferianos,* 19, Nicene and Post Nicene Fathers, Series II, 6:329.

25 Athanasius, *De Synodis*, 6, *Nicene and Post Nicene Fathers*, Series II, 4:453.

26 I credit one of my students, Michael Porter, with this phraseology.

27 Robert Vaughn, *The Life and Opinions of John de Wycliffe* (London: Holdworth and Ball, 1831), 313. See 312-17 for a summary of Wycliffe's doctrine of the sufficiency of Scripture.

28 Augustine, *To Maximim the Arian*, as cited by George Salman, *The Infallibility of the Church* (Grand Rapids: Baker Book House, 1959), 295.

Chapter Nine

Reply to Mr. White's Critique of My Book, *The One-Minute Apologist*: Regarding Deacons as the Equivalent of Pastors and Elders in Some Denominations
[16 June 2007]

Many of Armstrong's suggested objections and answers are either aimed at the most dismally ignorant of those who oppose Rome's claims (a common element of much of the literature produced by the wide spectrum of their apologists) or against people I honestly have never met or heard of. So a number of the sections really are not relevant to a serious non-Catholic reader. It is hard to decide which are which, because of some of the tremendously obvious errors Armstrong makes. For example, on page 17, Armstrong attempts to present a "Protestant" objection relating to the offices of the church:

> The Bible teaches that bishops, elders, and deacons are all synonymous terms for the same office: roughly that of a pastor today. It doesn't indicate that bishops are higher than these other offices.

Just who believes this, I wonder? I have never read any work by any Protestant theologian of any note who has ever made this argument. So, is Armstrong just ignorant of Protestant ecclesiology, or, has he run into some tiny sect someplace that has come up with some new wacky viewpoint? Given that he was once non-Catholic, it is hard to believe he could be so ignorant of the reality regarding the fact that bishop and elder refer to the same office and are used interchangeably in the New Testament, but that this office is clearly distinguished from that of the deacon. But, he does not show any knowledge of the biblical arguments in his presentation in this book . . .

This is a case of a poor choice of one word (minor point) on my part, in the midst of a perfectly valid overall argument (major point); in other words, "majoring on the minors" (something White is extremely good at doing, as a first-rate sophist and obscurantist). It is true that this was an unwise use of "deacon". If I had left out that word, the argument, coming from the hypothetical Protestant, would have been virtually identical to White's *own* ecclesiology, since we see above that he equates elder and bishop (and has done so before, notably in this quote):

> I am an elder in the church: hence, I am a bishop, overseer, pastor, of a local body of believers.

(correspondence with me: 10 January 2001)

In fact, this utterance is the reason why I have taken to often calling White "*Bishop* White." *He* said it; I am simply following his own protocol when I use the title. I believe what I had in mind was somewhat related to the thought that I have expressed in my book, *A Biblical Defense of Catholicism* (Manchester, New Hampshire: Sophia Institute Press: 2003):

> As is often the case in theology and practice among the earliest Christians, there is some fluidity and overlapping of these three vocations (for example, compare Acts 20:17 with 20:28; 1 Timothy 3:1-7 with Titus 1:5-9). But this does not prove that three offices of ministry did not exist. For instance, St. Paul often referred to himself as a deacon or minister (1 Cor. 3:5, 4:1; 2 Cor. 3:6, 6:4, 11:23; Eph. 3:7; Col. 1:23-25), yet no one would assert that he was merely a deacon, and nothing else. (p. 252)

The argument in the present context would then be that *some* Protestants (I am not implying in any of my vaguely *Summa*-like "objections" in the book that *all* Protestants would believe what is portrayed; that is rarely the case with *anything*) adopt this more fluid and primitive New Testament ecclesiology and use the terms interchangeably, whereas Catholics follow a far more developed ecclesiology. But I concede that "deacons" should not have been in this statement of the "objection" because most, if not all Protestants, *do* distinguish their office, as White pointed out. And I recognized the distinction *myself* (so much for the claims of my profound ignorance), in the same section of the above book (completed in 1996):

> Bishops are always referred to in the singular, while elders are usually mentioned plurally. The primary controversy among Christians has to do with the nature and functions of both bishops and elders (deacons have largely the same duties among both Protestants and Catholics).

I recently pointed out a basic, simplistic error in Dave Armstrong's new book: he claims Protestants (he makes no distinctions) think elders, bishops, and deacons are all one office.

This is sophistry and misrepresentation of opponents at their "finest." First of all, I never claimed that *all* Protestants believed in such a thing in the first place, and it is ridiculous to contend that I did so in this book. The standard format in every two-page section has a second portion entitled "A Protestant Might Further Object". Now, obviously, anyone who has even a fleeting acquaintance with comparative theology (and presupposing that they have an IQ higher than a box of nails) understands that this is either a generalization, or (as here) a presentation of *one strain* of Protestant belief, and how it would object to some Catholic view.

Moreover, it is quite difficult in particulars to speak of beliefs that all Protestants share. This is especially the case in the area of ecclesiology, which is what this section was about, since it is well-known that Protestants have great and serious disagreements in that area. So how would it be possible in a three-sentence hypothetical objection, to somehow represent *all* Protestant thought? It's not, and this is patently obvious. If it were not already plain, then it would be if White had troubled himself to read my Introduction, where I state:

> It should be noted here that my use of the word "Protestant" is very broad. In most cases, I have in mind traditional, conservative, or evangelical Protestants, but in a few instances, the term applies (in context) to more "progressive" strains of the spectrum, encompassing an array of belief that includes theologically liberal denominations . . . (p. xiv)

All of this being the case, much of White's derisive argumentation against me is entirely moot; irrelevant. I never claimed that Protestants *en masse* (with "no distinctions") believed such a thing. They obviously do *not*, and I know this full well, as I proved in my first reply. Therefore, my present burden is rather simple: all I have to do is show that *any* strain of Protestantism believes something along these lines.

If I can do that, White's objection utterly collapses, and he is shown to be ignorant of (at least some) fellow Protestants, which is far more scandalous than any shortcoming of knowledge he fancies that I suffer from, since he has made out that *no* Protestant sub-group believes this, or else that if anyone does, it must be a "tiny sect" with a "wacky viewpoint".

In any case, Armstrong made a mistake on the level of my saying Catholics think Cardinals and acolytes are the same office. It's just wrong. He can't blame it on a typo.

I didn't claim it was a typo, but rather (in retrospect), a poor choice of words.

He really believed that we make no distinction between the two offices despite the fact that there are two lists of qualifications for the two offices in Scripture! And this from a man who is a former Protestant. This speaks to how solid his "Protestant" credentials really were, and he knows it.

Nice try. Oh, he's trying *so* hard to decimate my reputation! But bad things happen when one sets out to do such unsavory things. What goes around comes around. You reap what you sow . . . Who is the "we" here? White is pretending that I am somehow referring to *all Protestants*. But I was not; it is simply one hypothetical objection that might come from any number of different sects of Protestantism, as explained in the Introduction. Then he foolishly tried to make out that I don't have the slightest idea of what I am talking about, and was an imbecile when I was a Protestant too! How desperate and ridiculous can he get?!

Now, the proper way to respond to the error is to say, "I'm sorry, I should have been more careful. I confess I do not know nearly as much about what Protestants believe as I pretend to." Of course, that won't do, because Armstrong considers himself an expert in Protestant beliefs.

I explained myself quite adequately in my first reply, but because White wished to press the issue, I have done so in even greater detail now, and it is only White's reputation for supposed invincibility in argument that will suffer, not mine.

You see, he may have made a "poor choice of one word" but you see, really, it's my fault anyway. Poor choice of one word? Poor choice of wording has to do with adjectives, not with completely blowing the Protestant view of the deaconate!

What "Protestant" view? I wasn't claiming to speak for *all* Protestant views; White is the only one doing that, and in so doing is merely setting himself up for a rather embarrassing fall and a serious case of log-in-the-eye deficiency.

When my point was that Armstrong's book includes misrepresentations of Protestant belief, how can a plain example of this be a "minor" point? By saying this was an "unwise" use of "deacon," would it follow that if I said "Catholics worship the

Pope" I could excuse it later by saying "that was an unwise use of the word Pope"? It is this kind of refusal to simply admit, "Okay, I was wrong," that leaves Armstrong without a shred of credibility. But it gets worse. If Armstrong would take the time to actually study the writings of those he critiques (rather than just proof-texting sources, often from secondary writings), he would know that Reformed Baptists have confessed the elder/bishop interchangeability since their inception; likewise, that we have always distinguished deacons from elders.

Here is another *non sequitur*. What makes White think I necessarily had only *Reformed Baptists* in mind in this instance? He doesn't know this; he simply assumes it. Now it is true that some of his own ludicrous statements in the past on ecclesiology probably influenced this entry of mine, but the hypothetical applies to any Protestant group who would believe something similar to what I wrote. I didn't mention Reformed Baptist or any other kind of Baptist in this hypothetical objection. In fact, I don't believe (I might be wrong) that I *ever* named a Protestant group in *any* of the objections.

And, he might actually have to deal with the reality that the Scriptures likewise use the terms interchangeably. *This is not even a debatable topic, to be honest. It is a given, but, clearly, Armstrong is ignorant of the facts of the case. This is why he calls me "Bishop White," though, of course, no one else does.*

Since the man called *himself* a bishop (and indeed this follows from the equation in his mind of elder and bishop: he being an "elder" at his church), then why should I *not* call him the same? Makes perfect sense to me . . .

He thinks it is funny, when all he is proving by using the phrase is that he is the one ignorant of the subjects he chooses to pontificate upon in his voluminous writings.

What does that say about *him*, then, since he was silly enough to call himself a bishop? White goes on to wrangle about bishops. Let us now examine the question of whether any Protestant group regards deacons as similar or identical in status to elders or pastors. Can it be done? I think so. White stated: "I have never read any work by any Protestant theologian of any note who has ever made this argument." I don't doubt his word, but only the scope of his knowledge of Protestant ecclesiology (and he wrote about how he contributed to a book of comparative ecclesiology, so he ought to know a wee little bit about that -- one would *hope*, anyway).

It so happens that there is a little old "tiny sect" with a "wacky viewpoint" called *Lutherans*. Has White ever heard of those guys? You know: Martin Luther and Philip Melanchthon and Martin Chemnitz et al? "Here I stand"? Augsburg Confession, etc.? I'll assume henceforth that White has heard of that group of Protestants, though judging by his above remarks and the smug dogmatism with which they were made, one might reasonably surmise that he hadn't.

Has Bishop White perchance heard of a man named C. F. W. Walther (1811-1887)? He was only the first president of the Lutheran Church Missouri Synod: one of the most traditional Lutheran bodies today (with 2.6 million members: just a "tiny sect"). What did Walther believe about deacons? Let's take a look-see. In a treatise entitled, *Comments on the Expulsion of a Lutheran 'Deacon'* [that I found online at the time: translation and by Mark Nispel; from *Der Lutheraner*, Jan. 1, 1867, v. 23, n. 9, p. 65-68], Walther stated (italics mine):

> The so-called system of bishops originally rested on this view of things in the times when the pure teaching still reined in the church. It was recognized that a *Bishop* set over the other ministers of the church was really nothing other than a *presbyter* (*Elder*), a *pastor*, who only for the sake of church order was set over the other ministers of the church and who had the additional authority given to him merely by human right. . . . This also applies then to the distinction between a pastor and a *Senior of Ministers* (6), a *president*, a *Superintendent*, a *Dean*, a *head pastor* (Oberpfarrer), or whatever they may be called who are set over one or more preachers. . . . But *since there is no*

distinction between such offices according to divine right, so likewise between them and a Lutheran Deacon, to whom the office of the Word is commended. For the call to preach God's Word publicly is truly the essence of the preaching office.

. . . A Deacon in the biblical sense is a man who only has a helping office to the ministry of the Word according to human arrangement. *But a Deacon* who is called to the preaching of the Word of God, as happens in the Lutheran Church, does not attend a helping office, but rather the highest office in Christendom. He *is nothing else and nothing less than what the Scripture calls a pastor, Presbyter (elder), or Bishop. He has the same authority and rank of office and the same jurisdiction* and the deacons in the biblical sense are also their servants. . . . in the Lutheran Church the *deacons* who are called for the preaching of the Word of God and for the Administration of the Sacraments are seen as *entirely equal to the pastors* . . .

Martin Luther himself appears to teach something very similar if not identical (which is why Walther in the same piece cited him in favor of his own view) (italics mine):

On this account I think it follows that we neither can nor ought to give the name priest to those who are in charge of Word and sacrament among the people. The reason they have been called priests is either because of the custom of heathen people or as a vestige of the Jewish nation. The result is greatly injurious to the church. According to the New Testament Scriptures *better names would be ministers, deacons, bishops, stewards, presbyters* (a name often used and indicating the older members). For thus Paul writes in I Cor. 4 [:1], "This is how one should regard us, as servants of Christ and stewards of the mysteries of God." He does not say, "as priests of Christ," because he knew that the name and office of priest belonged to all.

330

(*Luther's Works*, Vol. 40: *Church and Minstry II*, edited by Conrad Bergendoff, Philadephia: Muhlenberg Press, 1958, p. 35; primary work: *Concerning the Ministry*, 1523, translated by Conrad Bergendoff)

St. Paul calls himself a "deacon" (i.e., Greek *diakonos*) in many places, as I noted in the book:

1 Corinthians 3:5: What then is Apol'los? What is Paul? *Servants* through whom you believed, as the Lord assigned to each.

2 Corinthians 3:5-6: Not that we are competent of ourselves to claim anything as coming from us; our competence is from God, who has made us competent to be *ministers* of a new covenant, not in a written code but in the Spirit; for the written code kills, but the Spirit gives life.

2 Corinthians 6:3-4: We put no obstacle in any one's way, so that no fault may be found with our *ministry* [*diakonia*], but as *servants* of God we commend ourselves in every way: through great endurance, in afflictions, hardships, calamities,

2 Corinthians 11:22-23: Are they Hebrews? So am I. Are they Israelites? So am I. Are they descendants of Abraham? So am I. Are they *servants* of Christ? I am a better one . . .

Ephesians 3:7: Of this gospel I was made a *minister* according to the gift of God's grace which was given me by the working of his power.

Colossians 1:23, 25: . . . the hope of the gospel which you heard, which has been preached to every creature under heaven, and of which I, Paul, became a *minister*. . . . of which I became a *minister* according to the divine office which was given to me for you, to make the word of God fully known, . . .

Compare Paul's similar use of *diakonia* as a description of what he does:

Acts 20:24: But I do not account my life of any value nor as precious to myself, if only I may accomplish my course and the *ministry* which I received from the Lord Jesus, to testify to the gospel of the grace of God.

Romans 11:13: Inasmuch then as I am an apostle to the Gentiles, I magnify my *ministry*

Romans 15:31: . . . that my *service* for Jerusalem may be acceptable to the saints,

2 Corinthians 4:1: Therefore, having this *ministry* by the mercy of God, we do not lose heart.

1 Timothy 1:12: I thank him who has given me strength for this, Christ Jesus our Lord, because he judged me faithful by appointing me to his *service*,

And also *diakoneo*:

2 Corinthians 8:19-20: and not only that, but he has been appointed by the churches to travel with us in this gracious work which we are *carrying on*, for the glory of the Lord and to show our good will. We intend that no one should blame us about this liberal gift which we are *administering*,

That is at least fifteen times (I may have missed some) that the Apostle Paul uses the term *deacon* or related term for himself (*diakonos*: 7; *diakonia*: 6; *diakoneo*: 2). Remember what the good Bishop White claimed:

. . . people I honestly have never met or heard of.

. . . not relevant to a serious non-Catholic reader.

. . . tremendously obvious errors Armstrong makes. For example, on page 17, Armstrong attempts to present a "Protestant" objection relating to the offices of the church:

Just who believes this, I wonder? I have never read any work by any Protestant theologian of any note who has ever made this argument.

So, is Armstrong just ignorant of Protestant ecclesiology, or, has he run into some tiny sect someplace that has come up with some new wacky viewpoint?

Armstrong made a mistake on the level of my saying Catholics think Cardinals and acolytes are the same office.

. . . completely blowing the Protestant view of the deaconate!

. . . misrepresentations of Protestant belief . . . leaves Armstrong without a shred of credibility.

I suppose, then, it follows (by White's "reasoning") that Walther and Martin Luther (only the *founder* of Protestantism) were either 1) exceptionally ignorant, as White claims I am; 2) wackos on the fringe of Protestantism, leading a tiny sect, or; 3) not Protestants, or 4) not theologians, etc. In case White missed the direct comparison, let's do a side-by-side:

Dave Armstrong:

"A Protestant might further object: . . . bishops, elders, and deacons are all synonymous terms for the same office: roughly that of a pastor today."

Lutheran theologian C.F.W. Walther:

"there is no distinction between such offices according to divine right, so likewise between them and a Lutheran Deacon"

"But a Deacon . . . is nothing else and nothing less than what the Scripture calls a pastor, Presbyter (elder), or Bishop. He has the same authority and rank of office and the same jurisdiction"

Martin Luther:

"According to the New Testament Scriptures better names [for priests] would be ministers, deacons, bishops, stewards, presbyters . . ."

Take your pick, or – as an infinitely superior option – throw out White's ludicrous argument . . .

Chapter Ten

Rebuttal of James White's Review of *The One-Minute Apologist*: On the Communion of Saints
[20 June 2007]

Under the broad topic of Mary and the Saints, Armstrong attempts to defend Rome's doctrine of prayer to saints.

The correct description is "asking saints to pray, or intercede for us. They, in turn, go to God, Who answers the prayer (or doesn't, as the case may be, if His answer is 'No'!)." The title of the section on pp. 120-121 is entitled "Praying to saints is wrong" precisely because this is how Protestants describe what we do (since the book dealt with the objections as the starting-point of each reply). If a Catholic says "I prayed to Saint So-and-So" he means (unless he is ignorant of his faith) "I asked him to *intercede*"; so it is a question of semantics. Just to get *that* straight right off the bat . . . but 90% of anti-Catholics refer to the doctrine as "prayer to saints."

Once again, we find no evidence that he is interested in responding to the strongest objections to his position, but only to the weakest.

Actually, the point of the book is to deal with (as the subtitle indicates) "*common* Protestant claims." These may be weak or relatively strong (in my experience, almost invariably the former), but my task as an apologist trying to equip the Catholic with answers to objections, is to meet these objections, whether

335

they are strong *or* weak. So if they are weak but rather common, then the degree of weakness or strength is irrelevant to deciding whether to *answer* them or not.

White, therefore, inadvertently proves that the standard garden-variety anti-Catholic or contra-Catholic rhetoric is exceptionally weak, since the most common arguments from that sphere are pitiful as can be. But he is here to provide us all with "strong" objections, which I will be more than happy to shoot down as well. And (very unlike him) I will actually *reply* to and refute his objections whenever they are offered.

But despite this, even in responding to the weakest argumentation, the number of circular arguments and simply false assumptions is [sic] great indeed.

He can *claim* this all he wants, but *demonstrating* it is another matter entirely.

Armstrong rightly lays out the objection: "The Bible forbids communication with the dead. It also tells us there is only one mediator between God and men: Jesus." Exactly, and, if he has taken the time to listen at all, he knows that the vacuous, yet nigh unto universal, argument of Roman Catholic apologists regarding asking a friend to pray for you (this is somehow taken as having relevance to Jesus' role as the sole mediator between God and men).

I kept waiting for the end of the sentence to come; it is incomplete and ungrammatical. Because of that, I'll pass on comment for the moment, hoping he will clarify later in his "review."

The fact that Jesus role as mediator is essentially and necessarily different is lost on those who use this facile argumentation, for Christ has a grounds upon which to stand as a mediator that no one, including Mary, possesses.

No one is *denying* that, so it is irrelevant, and no point of contention between us.

This has been explained many times, but Roman apologists continue repeating their simplistic argument as if no one has ever responded to it.

We don't disagree that Jesus' mediatorship is absolutely unique and "essentially and necessarily different"; we are saying that asking a dead saint to pray is no different in essence than asking a living friend to pray for us or someone else. It is biblically challenged Protestants who make the rather dumb objection that asking others to pray for us is the equivalent of denying that Jesus is sole mediator. That is where the dense incomprehension lies, and why we keep saying what we do, that White alludes to. I think I have provided more than enough biblical support for the notion in many portions of my apologetics.

Armstrong's "one-minute" reply is that James 5:16-18 tells us that "the prayers of certain people are more effective than those of others." Of course, what James 5 tells us is that "the prayer of a righteous man has great power." From this, it seems, you can create a direct proportion statement, so that the saints, being perfected, have the greatest "prayer power co-efficient" possible.

Good; White shows that he at least *comprehends* my argument. That's a start. But as we'll see, he goes off into fallacy-land right away   .   .   .

But please notice, there is nothing in James 5 about dead people praying for us. Nothing at all, in fact, just the opposite.

That's irrelevant to the argument. It only is relevant if one is claiming that this verse itself contains all the components of the Catholic doctrine of the communion of saints. I have not claimed that it does. It establishes the principle that lies *behind* why

Catholics pray as they do. The Catholic chain of reasoning is as follows:

1. We ought to pray for each other (much biblical proof).

2. The prayer of a righteous man has great power in its effects (James 5:16-18).

3. Therefore it makes eminent sense to ask more righteous people to pray for us (implied in same passage).

4. Dead saints are more alive than we ourselves are (e.g., Mt 22:32).

5. Dead saints are aware of what happens on the earth (Heb 12:1 etc.), and indeed, are portrayed as praying for us in heaven (Rev 6:9-10).

6. Dead saints are exceptionally, if not wholly, righteous and holy, since they have been delivered from sin and are present with God (21:27; 22:14).

7. Therefore, it is perfectly sensible and wise to ask them to pray on our behalf to God.

James 5:16-18 only provides a *portion* of the entire biblical argument necessary (#2 and #3 above, with #1 implied as the background premise). Other biblical passages support propositions #4-6, with #7 following, based on James 5, provided that #4-6 are established on other biblical grounds. Therefore, it is a complete *non sequitur* for White to "object" that James 5 doesn't mention dead saints, because it was never my claim in the first place. It's based on his dumbfounded misunderstanding of how the argument works.

The example Armstrong relies on specifically says, "Elijah was a man of like nature with ourselves." Yes, he was...and that likewise means he was alive!

. . . which is perfectly irrelevant, per the above, but (to get back to the land of relevance) Abraham, Isaac, and Jacob are "alive" *too*, according to Jesus (!!).

From this Armstrong recalls the examples of Abraham and Moses who interceded with God, which is, again, quite true. But it is likewise irrelevant since, obviously, they were both alive at the time of their intercession with God.

. . . another *non sequitur*, flowing from White's apparent inability to grasp how my argument is logically structured (a not uncommon occurrence with him). But one gets used to it after so many years, like a spouse snoring or a child who lisps or whines. One must accept the deficiencies in others and exercise patience.

Then we have the statement,

> If, then, the Blessed Virgin Mary were indeed sinless, it would follow (right from Scripture) that her prayers would have the greatest power, and not only because of her sinlessness but because of her status as Mother of God. So we ask for her prayers and also ask other saints, because they have more power than we do, having been made perfectly righteous (according to James 5:16-18).

You will remember that back in the days of the Reformation a common complaint made by the Reformers was that Rome's defenders were sophists, men who tried to look wise while promoting the most amazingly incoherent statements. Little has changed over the centuries. You take the statement that a righteous man's prayers have great power, which is said only of the living, transport this into another context, attach it to Mary (assuming her alleged sinlessness), and then "follows" "right from Scripture" (!!) that her prayers would have "the most power."

Again, the same incomprehension of how my argument works leads White to caricature it and present a twisted version of what my argument supposedly *is* in the first place, as something he then shoots down (the proverbial "straw man" of illogical argumentation). Also, it is true that here I *assumed for the sake of argument* that Mary was sinless:

> *If*, then, the Blessed Virgin Mary were indeed sinless, it would *follow* . . .

Assuming things for the sake of argument means, in effect, saying, "I won't digress to argue that point at the moment [it's almost like a footnote], in the midst of this argument, because it is another topic; we will *assume* it here and argue it *elsewhere*." That is exactly what I did. In this book, my argument for Mary's sinlessness occurs in pages 108-109. I've defended that doctrine in much greater depth elsewhere in books and on my blog.

But note how White twisted and distorted the very nature of my argument. This is first-rate sophistry. He is accusing me of being the sophist, and of being incoherent. Yet what I did was completely coherent and therefore not sophistry at all. I assumed the hypothetical (Mary's sinlessness). I didn't *argue* it in this particular section (one can't digress when one has two pages to work with). But White completely blows it; he doesn't *get* it. Let me illustrate how he engages in this sophistry with a comparison. This is the structure of my *actual* argument:

> 1. The prayer of a righteous man has great power.

> 2. *If* Mary is sinless [biblical arguments having been made *elsewhere* favoring this], it would follow that her prayers have the greatest power.

> 3. Assuming the hypothetical in #2 for the sake of argument, it follows *"right from Scripture"* that her prayers would have the most effect, based on the logical relationship of "more holy = more effective prayer" to "holiest of all = most effective prayer of all."

But here is how White twists the very nature of my argument in order to mock and "refute" it: 1) The prayer of a righteous man has great power; 2) Assume that Mary is sinless (without argument, biblical or otherwise); 3) Assume ("right from Scripture") that her prayers have the greatest power; 4) Thus, the Catholic claim has no biblical support and is altogether incoherent and circular.

In other words, White wants to pretend that I am making an authoritative, dogmatic claim based on nothing at all. That's why he thinks my reasoning is circular: because he doesn't understand how the argument works in the *first* place. This recurrent logical deficiency in White's anti-Catholic apologetics (I've observed it countless times through the years) causes great flaws to appear in the very heart of his arguments. Anyway, what I was specifically referring to as "right from Scripture" was a purely *logical* relationship:

From the proposition:

"more holy = more effective prayer"

it follows that:

"holiest of all = most effective prayer of all."

That follows "right from Scripture." This is what I meant. I didn't assume Mary's sinlessness with no argument whatsoever. I assumed it in this context for the *sake of argument*, while providing arguments for her sinlessness elsewhere.

Then, you throw in the other saints, who now have more power (because the prayers of a living righteous man have great power), and tie it all up with another reference to James 5, and voila! the Roman position. Not compelling? Of course not. It really isn't meant to be. It is meant to have just enough appeal to it to keep the person who wants to believe it in a state of faith.

Of course it is not compelling because this is not the Catholic argument in the first place! It is a pathetic caricature of a stereotype of Catholic faith: what White *mistakenly thinks* that we teach, rather than what we *actually* believe.

This is then followed by the constant false appeal to inter-Christian prayers as if they are relevant. "Most Protestants are quite comfortable asking for prayers from other Christians on earth; why do they not ask those saved saints who have departed from the earth and are close to God in heaven? After all, they may have passed from this world, but they're certainly alive -- more than we are!" That sounds so nice, but it is double-talk. Passed from this world = dead to us. *Alive to God? Of course. Spiritually alive? Completely. But the prohibition of contact with the dead **is*** specifically in the context of people living on earth seeking to have contact with those who have "passed from this world"! *This kind of argumentation leaves the prohibition of contact with the dead meaningless and undefined.*

But White is assuming here something that is quite unbiblical itself: the notion that God wants us to have *no contact at all* with those who have died. Why would he think this? According to the Bible it is patently untrue:

> A) **1 Samuel 28:12,14-15 (Samuel):** the prophet Samuel appeared to King Saul to prophesy his death. The current consensus among biblical commentators (e.g., *The New Bible Commentary, The Wycliffe Bible Commentary*) is that it was indeed Samuel the prophet, not an impersonating demon (since it happened during a sort of seance with the so-called "witch or medium of Endor"). This was the view of, e.g., St. Justin Martyr, Origen, and St. Augustine, among others. Ecclesiasticus (Sirach) 6:19-20 reinforces the latter interpretation: "Samuel . . . after he had fallen asleep he prophesied and revealed to the king his death, and lifted up his voice out of the earth in prophecy, to blot out the wickedness of the people."

B) **Matthew 17:1-3 (the Transfiguration: Moses and Elijah):** . . . Jesus took with him Peter and James and John his brother, and led them up a high mountain apart. And he was transfigured before them, and his face shone like the sun, and his garments became white as light. And behold, there appeared to them Moses and Elijah, talking with him. (see also Mark 9:4 and Luke 9:30-31)

C) **Matthew 27:52-53 (raised bodies after the crucifixion):** . . . the tombs also were opened, and many bodies of the saints who had fallen asleep were raised, and coming out of the tombs after his resurrection they went into the holy city and appeared to many.

D) **Revelation 11:3, 6 (the "Two Witnesses"):** And I will grant my two witnesses power to prophesy for one thousand two hundred and sixty days . . . they have power to shut the sky, that no rain may fall . . . and they have power over the waters to turn them into blood, and to smite the earth with every plague . . .

These two witnesses were killed (11:7-9), raised after "three and a half days" and "stood up on their feet" (11:11), and then "went up to heaven in a cloud" (11:12). Many Church fathers thought these two were Enoch and Elijah, because both of them didn't die; thus this would explain their dying after this appearance on earth. Some Protestant commentators think the two witnesses are Moses and Elijah, because of the parallel to the Transfiguration, and also similarities with the plagues of Egypt and the fact that Elijah also stopped the rain for three-and-a-half years (James 5:17).

We must conclude, based on the above passages, that contact between heaven and earth is God's will; otherwise He wouldn't have permitted it in these instances. The Catholic belief in more interconnection between heaven and earth cannot be ruled out as "unbiblical." One has to try other arguments to refute our beliefs in this regard. It sounds, then, like James White is the one making the circular arguments: assuming things but not proving them. I have made the biblical argument. Let him deal with Holy Scripture.

Further, there is a substantive, clear difference between asking a fellow believer to pray for you, and the prayers that are addressed to Mary and the saints. I have never asked anyone to save me from the wrath of Jesus, and yet that is what we read in this famous prayer:

> O Mother of Perpetual Help, thou art the dispenser of all the goods which God grants to us miserable sinners, and for this reason he has made thee so powerful, so rich, and so bountiful, that thou mayest help us in our misery. Thou art the advocate of the most wretched and abandoned sinners who have recourse to thee. Come then, to my help, dearest Mother, for I recommend myself to thee. In thy hands I place my eternal salvation and to thee do I entrust my soul. Count me among thy most devoted servants; take me under thy protection, and it is enough for me. For, if thou protect me, dear Mother, I fear nothing; not from my sins, because thou wilt obtain for me the pardon of them; nor from the devils, because thou are more powerful than all hell together; nor even from Jesus, my Judge himself, because by one prayer from thee he will be appeased. But one thing I fear, that in the hour of temptation I may neglect to call on thee and thus perish miserably. Obtain for me, then, the pardon of my sins, love for Jesus, final perseverance, and the grace always to have recourse to thee, O Mother of Perpetual Help.

Well, of course there is a difference between asking Mary, the Mother of God to pray for us and asking Pastor Doe or Grandma Smith. This is the whole point. We think Mary is the highest creature that God ever made. Everything she is, is because of God's free, unmerited grace. So her prayers are the most powerful of any human being. We could ask God for something, or we could ask Mary to ask God for the same thing. If indeed Mary is what we believe she is (sinless and God's highest creation) then clearly, her prayers would have far more effect than ours, based on James 5:16-18). That's precisely why we "go to her" instead of going right to God (but we can do that, too, anytime we want, and the Church doesn't require us at all not to approach God directly).

White cites this Marian devotion because he knows most of his readers (even more uninformed or misinformed than he is on such matters) will recoil with horror just as he does. But the properly informed Catholic understands the overall *Christological context* of Marian piety and Mariology.

I went through this fundamental spade work with two other anti-Catholics who wanted to go after St. Alphonsus Liguori by presenting a cynically selective, distorted view of what he taught. They would cite all the flowery language of Marian devotion while conveniently overlooking and not considering the many statements from the same saint about *Jesus* that are always assumed as lying behind the Marian expressions.

White's primary aim is always to play to his followers (preaching to the choir); to find the most "outrageous" things (i.e., from the warped anti-Catholic perspective) that will cause them to think that anyone who espouses such things is a nut and biblically illiterate; in spiritual darkness. But it is absurdly presented so selectively that it amounts to a half-truth, which is no better than a lie (in both a legal and logical sense).

If one doesn't understand the Christological emphasis *behind* Catholic Mariology (doesn't even *try* to do so), then one has no hope of understanding the Mariology itself. It's as simple as that. White sees to it that he never presents the full, balanced picture, because that would work against his purpose of making the Catholic look like a nutcase idolater who doesn't even know that Jesus is the one Who saves, etc., etc.

When Mr. Armstrong finds me bowing down in front of one of my fellow believers, rocking back and forth mouthing prayers while fingering a string of beads, and placing a lit candle before them, then we can talk about parallels.

One doesn't have to do that with living people (i.e., those still on earth with us, not having died), but plenty of folks bow down before the grave of a loved one, or at the place where they were killed in a car crash. People light candles in memory of people who died (look at, for example, what happened after the deaths of John Lennon and Princess Diana, or, for that matter, 9-11). I've seen many people kiss dead bodies in caskets. They are no longer there; it's just a dead body. So is that some abominable idolatry too? There are plenty of statues of people we regard as heroes.

Humorously and ironically enough, on the very same day that White issued this critique, he posted a picture of "the famed Reformation Wall" in Geneva: huge statues of "reformers" Farel, Calvin, Beza, and Knox. Statues honor the memory of people we admire for some reason or other. Otherwise, why have them at all (just for pigeon toilets?)?

If White would get sufficiently biblical, he could bow before one of these statues and ask one of these men (represented by the statue, for a visual and devotional aid) to pray for him, too (assuming they are out of purgatory yet, and assuming they were granted the grace to even *get* to purgatory). After all, even John Calvin held that dead saints pray for us (*Institutes*, III, 20, 24), though he denied (without reason and against the evidence of Scripture) that they observed what happened on the earth or should be *asked* to pray.

I'd much rather see Mr. White rocking back and forth in a rocking chair with an introductory textbook on logic. Most of the prayers of the Rosary are straight from the Bible: the "Hail Mary" was uttered by an angel of God, Gabriel (Luke 1:28). The next part of the Rosary was uttered by Elizabeth, and recorded in Scripture (Luke 1:42). Would White counsel Christians to refrain from praying biblical prayers that came from the mouth of an angel and from Elizabeth, the mother of John the Baptist? That would be odd. But this is just another of White's tactics to divert attention from my actual apologetic that he is supposedly "refuting."

But then we find the paragraph that drew my attention to this section. I quote it in full:

346

If it is objected that the dead saints cannot hear us, we reply that God is fully able to give them that power -- with plenty of supporting biblical evidence: 1) the "cloud of witnesses" that Hebrews 12:1 describes; 2) in Revelation 6:9-10, prayers are given for us in heaven from "saints"; 3) elsewhere in Revelation an angel possesses "prayers of the saints" and in turn presents them to God; 4) Jeremiah is described as one who "prays much for the people" after his death in 2 Maccabees 15:13-14. The saints in heaven are clearly aware of earthly happenings. If they have such awareness, it isn't that much of a leap to deduce that they can hear our requests for prayer, especially since the Bible itself shows that they are indeed praying.

(p. 121)

Let's examine this argumentation. First, the objection would be based upon a lack of biblical evidence, along with the positive biblical prohibition against contact with the dead.

We have seen how there is a quite permissible "contact with the dead" of some sort illustrated in the Bible, by four explicit, undeniable examples. I have condemned what is *not* permitted, right along with White, in the same section he is critiquing:

A Protestant Might Further Object:

It is not clear how these Catholic practices are any different from the séances, magic, witchcraft, and necromancy forbidden by the Bible. When you come down to it, Catholics are still messing around with dead spirits.

The One-Minute Apologist Says:

Catholics fully agree that these things are prohibited, but deny that the Communion of Saints is a practice included at all in those condemnations.

The difference is in the source of the supernatural power and the intention. When a Christian on earth asks a saint to pray for him (directly supported by the biblical indications above), God is the one whose power makes the relationship between departed and living members of the Body of Christ possible. The medium in a séance, on the other hand, is trying to use her own occultic powers to "conjure up" the dead -- opening up the very real possibility of demonic counterfeit. Catholics aren't "conjuring" anyone; we're simply asking great departed saints to pray for us. If they are aware of the earth, then God can also make it possible for them to "hear" and heed our prayer requests. If this weren't the case, then saints and angels in heaven wouldn't be portrayed as they are in Scripture: intensely active and still involved in earthly affairs.

(p. 121)

To reply, "Well, God is fully able to give them that power" is not, in fact a response. Of course God can do so. God has all power, and since that is not a point in dispute, this is a classic example of a red herring. If God had wanted to arrange things so that Mary is the mediatrix of all graces, and so that saints intercede on our behalf in a Christianized pantheon of gods in heaven, He could have done that. The question is not "does God have the power to do so," the question is "has God done so?"

There is indeed biblical evidence for this. The Bible plainly teaches us these things:

1. Dead saints are alive.

2. Dead saints are aware of earthly affairs.

3. Dead saints have specifically come back to earth and have had contact with human beings.

4. Dead saints pray for us in heaven.

Those things are beyond dispute. They're explicitly biblical. White seems to deny #4 ("saints intercede on our behalf in a Christianized pantheon of gods in heaven"). He describes this as an example of a red herring and denies that God has brought this state of affairs about. But he is contradicted by the explicit example of Revelation 6:9-10, that I cited in the very paragraph he noted in his own critique. It is a curious methodology that ignores explicit biblical proofs while wishfully fancying that there are none:

> When he opened the fifth seal, I saw under the altar the souls of those who had been slain for the word of God and for the witness they had borne; they cried out with a loud voice, "O Sovereign Lord, holy and true, how long before thou wilt judge and avenge our blood on those who dwell upon the earth?"

Is it true that the Bible doesn't explicitly state that we should ask these same dead saints to pray for us? Well, yes and no. It's not absolutely explicit, yet the Bible does present angels in heaven having something to do with "prayers of the saints." I presented this in *A Biblical Defense of Catholicism* (p. 112):

> **Revelation 5:8:** "The four living creatures and the twenty-four elders fell down before the Lamb, each holding a harp, and with golden bowls full of incense, which are the prayers of the saints."

> **Revelation 8:3-4:** "And another angel came and stood at the altar with a golden censer; and he was given much incense to mingle with the prayers of all saints upon the golden altar before the throne; and the smoke of the

incense rose with the prayers of the saints from the hand of the angel before God."

I ask Mr. White and anyone else who believes as he does: "what are men or angels (or both) in heaven *doing* with the 'prayers of the saints'? What sense does this make in the Protestant worldview?" Our prayers, according to that theology, go right to God without any intercessory "mediator." How, then, is this explained? Perhaps White can tell us how it fits into his Baptist tradition. I'll follow the teaching of the Bible rather than man-made traditions.

Now, back to what I was arguing above. The missing "plank" there was an example of biblical sanction of our asking saints to pray for us. I have just presented two biblical instances of creatures in heaven having something to do with our prayers. If they have received our prayers, then it follows logically that either:

1. human beings asked them directly,

or

2. God sent them their way, just as one post office might send a load of mail to another to "sort", before the ultimate destination (back to the original one).

Or

3. Prayers automatically get channeled through creatures before they get to God.

In any of these scenarios, intercession of the saints is involved, and White stands refuted from the Bible. It's not just "me 'n' God." Others are involved in the process of prayer.

Moreover, even if these proofs are somehow rejected or discounted, it follows from common sense that if #1-4 above are true (the "chart" further above about dead saints), that we can ask them to intercede, since if they are aware of earthly happenings and even pray for those on the earth, then common sense would seem (at least to me) to dictate that they can, most likely, "hear" our prayers as well. It's two different lines of argument: one explicitly biblical and the other a straightforward and plausible deduction from explicitly biblical data.

But what kind of supporting biblical evidence are we offered?

. . . evidence of the sort that I have just outlined above, that I had already provided in my first book. In the present book, I had only two pages of space to defend each belief, so I obviously couldn't provide the depth that I could in my first book, where, for example, I devoted seventeen pages to communion of saints. In *The Catholic Verses* (Sophia: 2004), I provided the reader with fourteen more pages on the topic.

I mean, if prayer, an act of worship in Scripture, is to be offered to anyone but God,

Asking saints to pray is not the same as praying *to* them (in the sense of expecting them to actually answer the prayer).

surely there will be overwhelming evidence found in the normative practice of the Christian church, and in the writings of the early leaders of that church, the New Testament. But is that what we find?

Yes. I have provided the biblical evidences. I won't spend more of my time delving into patristics, as this is, ostensibly, a review of my book (mostly biblical arguments). But it's assuredly there, if White wants to argue about patristic beliefs.

The first text given is Hebrews 12:1, "Therefore, since we have so great a cloud of witnesses surrounding us, let us also lay aside every encumbrance and the sin which so easily entangles us, and let us run with endurance the race that is set before us." Armstrong assumes that the "great cloud of witnesses" refers to saints in heaven observing events on earth. However, given that this is a transitional statement following the chapter on the faithful men and women of old, it is far better to understand this

351

text as referring to them and to recognize that a witness is not one who is observing events (as in Western thinking) but one who testifies, witnesses, by their life. The faithful of old are the ones who have witnessed to God's faithfulness by their own lives, and, since we have their testimony, we are to run the race with patience and joy. There is no reason, in the context of Hebrews, to conclude that the writer was positively teaching that saints in heaven observe earthly events, a concept that would be completely irrelevant to his point.

Well, that is Bishop White's opinion. He is entitled to it, but he has to argue for it and establish why it is the most plausible exegetical position, just like anyone else. He can't simply expect everyone to accept his word as if from on high because *he* said it. Many others disagree with him on this. I have myself found at least three non-Catholic language references (Thayer, Vincent, and Kittel) that confirm that the element of "spectatorship," which lends itself to the Catholic notion of communion of saints, where saints in heaven are aware of, and observe events on earth. This is present in Hebrews 12:1, and cannot be ruled out simply on the basis of a prior doctrinal bias. Witness is the Greek word *martus*, from which is derived the English word *martyr*.

Chapter Eleven

Answers to James White's Top Ten Questions for "Romanist" Converts
[4 September 2007]

Last week I received the following e-mail, and I felt it would be best to share my response here on the blog.

> Dear Mr. White, For someone considering converting to Catholicism, what questions would you put to them in order to discern whether or not they have examined their situation sufficiently? Say, a Top 10 list. Thanks.

When I posted this question in our chat channel a number of folks commented that it was in fact a great question, and we started to throw out some possible answers. Here is my "Top Ten List" in response to this fine inquiry.

10) *Have you listened to both sides? That is, have you done more than read* Rome Sweet Home *and listen to a few emotion-tugging conversion stories? Have you actually taken the time to find sound, serious responses to Rome's claims, those offered by writers ever since the Reformation, such as Goode, Whitaker, Salmon, and modern writers? I specifically exclude from this list anything by Jack Chick and Dave Hunt.*

This is actually a decent observation, and one that I would pretty much agree with (since I am well-known for doing debates with many folks and presenting both sides on my blog so that people can see both sides presented by advocates, and make up their own minds). My book, *Pillars of Sola Scriptura* was precisely a point-by-point rebuttal of both Goode and Whitaker. I do, nevertheless have a few relevant criticisms to offer:

1) White implies that if someone did this, then he would respect their decision, but we know that he does *not* in actual cases. For example, look at how he treats Scott Hahn (no differently than any *other* Catholic convert: with considerable scorn and mockery. White knows full well that Scott, a former Presbyterian pastor, voraciously read everything he could get his hands on, prior to his own conversion (literally, several hundred books). Ironically, he mocks Scott's conversion story as lightweight (above, by strong insinuation), yet Scott did the very thing that White calls for, and it makes no difference. White will show disdain for any convert, no matter how much he studied both sides. This objection looks great as rhetoric, because it contains a significant amount of wisdom and truth, but *in practice* it makes no difference as far as *he* is concerned.

2) Many former pastors and theological professors (or former Protestant missionaries / apologists, such as myself) have converted to Catholicism. White would have to maintain that all of them were unacquainted with Protestant arguments, despite their seminary or theological educations, or (as, again, in my case) their own wide reading. This is far too simplistic, in that it would require the absurd scenario whereby any pastor / professor / missionary who becomes a Catholic must have been abominably ignorant of his own former Protestant belief-system and good reasons in favor of it.

3) Another example of the same hypocrisy is how White approaches my own case. During the course of a "critique" of my book, *The Catholic Verses*, he started making out that I was an ignorant Protestant who hadn't read anything (Protestant) of any worth, and that this is why I converted (he tried to make this argument in our very first written debate, in 1995, too). Well, I took the time to list the books that I had read as a Protestant.

Now, did this make a whit of difference? Did it show White that I was sufficiently acquainted with my former Protestant belief-system, to have made a decision to become a Catholic without being accused of ignorance? No, of course not. It not only made no difference at all; White upped the ante and immediately accused me of "knowing deception." This charge of dishonesty and intentional deception, by the way, is standard practice among anti-Catholics.

4) This can easily be flipped around and it can be demonstrated that it is far more characteristic of *former Catholics who become Protestant* (especially those -- many in number -- who become *anti-Catholic*, as part and parcel of their newfound Protestantism). I've seen it myself a hundred times or more (when I question folks to see what they have read). One doesn't find White chiding former Catholics for a lack of Catholic reading (if I missed it, I'd love for him to direct me to such a piece). He doesn't urge them to get up to speed with Catholic apologetic arguments, so that they can have a sufficiently informed Protestant faith, with robust confidence. No; any argument against Rome at all is fine with White. He need know nothing further of a new Protestant convert, other than the fact that they rejected Catholic teaching in some respect. That immediately proves they are wise, regenerate, and on the side of the angels. But in fact it is yet another double standard on his part.

5) Nor can White so flippantly dismiss the more extreme, dumb anti-Catholic polemicists, such as Jack Chick and Dave Hunt. The fact is, that most of the contra-Catholic / anti-Catholic polemical literature out there is almost as irrational and fact-challenged as the Chick garbage. Granted, folks like White and Ankerberg and MacArthur and Sproul are far more sophisticated than Chick, and generally omit the super-stupid conspiratorialism and Know-Nothing aspects of a guy like Chick, but scarcely less insulting, and with almost as many glaring fallacies and deficiencies in their work, as seen when one reads *both sides* with regard to one of *their* presentations. For every Norman Geisler, who offers an amiable, charitable, non-anti-Catholic

355

(ecumenical), serious sustained critique of Catholicism from an evangelical Protestant perspective, there are a hundred Whites who offer misinformation and sophistry.

9) *Have you read an objective history of the early church? I refer to one that would explain the great diversity of viewpoints to be found in the writings of the first centuries, and that accurately explains the controversies, struggles, successes and failures of those early believers?*

White doesn't offer an example of such an "objective history." Of course, it would probably be a Protestant historian that he has in mind. But this is by no means the slam-dunk for his side that he supposes. For example, I have cited historian Philip Schaff many dozens of times in my treatments of the fathers, and that is because he is a *fair and accurate historian*. He is thoroughly Protestant in affiliation, and makes no bones about it (often running down various Catholic beliefs in an openly partisan fashion), yet he gives *the facts of history*, whether they are "Catholic" or (as he sees it) more in line with later Protestantism. Thus, he is a valuable ally in my apologetic efforts of presenting the fathers as they actually were.

I encourage anyone to read serious historical scholarship concerning the early Church, whether written by a Catholic or a Protestant. The Catholic position will always benefit from that. One could easily become a Catholic on historical grounds, simply from reading Schaff, and other learned Protestant historians such as Pelikan, Kelly, Latourette, and Oberman. One wouldn't even have to use Catholic sources (that White would accuse of being severely slanted and biased). I would agree that many on either side of the aisle never trouble themselves to read such works, but I would direct anyone in a second to Schaff or the others I have mentioned. And that is because historical arguments from the fathers overwhelmingly favor a "Catholic" interpretation.

8) *Have you looked carefully at the claims of Rome in a historical light, specifically, have you examined her claims regarding the "unanimous consent" of the Fathers, and all the* *evidence that exists that stands contrary not only to the universal claims of the Papacy but especially to the concept of Papal Infallibility? How do you explain, consistently, the history of the early church in light of modern claims made by Rome? How do you explain such things as the Pornocracy and the Babylonian Captivity of the Church without assuming the truthfulness of the very system you are embracing?*

"Unanimous consent" means, of course, "significant consensus" rather than absolute unanimity. That is simply a matter of semantics. Such consensus in favor of Catholic positions is indeed what we consistently find, so this poses no problem at all. Speaking for myself, this was a central concern of mine, and I *did* read at least some sources that White champions, such as the Anglican anti-Catholic George Salmon, whom we see him mentioning above. And I read Catholic liberal dissidents like Hans Küng, who reject infallibility.

But then I also read (given my love for hearing both sides of any story) John Henry Cardinal Newman, and he helped me a great deal to precisely understand "the history of the early church in light of modern claims made by Rome." But of course White wouldn't recommend that anyone reads *his* works. That would be too dangerous. Newman can only be *mocked*, never dealt with seriously.

Evidence for the early existence of a strong papal authority is also abundant. I strongly urge folks to read both sides. There is also considerable biblical support for the papacy.

Various sins and rough periods in Church history are instances of, well, *sin*! White thinks this is supposed to be some surprise or disproof of anything? It's responded to by pointing out that there will always be sinners in the Church, and by showing that the supposedly pure early Protestants were no different in this regard (if not worse). We expect to find sin in any environment, even Christian places. Jesus and Paul told us it would be so, so this is no "argument" at all, and has no bearing on truth claims.

7) *Have you applied the same standards to the testing of Rome's ultimate claims of authority that Roman Catholic apologists use to attack* sola scriptura*?*

Many Catholic apologists have dealt with anti-Catholic arguments along these lines, yes. I wouldn't expect every new convert to be familiar with every jot and tittle of current Catholic-Protestant argumentation. It's getting harder and harder all the time for someone to see both sides on the Internet, since very few anti-Catholic apologists lower themselves to actually engage Catholics in debate anymore. But there are more than enough of debates from the past that remain online, for folks to do the comparison themselves. I have many scores of such debates on my own blog.

How do you explain the fact that Rome's answers to her own objections are circular?

This assumes what it is trying to prove, which is itself circular logic (strange, since it is objecting to the same thing that it is doing).

For example, if she claims you need the Church to establish an infallible canon, how does that actually answer the question, since you now have to ask how Rome comes to have this infallible knowledge.

This confuses the issue. It is indisputable that Church authority was necessary to definitively establish and verify (not create!) the canon. That is simply historical fact that no one can deny. Questions of how this authority came about are secondary to the fact. They are worthwhile in and of themselves, but merely pointing to them does not alleviate the Protestant difficulty of having to rely on a human institution for a binding decree regarding the canon (it's a problem because for Protestants, the Bible is the only infallible authority).

This is one example (of many) of White's unreasonable demands. The fact is, that *any* Christian position *requires faith*, for the simple reason that Christianity is not merely a *philosophy*, or exercise in epistemology. White's view requires faith; so does the Catholic outlook. One exercises faith in the Catholic Church being what it claims to be: the One True Church, uniquely guided and led by the Holy Spirit, with infallible teaching. Hopefully, one can give cogent reasons for why this faith is *reasonable*, but it is still faith in the end: reasonable, not blind.

White's Protestant friends have the same exact problems that need to be worked out for their systems, too. But there we have countless self-contradictions. What denomination is right? Who teaches correctly on baptism or free will or predestination? Etc. If they really agree, then why are they institutionally separate (the sin of schism)? If they disagree, then error is inevitably present somewhere, and the devil is the father of lies and falsehood, so millions of Protestants are in bondage to a pack of lies. It must be, where contradiction is present.

In any event, why does White require every Catholic convert to instantly know the answers to all these questions, lest their conversion be doubted in its knowledge, and/or sincerity? Conversion is an extraordinarily complicated and personal process. If I wanted to play this unfairly, as White does, I could easily take apart a hundred former Catholics in his chat room, if I was allowed to grill them with all of these sorts of questions.

I guarantee that none of them would pass with a 100% mark, under questioning of how much of both sides they have read and understood, etc. But White acts as if the validity of religious faith utterly depends on passing such a quiz and having exhaustive knowledge on these sorts of topics, that only experienced, trained apologists (or clergymen or philosophers or theologians) can reasonably be expected to possess.

Or if it is argued that sola scriptura *produces anarchy, why doesn't Rome's magisterium produce unanimity and harmony?*

It does. I deny that it does not. We have one teaching, and everyone knows what it is. The fact that we are plagued by dissidents in our ranks proves nothing against our doctrine. Their very label as dissidents proves that they dissent from the official teaching. Everyone knows what the latter is. Even White refers to "wild-eyed liberal wackos who parade under the banner of 'Roman Catholic scholarship'." He knows the method of liberals, because they do the same thing in Protestant denominations. I agree, however, that all these issues require vigorous discussion. White and virtually all of his anti-Catholic friends don't want to have a serious discussion of that sort. They would rather mock, run from critiques and debate challenges, and pick on new converts.

And if someone claims there are 33,000 denominations due to sola scriptura, *since that outrageous number has been debunked repeatedly, have you asked them why they are so dishonest and sloppy with their research?*

Speaking for myself, I agreed several years ago that this number is based in part on fallacious categorization, and I no longer use it, or anything remotely approaching it (I will usually say "hundreds of competing denominations"). White and Protestants, however, are by no means free from their severe difficulties, since, as I point out, *any* number of "churches" beyond one is a blatantly unbiblical concept and scandalous.

6) *Have you read the* Papal Syllabus of Errors *and* Indulgentiarum Doctrina? *Can anyone read the description of grace found in the latter document and pretend for even a moment that is the doctrine of grace Paul taught to the Romans?*

Most new converts have not. Most longtime Catholics have not. But so what? Does White want to contend that most Calvinists have read Calvin's complete *Institutes* or all of the many confessions? Most have not. Does that mean they are illegitimate Calvinists? No, and clearly so. Not everyone is required to have exhaustive knowledge of everything. I think it is sad that White makes such arguments because he perpetuates the stereotype that we apologists are burdened with: as intolerable know-it-alls. I would never say that a Catholic has to instantly know all of this stuff in minute detail before they could be accepted into the Church in good standing. White doesn't require similar knowledge of his Calvinist friends. *The Syllabus of Errors*, of course, deals with many different things. Each would require a lengthy discussion, but White is unwilling to do that. So it is hardly impressive that he simply assumes that it is a false document, with no argument.

As for Indulgences, they are based on explicit biblical (Pauline) evidence (1 Corinthians 5:1-5 and 2 Corinthians 2:6-11), that I have presented in my first book. But will White engage in that discussion? No . . .

I'm all for folks knowing as much about their religious faith as the can: the more the merrier. But I would never require what White requires. He wants to set the bar so high that virtually *no one* would pass the test; therefore there are no legitimate Catholic converts on the face of the earth. But that is what White *already believed*, before he ever dreamt-up this list in the first place. So it's simply rationalization after the fact.

5) *Have you seriously considered the ramifications of Rome's doctrine of sin, forgiveness, eternal and temporal punishments, purgatory, the treasury of merit, transubstantiation, sacramental priesthood, and indulgences? Have you seriously worked through compelling and relevant biblical texts like Ephesians 2, Romans 3-5, Galatians 1-2, Hebrews 7-10 and all of John 6, in light of Roman teaching?*

This is more of the excessively unrealistic demands for a new convert. One can study theology and apologetics over a lifetime and always have more to learn. I've been doing apologetics for 32 years now (Catholic apologetics for 23), and it's endless; I feel that I have only scratched the surface, and I am known as one of the more voluminous apologists.

But in any event, I could simply flip this around and find passages that are relevant to distinctive Protestant beliefs, and ask former Catholic Protestants if they had studied all of that in depth, enough to face the equivalent of a White cross-examination. God doesn't expect everyone to know everything. He does expect a great degree of understanding of at least the basics of one's faith, though.

In the end, all have to exercise faith. White knows this full well; in fact, the presuppositionalism (of Greg Bahnsen et al) that he himself follows, particularly requires it. Calvin (as White also knows full well) writes about an inner subjective assurance that cannot be reduced to mere philosophy and epistemology. Calvinist presuppositionalism does not require that level of mere philosophical "certainty." Nor does Catholicism.

White, then, is operating on a double standard, or else he is too ignorant of Catholic apologetics to know that we don't require what he seems to feel is necessary.

4) *Have you pondered what it means to embrace a system that teaches you approach the sacrifice of Christ thousands of times in your life and yet you can die impure, and, in fact, even die an enemy of God, though you came to the cross over and over again?*

I replied to White regarding the Sacrifice of the Mass, but he fled, as always, and never counter-replied. We can give quite adequate answers to these objections.

And have you pondered what it means that though the historical teachings of Rome on these issues are easily identifiable, the vast majority of Roman Catholics today, including priests, bishops, and scholars, don't believe these things anymore?

Why should anyone ponder it? It is irrelevant. Because liberals infiltrate every Christian communion and try to subvert them, has no bearing at all as to whether the teaching of that group is true. It is neither a disproof of any Protestant denomination, nor of Catholicism. White himself carps on and on about how there are hardly any real evangelicals or true-blue (Calvinist) Protestants around anymore. Yet we don't see him advancing that fact (real or imagined) as a disproof of his *own* views. No; that level of tomfoolery is reserved for his anti-Catholic polemics.

3) *Have you considered what it means to proclaim a human being the Holy Father (that's a divine name, used by Jesus only of His Father) and the Vicar of Christ (that's the Holy Spirit)?*

Is White serious? All one has to do here is note that there are such things as "holy men" referred to in the Bible. The writer of Hebrews calls the recipients of his epistle "holy brethren" (RSV; also the same in White's favorite: the NASB). Peter refers to a "holy priesthood" (1 Peter 2:5; same in NASB) and "holy women" such as Sarah (1 Peter 3:5; same in NASB) and "holy prophets" (2 Peter 3:2; same in NASB; cf. Acts 3:21 [also Peter]; Zechariah's prophecy in Luke 1:70). John the Baptist is referred to as a "righteous and holy man" in Mark 6:20 (same in NASB). Jesus refers to a "righteous man" in Matthew 10:41. Therefore, men can be called "holy" in Scripture. That solves half of this "pseudo-problem." Can they also be called "father"? Of course!:

> **Acts 7:2:** And Stephen said: "Brethren and *fathers*, hear me. The God of glory appeared to our *father* Abraham, . . ."

> **Romans 4:12:** . . . the *father* of the circumcised . . . our *father* Abraham . . .

> **Romans 4:16-17:** . . . Abraham, for he is the *father* of us all, as it is written, "I have made you the *father* of many nations . . ." (cf. 9:10; Phil. 2:22; Jas. 2:21)

> **1 Corinthians 4:15:** For though you have countless guides in Christ, you do not have many *fathers*. For I became your *father* in Christ Jesus through the gospel.

That solves the other half of White's "objection." If a man can be called "holy" and also (spiritual) "father," then we can call a person both *together*, and the "problem" vanishes into thin air. As for "Vicar of Christ" this is an equally ridiculous trifle. I don't believe "vicar" appears in the Bible (at least it doesn't in the KJV and RSV, that I searched), yet somehow Bishop White has this notion that this phrase can only denote the Holy Spirit. Where does he come up with this claptrap? *Merriam-Webster* online defines a "vicar" as "one serving as a substitute or agent; *specifically* : an administrative deputy."

Now, is this some blasphemous way of speaking about disciples of Jesus? Again, absolutely not, for it is the sort of language (substitutes, agents, ambassadors, etc.) that Jesus *Himself* used, in referring to His disciples (the word *disciple* itself is not far in meaning from *vicar*):

Matthew 10:40 He who receives you receives me, and he who receives me receives him who sent me.

John 13:20 Truly, truly, I say to you, he who receives any one whom I send receives me; and he who receives me receives him who sent me.

John 20:23 If you forgive the sins of any, they are forgiven; if you retain the sins of any, they are retained.

Jesus even goes further than that, extending this representation of Himself to children and virtually *any* human being:

Matthew 18:5 Whoever receives one such child in my name receives me.

Matthew 25:40 Truly, I say to you, as you did it to one of the least of these my brethren, you did it to me. (cf. 25:45)

Mark 9:37 Whoever receives one such child in my name receives me; and whoever receives me, receives not me but him who sent me.

Luke 9:48 Whoever receives this child in my name receives me, and whoever receives me receives him who sent me; for he who is least among you all is the one who is great.

Then we see instances of radical identification with Jesus, such as the term "Body of Christ" for the Church, or Paul partaking in Christ's afflictions (Col 2:8; cf. 2 Cor 1:5-7; 4:10;

11:23-30; Gal 6:17), or our "suffering with Christ" (Rom 8:17; 1 Cor 15:31; 2 Cor 6:9; Gal 2:20; Phil 3:10; 1 Pet 4:1, 13).

Where's the beef, then? Jesus routinely refers to something highly akin to "vicar" in these statements (and the Apostle Paul picks up on the motif in a big way). So the pope represents Christ to the world, in a particularly visible, compelling fashion. Big wow. This is not outrageous blasphemy; it is straightforward biblical usage. Who is being more "biblical" now?

Do you really find anything in Scripture whatsoever that would lead you to believe it was Christ's will that a bishop in a city hundreds of miles away in Rome would not only be the head of His church but would be treated as a king upon earth, bowed down to and treated the way the Roman Pontiff is treated?

I see *plenty* about Petrine and papal primacy and headship; yes (see my Papacy web page and book, *Biblical Proofs for an Infallible Church and Papacy*, for lots of biblical argumentation). Would White like to actually have a *discussion* about it, rather than taunting new converts?

2) *Have you considered how completely unbiblical and a-historical is the entire complex of doctrines and dogmas related to Mary? Do you seriously believe the Apostles taught that Mary was immaculately conceived,*

No, because that was a development of the notion of her sinlessness that came to fruition hundreds of years later, just as the canon of Scripture was a development that came to fruition hundreds of years later, and just as the Two Natures of Christ was a development that came to fruition hundreds of years later. The disciples would have understood that she was sinless, as seen in Luke 1:28, closely examined.

and that she was a perpetual virgin (so that she traveled about Palestine with a group of young men who were not her sons, but were Jesus' cousins, or half-brothers (children of a previous marriage of Joseph), or the like?

There are plenty of biblical and historical arguments for that (see the appropriate section on my Blessed Virgin Mary web page). Luther, Calvin, and Zwingli, and many many Protestants throughout history (such as John Wesley) were as stupid as Catholics, since they, too, firmly believed in this doctrine.

Do you really believe that dogmas defined nearly 2,000 years after the birth of Christ represent the actual teachings of the Apostles?

Development is not creation. But true creation of doctrines *ex nihilo* can only be seen in such Protestant novelties / corruptions as *sola Scriptura* and *sola fide* and denominationalism and purely symbolic Eucharist and baptism, that cannot be traced to the fathers *at all*.

Are you aware that such doctrines as perpetual virginity and bodily assumption have their origin in gnosticism, not Christianity,

No. If White wishes to call biblical evidences Gnosticism, he may do so. I don't think he will impress many people with such an "argument," though.

and have no foundation in apostolic doctrine or practice?

Really? That's news to me.

How do you explain how it is you must believe these things de fide, *by faith, when generations of Christians lived and died without ever even having* heard *of such things?*

Biblical and historical arguments, and consideration of development of doctrine more than amply explains it.

And the number 1 question I would ask of such a person is: if you claim to have once embraced the gospel of grace, whereby you confessed that your sole standing before a thrice-holy God was the seamless garment of the imputed righteousness of Christ, so that you claimed no merit of your own, no mixture of other merit with the perfect righteousness of Christ, but that you stood full and complete in Him and in Him alone, at true peace with God because there is no place in the universe safer from the wrath of God than in Christ, upon what possible grounds could you come to embrace a system that at its very heart denies you the peace that is found in a perfect Savior who accomplishes the Father's will and a Spirit who cannot fail but to bring that work to fruition in the life of God's elect? Do you really believe that the endless cycle of sacramental forgiveness to which you will now commit yourself can provide you the peace that the perfect righteousness of Christ can not?

By denying the false assumptions and categorizations present in this hyper-loaded question. Catholics accept *sola gratia* every bit as much as Protestants do, so it is a non-issue. We deny (solely) imputed justification, but that is distinct from *sola gratia*. White's disdain of sacramentalism puts him at odds, of course, with the vast majority of Protestants throughout history, let alone Orthodox and Catholics. I have shown that by using his criteria of "sacramentalism vs. grace" Martin Luther himself could not even be regarded as a Christian; nor could St. Augustine (and White loves him even more than Martin Luther).

White has far more insuperable problems to resolve than any Catholic convert has: a host of viciously circular, incoherent, logically inconsistent beliefs to account for. I've highlighted many of them, but they are by no means a complete list. In White's worldview consistently applied, virtually no one can be a regenerate Christian at all except for Calvinists.

Chapter Twelve

Critique of James White's Exegesis of James 2 in Chapter 20 of His Book, *The God Who Justifies*
[9 October 2013]

I've deliberately refrained from documenting Mr. White's innumerable personal attacks, in order to stick to substance and save readers from the agony of an avalanche of juvenile tedium and foolishness. But lest anyone thinks he doesn't engage in that sort of thing, I will retain just one example that forms the backdrop of this chapter. It's quite illustrative and typical of White's attacks.

On his *Dividing Line* webcast of 19 February 2008, White incessantly mocked and ridiculed, laughing and yucking it up like a drunk middle-schooler, playing clips of the songs *Liar* (Three Dog Night) and *Honesty* (Billy Joel) and just having a grand old time conveying to his fawning audience what an idiot, imbecile, and all-around ignoramus I supposedly am.

White was "critiquing" (if we can call it that) a radio interview I did on 15 February 2008, on the *Spirit Morning Show*, with Bruce and Kris McGregor. It was mostly about my book, *The One-Minute Apologist*. He played little clips of my comments and then proceeded to ridicule and mock them, in his inimitable, obnoxious "style" that he reserves particularly for Catholic apologists. Around the 20 minute mark, he went after some comments I made on James 2. Here is what he said:

> I don't know how long I spent, writing the chapter on James 2 in *The God Who Justifies*. . . . I've never seen a

meaningful refutation or even an attempted refutation of that chapter . . . and I'll tell you one thing. Dave will call this mocking. This isn't mocking; this is a simple fact. *That* man is not up to even trying. He doesn't have the skills; he doesn't have the background; he doesn't have the training; . . . Roman Catholic apologists . . . don't keep up with what anyone else is saying, who's providing a response to them . . .

White was ranting about how we Catholic apologists don't read his books or bother to refute them, and allegedly don't interact with our best opponents. That's news to me. I guess that's why I wrote *Pillars of Sola Scriptura*, my book that examined in great depth the two men that Protestants consider the best historic defenders of *sola Scriptura*: William Whitaker (1548-1595) -- White has written that he was one of "a few godly servants of the truth have invested the time and effort necessary to produce for God's people a full-orbed defense of Scriptural sufficiency" -- and William Goode (1801-1868). These guys are considered (including by White and his anti-Catholic cronies) the cream of the crop. I did a 310-page book in response to them, massively citing them.

I guess that's why his two big buddies, David T. King and William Webster (supposedly, profound Protestant apologists), have never responded to any of the several in-depth critiques I have done of their work. King has been smarting since way back in 2002, when I blew out of the water his contention that Pope St. Pius X thought Blessed John Henry Cardinal Newman was a theological liberal, who espoused evolution of dogma rather than development of doctrine. Once I produced a letter from that saintly pope to the contrary, that was all over, and King -- clearly embarrassed, since he had been saying on a discussion board that Catholics were so stupid for not knowing that Newman was heterodox -- has utterly ignored me ever since (except for vehement insults).

I replied to Webster's historically absurd arguments at great length in 2000 and in 2003. I've never heard a peep from him, ever. Zero, zilch, nada. Later, I showed how King and

Webster's big three-volume set about *sola Scriptura* was self-published (White has been mocking my self-published books -- which are not *all* of my books -- for many years now).

I guess, too, my desire to ignore the most able critics of Catholicism is why I did a 388-page book in which I responded line-by-line to the entirety of Book IV of *Institutes of the Christian Religion*, by John Calvin. The book is called *Biblical Catholic Answers for John Calvin*. I did a follow-up in which I dealt with large portions of Books I-III of the *Institutes*, too: *A Biblical Critique of Calvinism*.

I guess this is why I have huge web pages devoted to both Calvin and Martin Luther, the founder of Protestantism, and a book about the latter (with scores and scores of their own words and arguments dealt with; why I have extensive papers taking on other Protestant figures of the period, like Chemnitz, Melanchthon, and Zwingli.

It's all, you see, because I want to *ignore* my best opponents. White talks about how his books are ignored by Catholics. Well, as of yet, I see no Protestants champing at the bit to come and refute any of these books of mine, nor a book that is a direct assault on one of the sacred pillars of Protestantism: my *100 Biblical Arguments Against Sola Scriptura*. (Catholic Answers: 2012). So two can play at *that* game.

But I am happy to make an exception to my usual rule of ignoring anti-Catholic polemics (in place since 2007). White thinks I ignore anti-Catholics now because I am so deathly afraid of their profound, sublime arguments. Let him think what he will. I'll be happy to take on a chapter of his book, just as I have taken on entire books written by Calvin, Goode, Whitaker, and other Protestant apologists.

Remember White's words: "*That* man [yours truly] is not up to even trying [to refute his chapter on James 2]. He doesn't have the skills; he doesn't have the background; he doesn't have the training . . ." Will he even reply to my critique, or this book? Probably not. I don't expect so, but maybe he'll pleasantly surprise all of us. Stranger things have happened.

White's book, *The God Who Justifies*, was published in 2001 by Bethany House (Minneapolis). Chapter 20 is entitled,

"James Attacks Empty Faith." It runs from pages 329-354. The great bulk of it is devoted to notions and aspects where Catholics and Protestants fully agree:

1) A person is saved by God's grace.

2) A person is saved by exercising faith (itself caused by God's grace).

3) True faith will manifest itself in good works.

4) A person demonstrates his genuine faith by performance of works.

I need not deal with these aspects since there is no disagreement. The main disagreement Catholics would have here would be the attempted removal of sanctification and works from the equation of salvation altogether (formal separation of justification and sanctification and merely imputed, forensic, external justification) and the notion that salvation is an already attained past event, after which the saved person does good works in gratefulness to God for his salvation, thus proving or manifesting evidence that he is saved. Reformed Protestants take it further and claim that this salvation can never be lost, once attained.

White asserts over and over in the chapter, that the person demonstrates or "shows" his faith (per James) by his works. That is true in most respects, but Catholics would argue that this is not the be-all and end-all of the purpose of James. We agree that a justified person can and does do works in gratefulness to God, but we deny that it is the *only* neat little "slot" that works can be placed in, as if they have nothing whatsoever to do with final salvation.

Moreover, we would quibble with White's argument that James refers to justification and faith and works in a sense altogether distinct from St. Paul, so that portions of Paul's writings about justification and faith cannot properly be cross-referenced with regard to James' treatment; moreover, that justification is an entirely past event in the believer's life (one who is doing good works), and is a one-time event. White argues in very standard, garden-variety fundamentalist Protestant exegesis of James (especially chapter two) that it's all about the outward show or "proof" of faith rather than the nature of faith in and of itself. Thus he starts the chapter with his "Synopsis," writing:

> The entire purpose of James 2:14-26 can be summarized by the words, "show me." . . . This exhortation of Christians is not addressing how the ungodly are declared righteous before God, but how that declaration is shown outwardly in the Christian life. (p. 329)

This is the way that fundamentalist Protestants -- exemplified in almost "self-parody" terms by White -- try to escape the seemingly obvious "Catholic" thrust of the book, insofar as it ties faith and works more closely together than many Protestants through history have been comfortable with (the most famous case being Martin Luther, who came very close to tossing James out of the New Testament -- as if he had any authority to do so in the first place).

White, in seeking to make his case that St. James is discussing issues vis-à-vis faith and works in a more or less completely different sense from St. Paul, then examines James 2:21 and especially the translation of same:

> **James 2:21** (RSV, as throughout, when I cite Scripture) Was not Abraham our father justified by works, when he offered his son Isaac upon the altar?

Since "justified by works" sounds so "Catholic" and foreign to Reformed Protestant thinking, White wants to stress different translations, so as to "soften the blow" of the passage, so to speak, for Protestants. He even lists a Catholic in order to do this (on p. 345): Luke Timothy Johnson, who translates the verse [*The Letter of James: A New Translation* (Garden City, New York: Doubleday, 1995) , p. 239], as:

Was not our father Abraham shown to be righteous on the basis of deeds when he offered his son Isaac on the altar?

He offers the evangelical-biased NIV as a second rendering:

Was not our ancestor Abraham considered righteous for what he did when he offered his son Isaac on the altar? (p. 345)

The problem is that these are non-literal translations, that don't even include the word or notion of "justification" in them (ostensibly, or speculatively, for fear of sounding "Catholic"). These are the translations what White chooses and highlights, with the utmost selectivity, for his polemical purposes.

His aim is to demonstrate that the thrust is to "show" or outwardly manifest the interior faith and that *this* is solely what the justification by works spoken of in James is referring to: not that good works (enabled by God's grace and flowing from the faith life of a regenerate person) are, or *could* ever be (in White's mind) organically connected with justification. Many other non-Catholic translations are very different from White's "favored few":

KJV / RSV / ASV / NASB / NRSV / NKJV . . . justified by works . . .

NEB / REB Was it not by his action . . . that our father Abraham was justified?

Beck . . . get to be righteous on the basis of works . . .

Goodspeed . . . made upright for his good deeds . . .

Moffatt . . . justified by what he did?

Wuest . . . vindicated by works [justified as to his claim to a living faith] . . .

The following (less literal) translations even (rather delightfully for our argument) include an element of "in *God*'s sight" that is *directly contradictory* to White's overall interpretation of James 2 (in *man*'s sight rather than God's):

Barclay Was it not because of his actions that he was accepted by God as a good man?

Phillips . . . his action which really justified him in God's sight . . .

Some translations have the "take" that White prefers, but they are clearly out of the mainstream. Williams has "shown to be upright." The Amplified Bible has "[shown to be] justified" but then it adds, "made acceptable to God -- by [his] works". Thus, the latter translation has one element that White favors ("shown") but also has the other that he seeks to deny: justification in God's eyes rather than merely outwardly in man's sight. Even the NIV's "considered righteous" doesn't make it clear whether it is man or God who does the considering.

Ignoring all of this overwhelming consensus of translation of James 2:21, White special pleads (as if repetition were rational argument):

James's use must be allowed to stand on its own. As a result, the translation . . . "shown to be righteous" or "considered righteous" (NIV) flows not from a precommitment to a theological perspective but from the context itself. (p. 346)

It's interesting, then, that 14 non-Catholic translations that I have found (to his two, plus Williams and Amplified) didn't think it necessary to add this notion of "shown" to the passage: that White seems to think is essential to its meaning or emphasis. White then bolsters his argument that James and Paul are talking about two different things:

But we have already seen that James is arguing against a use of the word "faith" (a deedless, dead, empty, useless faith that exists only in the realm of words and not of action) that is *not* paralleled in the Pauline passages that speak of how one is justified. Second, Paul speaks of justification "before God" (. . . Galatians 3:11) or "in His sight" (. . . Romans 3:20), while the context of James is . . . "show me." (p. 346)

Earlier in the book, in discussing Romans 3, White had stated:

To be justified before men is something obviously very different than to be justified before God. . . . This is important in considering James 2:14-26 . . . (p. 181)

The problem with this is that it doesn't accurately portray the totality of what St. Paul teaches about works. He, too, aligns them with faith, just as James does, and not simply in this "demonstration" sense for which White contends. For example:

Romans 2:13 For it is not the hearers of the law who are righteous before God, but the doers of the law who will be justified.

Paul is simultaneously discussing those who are justified or "righteous before God" and the relationship of works to that justification. A few verses earlier he had been discussing the final judgment (and eschatological salvation or justification), and presenting it in terms of good works or lack of same, rather than faith alone without works (he never mentions faith at all in the passage). For Paul, then, works are central in the equation in terms of God's judgment of who is saved and who isn't:

Romans 2:5-10 But by your hard and impenitent heart you are storing up wrath for yourself on the day of wrath when God's righteous judgment will be revealed. [6] For he will render to every man according to his works: [7] to

376

those who by patience in well-doing seek for glory and honor and immortality, he will give eternal life; [8] but for those who are factious and do not obey the truth, but obey wickedness, there will be wrath and fury. [9] There will be tribulation and distress for every human being who does evil, the Jew first and also the Greek, [10] but glory and honor and peace for every one who does good, the Jew first and also the Greek.

It's the "doers" who *will* be justified in Romans 2:13. This is backwards, according to White's own soteriology. Paul needs to spend time reading more of Bishop White's books (or his Internet and *Dividing Line* rantings), to get up to speed. What he *should* have written, getting the chronology and the main categories correct, was:

> **Romans 2:13** (RFV: Revised Fundamentalist Version) For it is not the doers of the law who are justified, but the hearers of the law who are declared righteous before God and then become doers in gratefulness for their justification.

Poor Paul. He just doesn't get it. But thankfully for our sakes, James White *does*. Paul doesn't just state his shocking conclusion of Romans 2:13 in isolation. He continues the supposedly exclusive theme of St. James in other passages:

> **Romans 6:22-23** But now that you have been set free from sin and have become slaves of God, the return you get is sanctification and its end, eternal life. [23] For the wages of sin is death, but the free gift of God is eternal life in Christ Jesus our Lord.

St. Paul again gets it backwards (it's frustrating and maddening how often he does this!). Somehow he mixes up justification and sanctification in a way that Catholics are notorious (in some circles) for doing. Eternal life and salvation isn't the end of sanctification, but of [imputed] *justification*. Thus, this passage is *supposed* to read (to make it consistent with White's fundamentalist Reformed soteriology, and non-troublesome):

> **Romans 6:22** (RFV) But now that you have been set free from sin and have attained eternal life as the end of justification alone, as slaves of God, the return you get is sanctification and its end, manifesting the proof of saving faith.

It's clear that if White is right in correcting Paul's soteriology, that he ought *also* to correct his epistles as well, so that the rest of us aren't led astray so often by him. St. Paul continues in his "Catholic" folly in his epistle to the Romans:

> **Romans 8:15-17** For you did not receive the spirit of slavery to fall back into fear, but you have received the spirit of sonship. When we cry, "Abba! Father!" [16] it is the Spirit himself bearing witness with our spirit that we are children of God, [17] and if children, then heirs, heirs of God and fellow heirs with Christ, provided we suffer with him in order that we may also be glorified with him.

Huh?! Here, Paul informs us that being "heirs of God" is conditional on a work that we must do in order to be glorified with Christ: *suffering* with Him. That's not faith alone. It's not imputed justification and merely being declared righteous in a forensic, external sense. It's *real* action and real *deeds*: suffering, which is directly tied to being glorified with Christ (i.e., saved in the end, with heaven and glorified bodies as our reward). St. Peter echoes this theme of suffering with Christ as a condition of salvation:

> **1 Peter 4:12-13** Beloved, do not be surprised at the fiery ordeal which comes upon you to prove you, as though something strange were happening to you. [13] But rejoice in so far as you share Christ's sufferings, that you may also rejoice and be glad when his glory is revealed.

378

Alas, White decided to skip over Romans 6 altogether in his book about justification and soteriology; and also Romans 8:15-17 (starting with Romans 8:28 in his chapter 14) and 1 Peter 4:12-13: despite devoting five chapters and some 115 pages to various portions of Romans. Paul again ties works to ultimate salvation:

1 Timothy 6:18-19 They are to do good, to be rich in good deeds, liberal and generous, [19] thus laying up for themselves a good foundation for the future, so that they may take hold of the life which is life indeed.

It is works that lay the "good foundation for the future, so that" a man may "take hold" of eternal life. This repeats what he wrote in 6:11-12, where he urges Timothy to "aim at righteousness, godliness" and "fight the good fight of the faith" so that he may "take hold of the eternal life" that he was called to when he confessed faith in Jesus. The confession is only the beginning. To "take hold" of the salvation requires works and strong perseverance.

To reiterate how important works are in the overall equation of salvation, Paul states: "I charge you to keep the commandment unstained and free from reproach" (6:14). This is another passage that White didn't find time to exegete in his book. Perhaps in the sequel . . . White moves along in James:

James 2:23 and the scripture was fulfilled which says, "Abraham believed God, and it was reckoned to him as righteousness"; and he was called the friend of God.

He comments:

. . . Abraham's confession of faith is recorded in Genesis 15:6. God justified Abraham upon the exercise of that faith. The reality of the faith Abraham had, upon which he was justified, is demonstrated in the offering of Isaac. (p. 349)

Here he will run into several serious difficulties, based on his assumption that justification is a one-time event only. White believes that for Abraham, that one-time event is described in Genesis 15:6; cited in James 2:23, and also by St. Paul in Romans 4:3. The conundrum for White and the false notion of one-time justification is seen in the book of Hebrews:

> **Hebrews 11:8-10** By faith Abraham obeyed when he was called to go out to a place which he was to receive as an inheritance; and he went out, not knowing where he was to go. [9] By faith he sojourned in the land of promise, as in a foreign land, living in tents with Isaac and Jacob, heirs with him of the same promise. [10] For he looked forward to the city which has foundations, whose builder and maker is God.

The entire chapter is devoted to faith and the heroes of faith, and is a great Protestant favorite, for that reason. It starts out:

> **Hebrews 11:1-2** Now faith is the assurance of things hoped for, the conviction of things not seen. [2] For by it the men of old received divine approval.

Now, the "faith" referred to here is clearly that which follows justification. It must be so -- particularly in Reformed soteriology --, since for them, no man who is unregenerate of unjustified can exercise true faith. But -- here's the rub -- Hebrews 11 is hearkening back to *Genesis 12*, not Genesis 15:

> **Genesis 12:1-4** Now the LORD said to Abram, "Go from your country and your kindred and your father's house to the land that I will show you. [2] And I will make of you a great nation, and I will bless you, and make your name great, so that you will be a blessing. [3] I will bless those who bless you, and him who curses you I will curse; and by you all the families of the earth shall bless themselves." [4] So Abram went, as the LORD had told

380

him; and Lot went with him. Abram was seventy-five years old when he departed from Haran.

The question then becomes: is this *saving* faith or *justifying* faith, that Abraham exercised at this juncture in his life? St. Paul seems to think so:

Galatians 3:8-14 And the scripture, foreseeing that God would justify the Gentiles by faith, preached the gospel beforehand to Abraham, saying, "In you shall all the nations be blessed." [9] So then, those who are men of faith are blessed with Abraham who had faith. [10] For all who rely on works of the law are under a curse; for it is written, "Cursed be every one who does not abide by all things written in the book of the law, and do them." [11] Now it is evident that no man is justified before God by the law; for "He who through faith is righteous shall live"; [12] but the law does not rest on faith, for "He who does them shall live by them." [13] Christ redeemed us from the curse of the law, having become a curse for us -- for it is written, "Cursed be every one who hangs on a tree" -- [14] that in Christ Jesus the blessing of Abraham might come upon the Gentiles, that we might receive the promise of the Spirit through faith.

This implies either a notion that justification can occur more than once, or some sense of ongoing justification, rather than one-time only. White shows awareness of this "particularly appealing" counter-argument, and mocks it by referring to "the ingenuity of man who is constantly attempting to find a way around God's way of justification" (p. 221). What is his response? Here it is:

The writer to the Hebrews says that Abraham acted in faith in responding to God's call to leave Ur of the Chaldees. However, saving faith always has an object, and the object of saving faith in Abraham's life was the promise given him in Genesis 15, not Genesis 12. (p. 222)

He digs in and ratchets up the polemics for effect:

> Justification, then, must be a point-in-time declaration, not a process that is repeated, or else Romans 4:1-8 is not inspired Scripture. To say otherwise is to make a complete mockery of the entirety of Romans 4. (p. 223)

Unfortunately for White, there is a lot of disagreement with him, even from within his own Reformed camp. And the disagreement and exegesis contrary to White's take is not, I submit, motivated by a disdain for St. Paul or desire to mock Romans chapter four. Phil Gons has a doctorate in theology (a *real* one; not a fake doctorate such as White possesses). He describes himself as "a theologically conservative evangelical Christian who is committed to the essence of Reformed Protestantism." Phil wrote a heavily researched Internet article, "When Was Abraham Justified?" He concluded:

> . . . virtually all the commentators and theologians that I have come across who deal with the issue are in agreement that Abraham was justified by the events recorded at the beginning of Genesis 12. Luther, Calvin, Brakel, and Spurgeon defend a Genesis 12 justification, as do O. Palmer Robertson and Brian Vickers. . . .

> The view that holds that Abraham was not saved until Genesis 15 finds virtually no support at all throughout church history (at least not that I have been able to find in hours of research in scores of commentaries and hundreds of journals) . . .

Very odd, isn't it? In a 20-page Word document accompanying the article, Gons assembles an impressive array of supporting sources for his contention. Here are some highlights, with my own added emphases in italics:

We must now notice the circumstance of time . Abram was justified by faith many years after he had been called by God; after he had left his country a voluntary exile, rendering himself a remarkable example of patience and of continence; after he had entirely dedicated himself to sanctity and after he had, by exercising himself in the spiritual and external service of God, aspired to a life almost angelical. It therefore follows, that even to the end of life, we are led towards the eternal kingdom of God by the righteousness of faith.

On which point many are too grossly deceived. For *they grant, indeed, that the righteousness which is freely bestowed upon sinners and offered to the unworthy is received by faith alone; but they restrict this to a moment of time*, so that he who at the first obtained justification by faith, may afterwards be justified by good works. By this method, faith is nothing else than the beginning of righteousness, whereas righteousness itself consists in a continual course of works. But *they who thus trifle must be altogether insane.* For if the angelical uprightness of Abram faithfully cultivated through so many years, in one uniform course, did not prevent him from fleeing to faith, for the sake of obtaining righteousness; where upon earth besides will such perfection be found, as may stand in God's sight?

Therefore, by a consideration of the time in which this was said to Abram, we certainly gather, that the righteousness of works is not to be substituted for the righteousness of faith, in any such way, that one should perfect what the other has begun; but that *holy men are only justified by faith, as long as they live in the world.* If any one object, that Abram previously believed God, when he followed Him at His call, and committed himself to His direction and guardianship, the solution is ready; that *we are not here told when Abram first began to be justified, or to believe in God; but that in this one place it is declared, or related, how he had been justified through his whole life* . For if Moses had spoken thus immediately on Abram's first vocation, the cavil of which I have spoken would have been more specious; namely, that the righteousness of faith was only initial (so to speak) and not perpetual. But now *since after such great progress, he is still said to be justified by faith, it thence easily appears that the saints are justified freely even unto death.*

(*Calvin's Commentaries*, Genesis 15:6)

The Lord, on the contrary, declares, that he imputed Abraham's faith for righteousness (Rom. 4:3), not at the time when he was still a worshipper of idols, but *after he had been many years distinguished for holiness. Abraham had long served God with a pure heart, and performed that obedience of the Law which a mortal man is able to perform: yet his righteousness still consisted in faith.* Hence we infer, according to the reasoning of Paul, that it was *not of works.* In like manners when the prophet says, "The just shall live by his faith," (Hab. 2:4), he is not speaking of the wicked and profane, whom the Lord justifies by converting them to the faith: his discourse is directed to believers, and life is promised to them by faith. Paul also removes every doubt, when in confirmation of this sentiment he quotes the words of David, "Blessed is he whose transgression is forgiven, whose sin is covered," (Ps. 32:1). It is certain that David is not speaking of the ungodly but of believers such as he himself was, because he was giving utterance to the feelings of his own mind. Therefore we must have this blessedness not once only, but must hold it fast during our whole lives.

(*Institutes of the Christian Religion*, III, 14:11)

Therefore *if you should ask whether Abraham was righteous before this time, my answer is: He was righteous because he believed God*. But here the Holy Spirit wanted to attest this expressly, since the promise deals with a spiritual Seed. He did so in order that you might conclude on the basis of a correct inference that those who accept this Seed, or those who believe in Christ, are righteous. *Abraham's faith was extraordinary, since he left his country when commanded to do so and became an exile*; but we are not all commanded to do the same thing. Therefore in that connection Moses does not add: "Abraham believed God, and this was reckoned to him as righteousness." But in the passage before us he makes this addition when he is speaking about the heavenly Seed. He does so in order to comfort the church of all times. He is saying that those who, with Abraham, believe this promise are truly righteous. Here, in the most appropriate place, the Holy Spirit wanted to set forth expressly and clearly the statement that righteousness is nothing else than believing God when He makes a promise.

("Genesis 15:6," *Lectures on Genesis: Chapters 15–20*, vol. 3, *Luther's Works*, ed. Jaroslav Jan Pelikan, trans. George V. Schick; Saint Louis: Concordia, 1961, 3:19–20)

New Bible Commentary

Abram accepted God's reassurance, he believed the LORD (6). *The verbal form suggests an ongoing activity, i.e. he kept believing the promise, he kept relying on the Lord.* So God credited it to him as righteousness. Righteousness is that state of acceptance by God which comes from perfect obedience to the law. Abram's failure to fulfil the law's demands completely is obvious in

Genesis, yet his faith in God's promise of a child is here said to count as righteousness. For Paul, this shows that faith, not works, is the prerequisite to acceptance by God (Gal. 3:6–14). *Jas. 2:18–24 and Heb. 11:8–9 point out that Abraham's faith was proved genuine by his good works.* This 'faith that works' is central to the Christian understanding of salvation and upright living.

(D. A. Carson, R. T. France, J. A. Motyer, and G. J . Wenham, eds., "15:1–21 The Covenant Promise," *New Bible Commentary: 21st Century Edition* [Leicester, England; Downers Grove: InterVarsity, 1994], Gen 15:1)

Allen P. Ross / *Bible Knowledge Commentary*

Genesis 15:6 provides an important note, but *it does not pinpoint Abram's conversion. That occurred years earlier when he left Ur.* (The form of the Heb. word for "believed" shows that *his faith did not begin after the events recorded in vv. 1–5.*) Abram's faith is recorded here because it is foundational for making the covenant. The Abrahamic Covenant did not give Abram redemption; *it was a covenant made with Abram who had already believed and to whom righteousness had already been imputed.*

(Allen P. Ross, "Genesis," *The Bible Knowledge Commentary: An Exposition of the Scriptures* , ed. John F. Walvoord and Roy B. Zuck [Wheaton: Victor Books, 1983–85], 1:55)

Gordon J. Wenham

The verbal form . . . "he believed" probably indicates *repeated or continuing action.* Faith was Abram's normal response to the LORD's words.

(Gordon J. Wenham, *Genesis 1–15* , vol. 1, *Word Biblical Commentary* [Dallas: Word, 2002], 329; comment on Genesis 15:6)

Charles Spurgeon

When he was comforted, Abram received an open declaration of his justification. *I take it, beloved friends, that our text does not intend to teach us that Abram was not justified before this time. Faith always justifies whenever it exists*, and as soon as it is exercised; its result follows immediately, and is not an aftergrowth needing months of delay. The moment a man truly trusts his God he is justified.

(Charles Haddon Spurgeon, "Justification by Faith—Illustrated by Abram's Righteousness," vol. 14, *The Metropolitan Tabernacle Pulpit Sermons* [Albany, OR: Ages Software, 1998])

Gons comments on Hebrews 11:

The author of Hebrews, in setting forth examples of faith to be followed, intentionally begins the story of Abraham with Genesis 12, when he "by faith" obeyed the Lord, believing His promises to him to be reliable. Had Abraham still been an idolater (cf. Joshua 24:2) and his faith something less than genuine, surely the author of Hebrews would have cited Genesis 15 or some point later in the narrative as the start of Abraham's exemplary faith.

Ironically enough, White's derisive comments against the Catholic view of ongoing or multiple instances of justification, also hit in large part the commentators above: Calvin, Luther, Spurgeon et al. They're all trumped by the Interpreter of all Interpreters, and the Final word in biblical exegesis: Bishop

James White. So much the worse for them. Here is White's opinion of views other than one-time forensic justification:

> . . . the argument carries weight for many who are seeking a way out of the biblical teaching on the subject.
> The fundamental error of the argument thus presented is really quite simple: it is not an argument *from* Scripture; it is an argument *against* Scripture. . . . To argue against an apostle of the Lord Jesus Christ only shows that one's theology is in error fro its very inception.
> . . . Paul's entire point is based upon justification being a forensic declaration that takes place one time in the believer's life. If, in fact, justification is ongoing, or repetitive, or iterative, then Paul's entire point collapses . . . (p. 222)

White gets to James 2:24 on his page 350:

James 2:24 You see that a man is justified by works and not by faith alone.

Once again, he wants to play the game of highly selective Bible translation, citing Luke Timothy Johnson, who translates, "shown to be righteous on the basis of deeds." And once again, in the interest of "full disclosure" and attempted objectivity, I will provide the reader with a much wider array of Bible translations for James 2:24:

KJV / ASV / Wuest . . . by works a man is justified . . .

RSV / NASB / NRSV / NKJV . . . justified by works . . .

Phillips A man is justified before God by what he does as well as by what he believes.

NIV . . . justified by what he does . . .

NEB . . . justified by deeds . . .

Williams . . . shown to be upright by his good deeds . . .

Beck . . a man gets to be righteous on the basis of his works . . .

Goodspeed . . . made upright by his good deeds . . .

Amplified . . . justified (pronounced righteous before God) through what he does . . .

Moffatt . . . by what he does a man is justified . . .

REB You see then it is by action and not by faith alone that a man is justified.

Barclay . . . it is in consequence of his actions that God reckons a man to be a good man, and not only in consequence of faith.

We see in several translations the idea that this justification by works (as well as by faith) is in the eyes of God, not just man, as White wants to argue and eisegete, according to his false fundamentalist presuppositions: Phillips: "before God," Amplified: "pronounced righteous before God," Barclay: "that God reckons a man . . ."

It's important to reiterate that Catholics do *not* believe in salvation by works. We deny salvation by faith alone and also by works alone. We assert salvation by grace alone through faith, expressed and "lived out" by the "obedience of faith" shown by faith- and grace-based good works. I wrote in the section of my book, *Bible Proofs for Catholic Truths* (Sophia Institute Press: 2009), entitled, "Salvation is not by works alone" (pp. 166-167):

This "justification by works" is not *by itself*, any more than faith is operative by itself. James writes of Abraham being "justified by works" (2:21) but this can't be ripped from context, so as to distort his meaning, since in the verse immediately before, he ties faith organically in with works, and he does the same in the verse immediately after, as he does in the larger context of 2:14, 17-18 and 2:26. They simply can't be separated.

Likewise, when justification by works is asserted again in 2:24, it is qualified in 2:26, by connecting faith with it, and in the larger context before the statement, also in 2:14, 17-18, 20, 22. The works can't possibly be interpreted as on their own, then, without doing massive violence to the contextual meaning and teaching.

The same applies to 2:25 and the statement about Rahab the harlot being "justified by works" -- it is qualified in the same way in context, by the consideration of 2:14, 17-18, 20, 22, 26. Moreover, salvation by works alone is flatly and explicitly denied by St. Paul in Ephesians 2:8-9 and 2 Timothy 1:9, and the same is strongly implied in Romans 11:5-6 (see the section "We are saved through grace").

For the Catholic, justification is not the same thing as salvation or the attainment of eternal life. It can be lost or rejected by means of human free will and disobedience. So, to assert "justification by works," even in a qualified sense, is not at all the same as asserting salvation by works. Therefore, it is scripturally improper to assert either salvation by works alone or salvation by faith alone. They are never taught in Holy Scripture, and are both denied more than once. Justification by faith or justification by works can be asserted in a limited sense, as Scripture does: always understood as hand-in-hand with the other two elements in the grace-faith-works triumvirate.

White takes note (p. 351) of the clause "you see." He argues (garden-variety polemical stuff here) that this proves some big change of category, compared to Pauline utterances on justification. He had expressed this more clearly in his comment on James 2:22:

Ironically, James says, "you *see* that . . .," showing the *demonstrative* element he is pushing into the forefront. . . . James wishes his hearers to *see* something from the example of Abraham's obedience to God in the offering of Isaac. We are to *see* Abraham's deeds . . . (p. 348)

This is equal parts silly and insubstantial. We need only go to St. Paul to show that there is no distinction here that White reads into the text for polemical purposes:

Galatians 3:6-7 Thus Abraham "believed God, and it was reckoned to him as righteousness." [7] So you see that it is men of faith who are the sons of Abraham.

That passage has to do with justification before God, as White himself agrees; yet it still contains the clause, "you see." Therefore, the latter is no proof in and of itself that James is discussing a different notion altogether: merely justification "before men" -- to be observed as the proof and fruit of genuine faith -- rather than before God.

White then makes short work of Rahab's stated "justification":

James 2:25 And in the same way was not also Rahab the harlot justified by works when she received the messengers and sent them out another way?

He merely assumes and states what he needs to prove (which is no rational argument, but rather, essentially mere "preaching"):

The evidentiary nature of this justification is again clearly seen: no one would argue that God justifies prostitutes on the basis of hiding spies. Instead, the faith she had come to possess in the God of Israel manifested itself in her willingness to act in accordance with her confession found in these words: "the Lord your God, He is God in heaven above and on earth beneath" (Joshua 2:11 NASB). (p. 352)

The obvious problem with this "exegesis" is that it is not exegesis at all; it is *eisegesis*: reading into Scripture what is not stated there. White is big on endlessly pointing this out if anyone else does it (and of course, according to him, Catholics always do). Earlier in his book he decried this sort of thing, noting:

> . . . the presence of human traditions that influence and often *determine* the reading of the text. (p. 129)

The text doesn't *say* she was justified based on her profession that he notes (though that is a quite reasonable supposition to hold; I'm just noting that the Bible doesn't directly *assert* it). The *text* says she was "justified by works when she received the messengers".

Thus, White has the choice of exegeting the text as it stands, or ignoring it. He chooses the latter, because his prior theological views disallow him to do any differently. He is doing exactly what he condemned in his statement above. It doesn't *matter* what the Bible says: he'll quickly discard that if it goes against his prior views, which lie external to the Bible, and in several places contradict it.

Catholics believe we are justified by faith and also by grace-based works done by the regenerate believer in conjunction with faith, as a co-laborer with God (1 Cor 3:9; 15:10; 2 Cor 6:1). White doesn't like the "works" part of that biblical equation, so he has to construct several desperate "arguments" in order to undermine it or explain it away at every turn. There is a word for that: sophistry. The Bible elsewhere freely places Rahab's faith and works together. They are of a piece: neither can or should be ignored:

Hebrews 11:31 By faith Rahab the harlot did not perish with those who were disobedient, because she had given friendly welcome to the spies.

Notice the "because" in the verse? Moreover, it is not foreign Scripture, to expressly state that works are the cause of justification or even a central criterion for eternal life. We've already noted this in Paul, above. Here it is again (repetition being a good teaching device):

Romans 2:13 For it is not the hearers of the law who are righteous before God, but the doers of the law who will be justified.

Indeed, final judgment in Scripture is always -- repeat, *always* -- associated with works (good and bad), and scarcely with faith at all. When we read Bible passages on the last judgment, it is works that are being discussed. I have collected fifty of these passages myself. So why are Protestants so reluctant to acknowledge this? Why can't they "go" where the Bible freely, easily does, so often?

Oftentimes the Bible discusses faith in isolation, in relation to justification and salvation. Other times, it discusses works in isolation, in the same way. Both are factors. So why does White feel the necessity of having to utterly ignore what James 2:25 plainly states, and skip over to another verse so he can preach his unbiblical, fundamentalist "faith alone" doctrine? How are Rahab or Abraham being "justified by works" in James fundamentally different from what the following five passages out of my collected fifty (four from Jesus Himself) assert?:

Matthew 25:31-46 "When the Son of man comes in his glory, and all the angels with him, then he will sit on his glorious throne. Before him will be gathered all the nations, and he will separate them one from another as a shepherd separates the sheep from the goats, and he will place the sheep at his right hand, but the goats at the left. Then the King will say to those at his right hand, 'Come, O blessed of my Father, inherit the kingdom prepared for you from the foundation of the world; for I was hungry and you gave me food, I was thirsty and you gave me drink, I was a stranger and you welcomed me, I was naked and you clothed me, I was sick and you visited me, I was in prison and you came to me.' Then the righteous will answer him, `Lord, when did we see thee hungry and feed thee, or thirsty and give thee drink? And when did we see thee a stranger and welcome thee, or naked and clothe thee? And when did we see thee sick or in prison and visit thee?' And the King will answer them, `Truly, I say to you, as you did it to one of the least of these my brethren, you did it to me.' Then he will say to those at his left hand, `Depart from me, you cursed, into the eternal fire prepared for the devil and his angels; for I was hungry and you gave me no food, I was thirsty and you gave me no drink, I was a stranger and you did not welcome me, naked and you did not clothe me, sick and in prison and you did not visit me.' Then they also will answer, `Lord, when did we see thee hungry or thirsty or a stranger or naked or sick or in prison, and did not minister to thee?' Then he will answer them, `Truly, I say to you, as you did it not to one of the least of these, you did it not to me.' And they will go away into eternal punishment, but the righteous into eternal life."

Luke 3:9 Even now the axe is laid to the root of the trees; every tree therefore that does not bear good fruit is cut down and thrown into the fire.

John 5:29 . . . those who have done good, to the resurrection of life, and those who have done evil, to the resurrection of judgment.

1 Peter 1:17 . . . who judges each one impartially according to his deeds . . .

Revelation 22:12 Behold, I am coming soon, bringing my recompense, to repay every one for what he has done.

I'd like to agree with a statement of White's in closing. Of course I'd *apply* it differently, but the statement itself remains true:

When Paul and James both address Christian behavior and Christian life, they speak as one . . . When we allow James to speak for himself . . . his intentions and purposes are clear. (p. 354)

Amen!